# WHO GOES WHERE?

by

STELLA RUTTER

A record of the families of
**BROUGHTON and  TOWLER**

Their work and personalities
and the autobiography of

**JOYCE ISABEL STELLA RUTTER**
nee Broughton

ISBN no. 978-0-9556642-0-5

Front cover designed by Stella Rutter
    Spitfire by Pat Owen, Aviation Artist
    Tree, Soldiers by Angela Thomas
    H.M.S. Belfast by Stella Rutter

People shown on leaves:
    John Knox the Reformer
    Cardinal Wolsey
    John Broughton
    Godolphin Arabian
    General Tom Thumb's Boots
    John Russell, 13th Duke of Bedford
        (by kind permission of His Grace the Duke of Bedford
        and the Trustees of the Bedford Estates)
    Jeffrey Quill
    R.J. Mitchell
    Joseph Smith
    Alan N. Clifton
    General Bernard L. Montgomery
    Major General D.A.H. Graham
    Air Marshal Sir Ivor Broom

Distributed by WGW Enterprise, Stanbury Close, Bosham PO ... 8NS

Printed by St Richard's Press, Chichester, 01243 539222

# Contents

# Foreword

I was delighted when Stella invited me to provide a Foreword for the fascinating book on her life and times from when she worked in the same Drawing Office at Vickers Supermarine as I did myself.

The Drawing Office comprised many Sections. My Section was relatively near to Stella, divided by an aisle. Social discussion between employees was not encouraged during working hours. Most people knew Stella, who was a striking looking young woman with a strong personality and her Section was known by many as 'The Special Branch'. Gerry Gingell, her Section Leader, on entering Supermarine as a young man in the Design Staff, worked with the legendary designer, R. J. Mitchell until his demise prior to World War II when he was succeeded by Joseph Smith, who became the Chief Designer.

Stella told me many years later of the special task she had undertaken involving a top security meeting leading up to the invasion of Europe in 1944 by Allied Forces on D-Day. Present were senior British Military Commanders including Major Generals, D.A.H. Graham, Rodney Keller, Thomas Rennie, Richard Gale and the American Commanders, Lieutenant General Omar Bradley and Major General Clarence Huebner.

At the conclusion of the War, most of us went our own ways and it was many years before Stella and I met again. This was a special occasion at the Southampton Museum of Aviation. Jeffrey Quill, one of the two Supermarine Chief Test Pilots, desired a book should be produced recording all the people who were associated with the development of the Spitfire and Seafire aircraft. I had the privilege of being one of the signatories, although the part I played was of a very junior nature. Stella is also included under her maiden name of Broughton.

Since then I have remained in touch with Stella, who has become a real friend. As more than sixty years have elapsed since we both worked together at Hursley Park memories are not quite as good as they were but I certainly remember Stella as will all the rest of the staff who knew her, many of whom, sadly, are no longer with us. I am sure all those who read this book will be amazed at its remarkable contents and she deserves every success in the publication of her book.

Signed,

The Earl of Gainsborough

# Acknowledgements

I must acknowledge with grateful thanks the invaluable help and encouragement I have received from those who have donated their time and expertise, unstintingly, to assist in my researches. Regretfully, many are no longer with us.

- Firstly to Harry Arch, a Vice President of the Bedford Family History Society who persuaded me to start writing my family history.

- To Miss Pat Bell for her commendation in the earliest stages on my writing ability and encouragement to continue enabling me to put my nose to the grindstone.

- Admiral Sir James Burnell-Nugent for his interest in my work for the Senior Service.

- To Air Marshal Sir Ivor Broom for his friendship and encouraging me to record the event of Saturday 3rd June 1944, prior to D-Day. He told me he 'Considered this event to be unique in military history.'

- To Field Marshal Bernard L. Montgomery for his trust in my discretion and integrity, allowing,

- Major General Douglas A. H. Graham to request me to be his hostess.

- To Brigadier Robert A. Phayre of the Essex Yeomanry in proving my involvement with the above.

- To Colonel Philip H. A. Brownrigg for his account of his Commanding Officer.

- My grateful thanks to people from all walks of life who have expressed interest including the following:

- To The Duke of Bedford for his approval of the paragraph regarding his grandfather.

- To Sir Martin Gilliatt for his support and friendship of many years.

- To Sir Henry Cooper for his comments on John Broughton.

- To Brigadier Roy Wilde, Clerk to The Worshipful Company of Tallow Chandlers for his correction of my text.

❁ To Squadron Leader Richard Ian Blair for providing me with a copy of his Citation. Also the poster depicting him which was produced for instructing public awareness of security.

❁ To Joseph Smith who succeeded R.J. Mitchell as Chief Designer for the Spitfire and for his trust in my integrity.

❁ To Geoffrey Quill and Alex Henshaw for their memories as Test Pilots.

❁ To Alan Clifton, Eric Lovell-Cooper, Jack Rasmussen, Jack Davis, Gerry Gingell and Dr. Gordon Mitchell for their recollections of Supermarine.

❁ To Peter Arnold, Spitfire Historian, for his collaboration in confirming my queries regarding details.

❁ To Mike Baylis for his work in producing copies of faded photographs, many of which were taken in the late 1880s and early 1900s.

❁ To those who have subscribed stories from their life such as Nurse Richards and members of Supermarine, Ken Miles, Jack Parnell, Bill Fisher and Alf Shorter.

❁ To old colleagues of Supermarine some of whom are also members of the Spitfire Society.

❁ To the poets, Paddy Anne Wilson, Joyce Lucas, Sir Edward Hamley and R.B. Bennett whose poems have been included.

❁ To George D. Davidson for his restoration of my autograph album and the family's books.

❁ To Irene Young whose story inspired me to write about Landladies.

❁ To Sir Matthew Hale for his letter to his son in the 17th Century.

❁ To various authors I am indebted for confirmation of facts. For example, Dr. Julian Litten, Nigel Tranter, Christopher Hibbert, Kenneth More, Tony Gee and Alfred Price. The latter for copies of photographs.

❁ To members of Libraries, Museums, County Record Offices, various journals, The Royal Mint, Eton College, Westminster Abbey Library, and The Guild of The Tallow Chandlers who gave of their time and expertise to search patiently for pieces of information. In addition allowing me to take relevant photographs. All of these have aided me to present my Scenario.

❁ To the Kent County Council Strategic Planning Department for accepting my evidence sent to Phil Harding of 'The Time Team' regarding the Aucheulian Handaxe.

- To Leicestershire Record Office for confirming my Father's work for the Wolsey Company.

- To Cecilia in particular, especially for her service in typing the text for publication.

- To friends who have helped, Bobbie, Anita, Joyce, Les, Janine, Leslie, Paul, Wayne, Jon, Joanna and the Lennox-Lambs.

- To the staff of St Richard's Press for their expertise and guidance.

# Introduction

If James I of Scotland had not executed his uncle Andrew Murdoch, the Duke of Albany, his sons Robert and Walter, Murdoch's father-in-law Duncan, the Earl of Lennox, on 25th May 1425 – and if John Knox the Reformer had not fallen for the charms of 'A young girl not above sixteen years of age' then the ancestry of my Mother would never have been written.

Who Goes Where is the record of two families – Broughton and Towler. The section 'Broughton Blood' records the family of Broughton from mid 1500's their work and characteristics. The Section 'Towler Treatise' records the ancestry from early times in Scotland. The Section 'Stella's Scenario' is the autobiography of Stella Rutter, nee Broughton, the younger daughter of the marriage between the two above families. As many of the people mentioned in the following pages are no longer with us, I hope their children and grandchildren will enjoy reading of their exploits and experiences.

My knowledge of my parents' antecedents, both of them being reticent concerning members of their respective families, was always sparse. Our ancestors had passed on verbal knowledge to all their descendants but no one had ever written it down. For instance, Father, grandfather and various uncles, aunts and great uncles had all told myself and my siblings the same story with the minimum of variation.

The discovery of distinguished and well known people acquainted with both families made my research fascinating and in fact easier. Crumbs of valuable information retained from early childhood and conversation with relatives combined with many years of checking facts has accumulated vast quantities of background material. The size of the task never daunted or deterred me. I felt like an athlete who gathers his second wind and goes racing on to reach the finishing line. With what glee I leapt from one fact to another to prove their acquaintance. With each visit to a family member, each book read, each journey, each telephone call I was a little nearer to discovering what I wanted to know. Rarely have I come away from my hours of research without finding some titbit or name which has added to my data.

My interest in family history was triggered by the birth of my first child. I realised that on my demise there would be no record of Father's reputation as a Modeller and Sculptor, Mother's talent for embroidery design and organising skills. Also my own work at Supermarine on the Spitfire and other Security incidents. Difficult as it is to write one's own memoirs, I felt driven to complete them.

# BROUGHTON BLOOD

# Words

by

Paddy Anne Wilson

The music of words is a wonderful thing.
A song to be sung by both peasant and king.
Keys to the mind which are turned by a pen
And hatched by a writer as eggs by a hen.
For ideas and stories by men long since dead
Lie treasures just waiting a chance to be read.

# How it all Began

It all started one Sunday lunchtime in August 1934. My brother, home from his first term at a London College, was expounding to our parents his activities during his free time from classes. Being nine years old and brought up to be seen and not heard in adult company, I was jolted out of this mode of behaviour by the sudden announcement that he was speaking of an unknown relative. His statement that he had found the tomb of John Broughton and his wife in Westminster Abbey was interesting  enough but he went on to say he was a 'Champion of England', a well known pugilist. Two other people by the name of Monk were buried above them in the same tomb! There was an immediate reaction to this statement. My Mother clattered the spoon in the vegetable tureen. A 'look' passed between Mother and Father. Before I could ask, 'What relation is he?' Mother stated, 'We do not talk about him' with such finality that no further comment was made by anyone.

Knowing so little about my parents' families and being of a naturally enquiring nature, I was determined to know more. Consequently I haunted the areas in the house where I might seize the opportunity to question my brother without my parents' knowledge. It was a couple of days before I managed to catch him on the upstairs landing. Keeping our voices to a whisper, I found out that John Broughton was known to be our Great-Great-Great-Grand uncle but no one had been able to find the exact date of his birth. 'What was a 'Champion of England? And what was a pugilist?' Bluntly I was told 'A boxer.', and that was all he would say. 'Who were the other people buried in the same tomb? Were they also family?' My brother was adamant –they were no relation. My curiosity was aroused. How was it possible for these people not to be family if they were buried in the same tomb?

 This question was stored in my mind to surface some fifty years later, when having retired I was in a position to make enquiries of my own. I thought it was possible for people other than relatives to be buried in any unoccupied spaces but believed this not to happen until two generations had passed when it could be safely assumed no members of that family were left. Even then I questioned the above assumption because filling up spaces could apply to parish churchyards in the 1800's and early 1900's, but did not think any tomb in Westminster Abbey would be so used. But I am wrong. On meeting with Dr. Julian Litten at the Victoria and Albert Museum, he drew my attention to a classic example:-

'A small vault beneath the Henry VII Chapel in Westminster Abbey contains Henry VII who died in 1509, his wife, Elizabeth of York who died in 1503 and James I who was buried between them in 1625'.

Just before I retired I visited my Father's sister Alice, who was living in Chard. Not having been able to see her for many years, I listened to her talking about her life with Uncle Frank Sidaway. She described a photograph which had been taken on them both at the time when they were living in a house, carved out of the Holy Austin Rock in Kinver. I took the opportunity to confirm the verbal knowledge which had been passed down the generations about the family and their friends. Alice had learned of various pieces of work which Father had done. He had spoken of them to his parents during visits after he left home as a young man. Some of these were commissioned during the latter part of World War II and before he obtained the position of Head of Modelling at The Southern College of Art, Portsmouth Centre. This stimulated me to try and record the sculpture, painting, modelling and teaching he had done throughout his life. This was a different side to the family man and I realised there was sufficient information to write a record of his achievements.

CAVE DWELLINGS      Kinver Edge

## Where to Start?

Where to start and who to start with? This was the problem. There were so many questions. Should I first write down what I remembered of episodes in my childhood? Consult other relatives for their memories of Father and Mother, or, just write off for copies of Birth, Marriage and Death Certificates? As the latter would involve some expense and money being very limited, I went for the first option.

Collecting all my photographs and indexing them into date order, I found several gaps which started my brain working. Pictures of holiday scenes were recalled but I could not instantly remember the year or place. Often on waking the next morning I exclaimed (not 'Eureka') but names of venues, people and remembrance of 'happenings' good and bad.

As times and places needed to be sorted into sequence there was no help but to make a time chart of my life. Gradually over a long period some semblance of order began to appear. Hours of reading in the local library brought to light snippets of facts, background information, times and places with which to make this book not only factually correct but interesting and informative to the reader. Now many years later all the bits of information gleaned from many sources have been put together and I found it necessary to make life charts of all the main characters to include details of their work, colleagues and meetings with my family members.

## Family Traits and Beliefs

It appears that family traits have been handed down through the generations. Their strong adherence to religious principles of right and wrong gave them the resilience to overcome and survive all troubles in a calm manner, reassuring their families whenever disaster befell them; John Broughton and Charles Henry Broughton being prime examples.

Over the years I have noticed these inherited traits on my visits to various members of our family. They also share many other traits in common, namely a generosity of spirit and natural courtesy on meeting with an innate desire to help those less fortunate with a warm and compassionate approach. There was an ability for reasoned thought and attention to detail involving lateral thinking, often in the field of invention with no thought of gain or personal benefit – a truly Christian precept.

Many members of the Broughton families appear to have certain talents in common – namely – artistic design and application, also an ability for precision drawing in architecture and engineering.

Physical characteristics have also spanned the years and are shown most markedly in the pictures of John Broughton, my father's great-great-grand uncle, father, myself and other members of the family, e.g. shape of skull, exceptional sturdiness of body, broad hands with short fingers, feet with high arches, facial contours, direct expressive eyes and vigorous health.

In comparison with John Broughton who had an exceptionally strong constitution and lived to a great age, it appears that I have also inherited these same traits.

Broughton men were innovative in that they invariably married intelligent women and allowed them the freedom to follow their own talents and pursuits to a degree which was unusual in their times. Broughton women were all hardworking and capable of organising commercial projects thereby ensuring their own daughters' individual prospects. As well as maintaining the household cupboards against all emergencies they also opened shops and kept accounts. Many of them became excellent needlewomen clothing their families with the minimum of expense. Obviously there were some who did not conform to this standard but they were in the minority.


## The Broughton Family

Whilst resident in London in the 1930's my brother completed his researches into the origin of our family. From his notes I see that he examined Parish Records of Burials at Arksey Church, Yorkshire, The Alumni Cantabrigienses and the Fawcett Index of Clergy. In the Yorkshire Archaeological Society's Journal he found an account by the Reverend Thomas Broughton, Bachelor of Art, Master of Art, born in 1639 at Bentley near Doncaster, in which he describes details of his father's life. His grandparents are not mentioned.

We begin with his father Thomas Broughton B.A., M.A, born circa 1597. In July 1614 he entered Christ's College, Cambridge as a Pensioner which means 'One who receives a payment as an undergraduate who pays for his own commons and other expenses.' In 1618 he qualified as a B.A. and in 1621 as a M.A.. In May 1622 he was ordained as a priest and became a clergyman at York. A year later he married Mary Wilbore and they had eight children, three of whom died in infancy. In 1627 he was a preacher at Bentley near Doncaster and by 1634 was the Rector of Chillesford, near Orford Ness in Suffolk. In 1642, presumably because he was a royalist and Suffolk was a Puritan stronghold, he was sequestered (banned from preaching) and in the following year was ejected from his living and imprisoned at Ipswich. During the next four years the family lived in a house at Orford in financial deprivation.

On his release in 1646 they returned to the area near Bentley, from which his family probably originated. Jeremiah Wilbore, his wife's brother, placed them in a house he owned in Arksey. There Thomas continued to teach until 'Oliver Cromwell prohibited all sequestered ministers from service or teaching in public schools or gentlemen's children in private houses.' Where he was buried is not stated.

Thomas Broughton B.A., M.A., born on 21st February 1628, son of Thomas above, was educated by his parents at Chillesford for seven years. He had one year at a school in Orford under Mr. Dodson, a fellow collegian of his father's at Christ's College, where he learnt Latin grammar. In 1642 at Arksey under Mr. Justice's last year of teaching, he began to learn Greek and continued his knowledge of Latin. Then he went to live with his uncle to 'assist him in his affairs of grounds, mercats and husbandry'. He continued his studies from such books as Mr. Marmaduke Cook, the schoolmaster of Doncaster School, used for his head scholars preparing for University. When he had time and during the evenings he began studying to acquire his skills in mathematics and read over all he had previously learned.

The political situation at that time meant there was little hope of him becoming a Scholar so his father and uncle considered apprenticing him to a druggist, but the fee required for the ten years was unacceptable. His uncle, being acquainted with the parents of a Scholar at Cambridge, was persuaded by them to put his nephew forward for entry and thereby using all endeavours he was entered as a Scholar at the house of Mr. Ralph Widdington, the President of Christ's College and University Orator.

At the age of 23 years which was old for an undergraduate, he was admitted as Sizar to Christ's College on 16th June 1652. A Sizar was 'an undergraduate admitted to the University of Cambridge who undertook menial tasks within his College and for which he received finance to enable him to study.' He obtained a B.A. in 1656 and a M.A in 1659. From the Fawcett Index of Clergy it is stated 'When he was Curate of Bishopwearmouth near Durham he kept the Parish registers with singular exactness'. On the first page of his second register, he wrote 'A commendation against all who shall deface or alter his said entree.'

On 23rd October 1660 in the year of the Stuart Restoration, he became the Vicar of Bishopwearmouth. Then on 8th January 1673 he was appointed Vicar of Bywell St. Peter, Northumberland, and continued in both appointments until his retirement in 1694. He married the daughter of McGregor of East Duddo near Ladykirk. They had seven children who were all baptised at Bishopwearmouth. After his wife's death he married for a second time Miss Elizabeth Pye on 2nd June 1690 and retired in 1694. He died, aged 66 years, on 15th September 1699 and was buried three days later.

John, his eldest son was baptised 14th August 1673 at Bishopwearmouth. He was admitted to Christ's College Cambridge as Sizar on 28th April 1690 at the age of sixteen. He obtained a B.A. in 1693 becoming a Fellow in 1694 and gained his M.A in 1697. In 1700 he is shown as Taxor, which means 'to check weights and measures and conduct of trade in victuals'. In the next year he became the Clerk (Clergyman) at St. Andrew's Church in Holborn London. He married Mary, nee Rutty, and they lived in Kirby Street, Holborn, where his sons Thomas and John were born. In 1712 was appointed as Vicar of Kingston on Thames. He achieved the status of Doctor of Divinity in 1716 and was Chaplin to the Duke of Marlborough until his death on 29th June 1720. He was buried on the 5th July as the Reverend Doctor Vicar!

Thomas, the son of the Reverend John of St. Andrew's Holborn above, was born on 5th July 1704 and baptised 25th July at St. Andrew's Holborn. He attended St. Andrews School and his father entered him at Eton as a King's Scholar in 1716. When his father died at an early age on 29th June 1720, Thomas was taken in charge by his uncle, believed to be his father's brother, who sent him to St. Paul's School for two years to complete his education. His predisposition was to follow the family tradition into the Ministry and on 1st April 1723 aged 18, he was admitted as Sizar at Gonville and Caius College, Cambridge. His tutor was Mr. Parham and he gained his B.A. in 1726. He is quoted as 34th Wrangler, which means 'His position was 34th in the students listed by the marks gained in the Mathematical Tripos.' In 1728 he was Curate of Offley in Huntingdonshire. He gained his M.A. in 1730 and in 1738 became a Lecturer at St. Ethelburga in London. The next year he was appointed Rector of Stibbington, Hunts. As Reader of the Temple Church in London, the Master of Temple Bishop Sherlock, proposed him as a Prebendary at Salisbury and in 1739 he became Vicar of Bedminster with the Chapel of St. Mary Redcliffe, Bristol.

He was an industrious writer on many kinds of compositions and is accredited with the translations of Don Quixote and Voltaire. In 1732 as 'a man of most Catholic tastes' he wrote 'Christianity Distinct From the Religions of Nature' and in 1742 'A Historical Dictionary of all Religions'. He also edited Dryden.

The Reverend Thomas Harris who lived in the precincts of Salisbury Cathedral, invited his friend George Frederick Handel to convalesce in Salisbury. Thomas, who was to marry Anne the daughter of Reverend Harris, was invited by Handel to write the Libretto for his Musical Drama, Hercules. Thomas drew the Broughton Owl emblem on the manuscript of this Libretto. In 1768 he wrote 'A Prospect of Futurity' and during these times he wrote a large number of Biographies in The Biographica Britannica. His wife died 21st September 1762 and he died on 21st December 1774.

Thomas Duer Broughton, born in 1778 was the eldest son of M.S. Broughton the Rector of Tiverton and of St. Peter's Bristol and the great-grandson of the Reverend Doctor Thomas Broughton of Bishopwearmouth. After attending Eton as a King's Scholar he went to India in 1795 as a Cadet and three years later experienced the siege of Seringapatum before becoming Commandant of the Cadet Corps. Then he was appointed as a Lieutenant in Madras. In December 1802 he became the Military Resident with the Mahrattas. On becoming a Major in 1814 he opened a bank account with Drummonds. He wrote a considerable number of works of literature, which are listed in The Gentleman's Magazine and amongst them is 'Letters From a Mahratta Camp'.

He married a daughter of John Chamier of Madras but they had no children. On returning to live in London he rose to the rank of Colonel. He was Honorary Secretary of the Royal Asiatic Society, an active Manager of the Mendicity Society and of the Mary-le-Bone Schools. In his retirement he travelled extensively until his death in Dorset Square on 16th November 1835.

Samuel Daniel Broughton was born on July 1787, the fourth son of M.S. Broughton the Rector of Tiverton and St. Peter's Bristol. After attending Bristol Grammar School he studied at St. George's Hospital and became the Assistant Surgeon of the Dorsetshire Militia. From the records of the Royal College of Surgeons I quote, 'He joined the 2nd Life Guards and in October 1812 he became the Assistant Surgeon with the temporary rank of Colonel in medical charge of the troops ordered abroad to the Peninsular War. The regiment was stationed in London from 1812 to 1837. Prior to 1745, when surgeons were given their own Company, they were regarded as inferior to Physicians and were considered to be no more than a barber'.

He was at the Battle of Waterloo under the command of the Duke of Wellington on the 18th June 1815. On the In 25th July 1821 he was promoted to the post of Chief Surgeon to the Regiment as a full Colonel. It is probable he bought his uniform and boots from Spurriers, later known as Henry Maxwell of Rupert Street, Dover Street and 181 Piccadilly. John Lobb of St. James's Street, Bootmakers, was not established at that time.

From 28th March 1817 having been made a Lieutenant, he visited Berry Bros & Co. of No.3 St James's Street, London every annual leave. Knowing this fact I called at No. 3 and met the present head of the firm, Simon Berry. He told me 'The Widow Bourne owned No 3 and was the founder of the present business. They sold tea, coffee, spices, groceries and wine. Her son-in-law, William Pickering, would have been the most likely person to have met John Broughton and one can assume he used the weighing scales for which the shop was noted. The building was remodelled in 1733 and the acquired a seat in 1765. The Berry family who owned a wine business in Exeter bought No.3 in 1790.

Samuel was in the habit of weighing himself on his annual leave on these scales which exist to the present day. On the first occasion he is recorded as weighing 11 stone 103/4 lbs in Boots. When wearing Boots he would have been in uniform with the exception of the 15th June 1826 where he is shown as wearing nankeens and shoes! The next year still in Boots but thereafter, to 1830, always in shoes which indicates his retirement from the Army.

During his life he was elected as a Fellow of the Royal Society and of the Geological Society and devoted his talents to writing many articles on physiological research. He gave valuable lectures on forensic medicine and toxicology jointly with Mr. Wilcox, barrister, a family member. His experiments on the effects of poison and his mode of ascertaining their presence after death proved illuminating.

In 1836 he had a fall injuring his leg which became diseased. On the 10th August 1837 the leg was amputated by the eminent surgeon, Robert Liston, but he died ten days later at the Regent's Park Barracks and was buried at Kensal Green Cemetery. The account of his funeral is graphically described in detail in The Gentleman's Magazine of 1837, Vol. VIII, page 432.

I JOYCE ISABEL STELLA RUTTER nee Broughton  younger
daughter of CHARLES HENRY BROUGHTON do hereby swear
that WILLIAM BROUGHTON my grandfather told me in
August 1937 that

> "JOHN BROUGHTON his father when a child had been
> told by his father JAMES BROUGHTON that WILLIAM
> BROUGHTON his father was the nephew of JOHN
> BROUGHTON the Champion Boxer of England and was
> nicknamed 'Jack the Dandy' and the reason was
> because he was always neat in his dress and wore
> clean white linen.  He had been to Eton could
> read and write and later became a Yeoman of the
> King's Body Guard."

In 1938 I asked my father about John Broughton the Boxer
and he gave me the same details as above which he said
had been told to him by his father and his uncle
Valentine when he was a boy.

In 1985 ALICE SIDAWAY my father's youngest sister told
me that

> "all my brothers and sisters my aunts and uncles
> had all known of the family connection with John
> Broughton the Boxer."

In 1996 my brother DOUGLAS ARTHUR BROUGHTON confirmed
to me that our father had given him the same information
when he was about twelve years old.

Recently LESLIE OLDNALL son of ETHEL OLDNALL my father's
sister said to me that he had heard about John Broughton
the Boxer from our grandfather when he was living with
his mother at 82 Exeter Road Smethwick Birmingham after
the death of our grandmother.

*Stella Rutter.*

*Sworn by Joyce Isabel Stella Rutter
at Bedford this 18th day of May 1999
before me*

*T. A. ...
Notary Public*

21

# John Broughton

My brother Eric, when lodging in London and studying to be an architect, researched our family tree back to Thomas Broughton, circa 1597. It appears all the eldest sons of each generation became Ministers of the Church. My great-great grandfather James had been told by his father William, that he was the grand-nephew of John Broughton, the famous pugilist, and brother of Thomas who was a Prebendary of Salisbury. They were the sons of John Broughton B.A., M.A., D.D. and Mary nee Rutty. This verbal knowledge has been passed down to all members of our family.

In the past there has been a premise about the date of John's birth for it has been assumed his brother Thomas was the elder. John's birth is recorded in the Records of Westminster Abbey as being 1703/4. He is buried in the West Cloister of the Abbey and it states he died on 7th January 1789 aged 86 years. This means he must have been born in the last two months of 1703 and before the 7th January 1704. His parents had at least twelve children and on checking my brother's research of all their birth and baptismal dates I have ascertained the two eldest daughters Elizabeth and Mary were named for their mother and grandmother. Therefore, it is logical the eldest son was named for his father.

His sister Mary, the second child, was not baptised until approximately five months after her birth and it is possible there was another child born between Mary and John, who did not survive. My brother did not find John's baptismal date but it is likely this took place at the grandparent's church before the family moved to Holborn in 1704 but Eton has his baptism recorded in 1706 at St. Andrew's!! All the following siblings, including a set of twins, were born at either 11 or 12 month intervals and were baptised at St. Andrew's Holborn. Taking into consideration all the above facts it is logical that John was born in 1703 and this makes sense of the anomaly.

At Eton John's classical education included Latin, Greek, Bible Catechism and Prayers, all learnt by heart. He would have had tuition in Algebra, Euclid and also Clerical Studies, Accounting and Estate Management! John and his brother were obliged to leave Eton at the end of term, their father's income ceasing when he died on 29th June 1720. Their mother having pre-deceased their father, all the children were taken into the care of their maternal grandmother Mary Young. It must have been a houseful but two years later, in November, she died and the children were put in the care of other relatives.

James Figg had arrived in London the year before and established himself as a master of all forms of self-defence and was responsible in giving pugilism respectability. He was a famous promoter and the owner of an Inn called 'The City of Oxford' later renamed the 'Two Blue Posts'. This was at the junction of the road to Tyburn, known today as Oxford Street, and the lane leading to the manor of Tottenheale, re-named Tottenham Court Road. A well-known villain, Jack Shepherd born in Bartholomew Close, was jailed nearby in Newgate Prison and due to be hanged on 29th October

1724 at Tyburn, now known as the site of Marble Arch. When the horse-drawn tumbrel climbed up the hill from Holborn it stopped at this corner to rest the horses. Here it has been recorded, James Figg brought out mugs of beer from his Inn for the prisoner and the guards.

John was physically very strong and agile. He was too young to have been in a position to use his fine educational background to obtain a clerical post and he would have been considered too old to be apprenticed. However, with no desire to enter the Church, similar to that of Field Marshal Bernard Law Montgomery, he took charge of his own life sublimating any ambition and accepted the offer by John Martin, Lighterman of London. On 31st May 1723 he appointed him to his brother, Thomas Martin, Waterman, for an apprenticeship of seven years to ply his craft from Hungerford Stairs on the River Thames. The Company of Watermen who carried

*George II*

people by boat across the river was formed in the early 1500's. Elizabeth I granted the Company its arms in 1585. In 1700 Lightermen, those who unloaded cargo and carried it on shore, joined them to become The Company of Watermen and Lightermen. John's younger brother William was apprenticed to the same Waterman.

John applied all his energy to his new occupation. His intelligent use of his strength and his courteous manner must have gained him a regular clientele. This could have been the root cause of resentment from other watermen resulting in a fisticuff fight which was observed by James Figg. He noticed John's physique and style and seeing his potential offered him the opportunity to improve his situation. The prospect of a place inside, out of the rain and cold, was too good to be missed.

In those days pugilism was one of the sports followed by the nobility. John's prowess soon came to the attention of William Augustus, Duke of Cumberland, the second son of George II. 'The rise of pugilism under aristocratic patronage provided scope for betting on a scale to suit all pockets and coincided with the Duke's young manhood. Horace Walpole said it attracted the Duke because it appealed to his gambling instinct which was born or bred in him.' Henry VII had created The Yeomen of the Guard in 1485 and they first appeared on duty at his coronation. The Duke, on 11th June 1727 on the occasion of his father's accession to the throne, secured John's entry in The King's Bodyguard of the Yeoman of the Guard.

In 1809 a fire broke out in St. James's Palace and the Yeomen were ordered to save the contents of the King's apartments. As a consequence some of the records of the

Yeomen were burnt but fortunately one page survived showing John as Bed Hanger and sufficient was left for Colonel Sir Reginald Hennell to write his book entitled 'The History of the King's Body Guard of the Yeomen of the Guard'. From his book I note the following:

'The name 'Yeomen' was a term in the 14th and 15th centuries to describe the prominence of the people who were neither upper class or labourers. These men were to be found in many of the personal attendants of the King, and in the armed personnel such as Archers, Cross Bowmen of previous centuries or the House Carls of long ago. For centuries the reigning Monarchs had collected men of courage, stature and good birth to be close to his person and these included duties of seeing to the tasks of the King's household. These were the personal and private guards of the Monarch and their duties died with the Sovereign's death.'

On the 7th February 1990 I visited St. James's Palace and met Sergeant Major Taylor, Officer of the Bodyguard who showed me the book by Colonel Sir Reginald Hennell in which was the page defining John as Bed Hanger to George II. On a second visit on 4th November 1998 I met Messenger Sergeant Major Dumon who allowed me to take a photograph of that page. He defined the duties of the Bed Hanger as being in charge of all camp equipment of the Sovereign. From the above mentioned book he also referred to the duties of the Bed Goer in making the Sovereign's bed, the placing of Sentries and Attendants from the Yeomen and ordering food and drinks.

When Henry VIII left the Tower for his coronation, he appointed twelve of his Yeomen as Warders. This body of men are now known as Yeomen Warders and have a separate entity and do not wear the crossbelt which distinguishes the Bodyguard.

George I after his accession having re-sworn the Guard and confirmed all their old privileges decided the Household Troops would take on all outside duties in guarding the palaces, whereas the Yeomen of the Bodyguard would perform all inside state duties.

George II, on his accession having re-sworn the Guard, decided that a selection should be made from amongst the Yeomen of a Special Guard to accompany him whenever he went to Holland.

'This Guard to be divided into three portions. Bed Hangers whose duties it was to look after the camp equipage. Bed Goers to look after the making of the King's bed and the remainder as actual Sentries and Attendants as 'Gardes of the King's Body'.'

In the Annual Register 'Recollections', a writer states, 'Duke William, as Broughton always called Cumberland, provided him with an annuity and assured for him his place among the Yeomen.' Shortly afterwards the Duke introduced John to his father who would have appreciated his general demeanour. When he came to the Court of St. James, his literacy and logistic capability was noticed, for he could not only read and write but could calculate and organise. As a result he was appointed to the position of Bed Hanger. In 1742 he is described as a Yeoman Waiter at a salary of £39.11s.3p and a further £10 per annum as Bed Hanger. In 1762 to his retirement in 1786 he served as an Usher.

John was popularly known as 'Jack The Dandy' for he had been brought up at

Eton to pay singular attention to his apparel and keep his linen clean and crisp. In his portrait this attention is apparent and his expressive eyes show that he probably he spoke little but always to the point, a family trait. For example, his comments to the Duke of Cumberland.

In his career he entered the Annual Race started by Thomas Doggett in 1715 on the 1st August 1730 and won the prestigious Doggett's Coat and Silver Badge. The Fishmongers' Company took over the organisation of this yearly event which was held on the first day of August from the time of the death of Thomas Doggett in 1721. An Advertisement placed in the Daily Advertiser by George Taylor, who had erected a Booth at Tottenham Court in November 22nd 1742 'Invited the professors of art to display their skill and the public to be present at the exhibition'. It was called 'The Great Booth'. In April 1741 an advertisement was published in the 'Flying Post' challenging all comers for title of 'Champion of England' and a contest was arranged with George Stevenson which is recorded in a painting by John Hamilton Mortimer. George was knocked out and because he died shortly afterwards John vowed he would never fight again but, two years later, he defeated George Taylor with whom he is reputed to have had a quarrel.

In 1723 Major John Hanway developed the site behind Oxford Street and created Petty Court, now Hanway Place, and John's Court, now John's Street. Prior to the middle of the eighteenth century parasols were a feminine accessory, but parish clergymen carried them to protect bare heads at funerals. These were bulky and cumbersome and usually made of leather. Another person of the name of Jonas Hanway, a traveller and philanthropist, had an ebony handled silk-covered, satin lined French parasol to protect his clothes from an afternoon deluge. It was nicknamed a 'Hanway'. Several decades passed before men followed his example, because carrying a brolly told the world you couldn't afford a carriage!

As James Figg had retired, John, having become a person of note and acquired some finance, set up his own Gymnasium at the far end of the inn yard behind the City of Oxford on the land which edged the marsh outside the boundary of the Parish of St. Pancras by the lane to Tottenheale. The Boundary posts defining the parish are still in place today along Hanway Street. Between the parish boundary and the edge of the marsh a terrace of small houses had been built. Two of these are still standing today with a small yard opening at the rear on to the lane called Petty Court.

On my visit on 7th September 2000 I consulted Colin Henderson, Head Coachman of The Mews, Buckingham Palace, and he gave his opinion as follows:

'The Duke of Cumberland would have driven up from St. James's Palace in his gig with his Tiger standing on a wooden platform set on the rear stanchions of the carriage framework.'

I assume he would have taken this route to avoid the crowds in Hanway Street for he could drive along Petty Court cross John's Court and go directly into the courtyard before the entrance of John's Gymnasium.

Some years ago, before the buildings were demolished I was allowed to view the upper gallery of this building which he had built as his Gymnasium. The double doors of six foot wide birds-eye maple led into the ground floor and the Prince and Noble Gentlemen would have ascended to the first floor to observe the bouts in the ring. Fortunately I was to be able to climb the stairs and enter the top floor where I found the original posts which were at six foot intervals supporting the galleries. These posts were fairly slender so it is possible the supporting pillars on the other floors were subsequently larger in proportion to support the floors above. It is logical to assume the ground floor pillars took the total weight of all the floors. The space which was centralised as the boxing ring had in the early 1990s been floored over when the building had changed from galleries to offices. The latrines were at the western edge of the building and drained directly into the marsh. The north wall had no windows and all the light came from the windows on the south side facing the courtyard.

When the building was demolished in 1998, the whole site from John's Street to the Tottenham Court Road was prepared for the present modern building of Sainsbury's. The north wall clearly showed the proportions of the pillars and floors of the building from the roof to the ground floor which I photographed.

It is not too surprising that Handel, in teaching the two princesses, met John in St. James's Palace and was probably introduced to his brother Thomas. When Handel was recovering from an illness he went to stay with the Harris family in Salisbury Precinct and met Thomas because he was courting the daughter. He was writing the Oratorio of Hercules and asked Thomas to write the Libretto which Handel took back to London on his recovery. It has been noted that Thomas had drawn the family emblem of an owl on the original Libretto.

A recorded entry states, on 20th September 1742 that:

'The eight Yeoman ordered to attend His Majesty abroad are armed with eight carbines and eight cartouche boxes and may appoint other Yeomen or other persons to do that duty whilst abroad with his Majesty.'

Before the Battle of Dettingen Cumberland took John to visit Berlin where he pointed out the Prussian Royal Guards and asked him 'How would he fancy one of those fellows for a set-to.' To which Broughton replied, 'He would take on the whole regiment if he could be provided with breakfast after every second bout!'

On Wednesday 27th April 1743 George II, acting as Elector of Hanover, and the Duke of Cumberland embarked at Gravesend for Holland with their entourage en route to Dettingen in Bavaria. Baron Jeffrey Amherst was a Cornet in Ligonier's Regiment and he served General Jean-Louis Ligonier who was a personal Staff Officer to George II and a close friend of The Duke of Cumberland.

'A combined British and Hanoverian army under Lord Stair, animated by the presence of George II was practically surrounded by the French and the King and his staff were in grave danger of attack by French cavalry and would have undoubtedly have been captured but for the timely rescue by a detachment of the 22nd Foot now the Cheshire Regiment. In recognition of this service the King presented the commander of the detachment with a sprig of oak leaves which he desired should be worn by the Regiment as a emblem every 12th of September. The Duke of Cumberland was wounded in the calf of his leg and this battle was the last at which an English Sovereign was present.'

After their return on Tuesday 15th November 1743, John introduced gloves called 'mufflers' of horse hair for sparring purposes to protect his pupils from the inconveniency of black eyes, broken jaws and bloody noses. Tony Gee in his book 'Up to Scratch' quotes this information and he has given a comprehensive account of John Broughton's career in the Oxford Dictionary of National Biography. He is remembered as the Father of Boxing who set out the rules in the Code Of Boxing on 11th April 1743 which were subsequently re-written after a hundred years by the Marquis of Queensbury. Sir Henry Cooper in his book 'Boxing' makes the comment 'I know whom to thank for the good looks I have today.'

Henry Hoare, the banker, probably met both John Michael Rysbrack and Louis Francois Roubillac in Slaughter's Coffee House in St. Martin's Lane which was the venue of Artists and Sculptors. Henry Hoare commissioned Rysbrack to sculpt a statue of Hercules to be placed in the Temple at Stourhead. Rysbrack chose John Broughton to pose for this statue and he used his hands, arms and shoulders for the statue. Several other boxers were models for the rest of the statue and these are listed in the George Vertue Papers. It took Rysbrack five years to complete the statue. George Vertue was a contemporary of Horace Walpole and Sir Joshua Reynolds.

In 1747 John placed an advertisement in the Daily Advertiser. He had opened his own Academy behind the Haymarket Theatre where it is likely he owned the house

beside the alleyway into the courtyard. The present site of Hobhouse Court has a opening on to Whitcomb Street. It would have been convenient for Noblemen in those days to have left their carriages in this street.

The Duke of Cumberland lost a bet of 10,000 guineas when John fought Jack Slack in 1750 and was beaten. From that time his friendship with John ceased.

On 21st January 1766 John married Elizabeth Willmott and at the same time took over the responsibility of bringing up his great niece Catherine, who was just four years old. They lived at Walcot Place, Southwark where Elizabeth died in December 1784. Catherine married Roger Monk who had been appointed Exon on 31st May 1805 to the Yeoman of the Bodyguard of the Sovereign.

John died at Walcot Place on 8th January 1789 aged 86 years. His coffin was first taken into Lambeth Church where it was carried on the shoulders of his boxing colleagues, namely Richard Humphries, Daniel Mendoza, Benjamin Brain, Jem Ward, Ryan and Tom Johnstone, all noted pugilists. The funeral was held there and a tablet with an epitaph in Latin was erected on the Church wall and was still there in the 1930's. Two days afterwards his coffin was taken from there to lie beside his wife in the Tomb in the West Cloister of Westminster Abbey. Roger Monk was interred in the same tomb and Catherine joined them on her demise in 24th October 1832 aged 70 years. This tomb was 8 feet in depth, and 5 feet 6 inches from the underside of the stone. It would have been brick lined with iron bars separating the later coffins, all buried with feet facing east, which left space for two more coffins!

Dean A.P.Stanley of Westminster Abbey, refused to have 'Champion of England' inscribed on John's tombstone. 'His daughter told Mr. Poole, who was Master Mason of the Abbey, that the empty line on Jack's gravestone should have read 'Champion of England' but the Dean objected.' This space was filled in 1989 with the words 'Prize Fighter of England' by the kind offices of the Reverend Ben Elliott. In recent years, due to its condition, the tablet on the wall of the cloister was removed for safety. Perhaps in the future I might be able to reinstate it?

As I talked with my Grandfather and other members of the family whom I could contact, I discovered verbal information had been passed down the generations but no one had actually written it down. This I am now trying to redress. John was my great great great granduncle!

In consultation with my second cousin and armed with copies of my brother's progress into the family tree with visits to known graves in Yorkshire I started with a visit to Westminster Abbey Library where I was given a print of John's portrait probably from the 1760's. They gave me details of his burial, his wife and those of Catherine and Roger Monk. This allowed me to formulate an Affidavit as to the verbal veracity of my forbears.

A portrait of John Broughton as a young man can be compared with the photograph of my father at roughly the same age and this shows a family likeness. Even more incredible is the comparison between the portrait of John held in Westminster Abbey Library records and a photograph of myself, both of mature years, not only in the shape of skull but in the physical stature and strength which has been passed down in the Broughton family. From these facts there is no question in my mind that the statements made by members of the Broughton family in my Affidavit, are irrefutable.

*John Broughton*

## The Worshipful Company of Tallow Chandlers – Roger Monk

From information received from the Worshipful Company of Tallow Chandlers I quote: 'Henry VI gave a Grant Of Arms to The Worshipful Company of Tallow Chandlers in 1456. The Guild dates from the 1200's, being incorporated by Charter on the 8th March 1462. The Old Hall was purchased in 1476. It was destroyed in the Great Fire Of London and the present Hall dates from 1672.' As wax candles were supplied to Churches from another Guild, the Tallow Chandlers dealt in tallow candles, vinegar, salt, sauces and oils.

John Broughton was a Yeoman of the King's Bodyguard and a Bed Hanger. He took Catherine, his great niece, to live with him in Walcot Place, Lambeth. When Roger Monk bought his commission to the Yeoman of the King's Bodyguard to George III at a sum in excess of the usual £3,500 he became a friend of John. Catherine was five years younger than Roger but soon they were married and had a long life together. On 24th June 1861 Queen Victoria cancelled the purchase of commissions to the Bodyguard of the Sovereign. Since that time the Yeomen have been chosen from retired Army personnel.

Roger Monk joined the Company on 2nd November 1784 as a Freeman when he was described as a 'weaver' of 10 Bowling Street, Westminster. On 12th July 1798 he became a Liveryman and in July 1826 he became the Master Tallow Chandler.

In the Guild of the Tallow Chandlers and during his life in St. James's Palace he progressed to the position of Exon. This title is derived from the French, 'Exonerer' and is a position enabling the officer to be exempt from his regiment in order to attend the Sovereign.

He had his portrait painted in his uniform and donated this full length picture to the Company. He also gave them a large painting of the marriage of Henry VII and Princess Elizabeth, the daughter of Edward IV by Mather Brown and full length portraits of Charles II by Sir Godfrey Kneller and another of Mary of Modena painted by John Riley. These all hang in the Hall of the Guild to this day. In addition he gave a considerable amount of money to the Company for the provision of pensions. Since his death Roger Monk is honoured for his service to the Company by the holding of a Dinner in the Hall every two years.

On my visit to the Tallow Chandlers I very much appreciated being allowed to take photographs and confirm the above family connection.


## Charles Henry Broughton – His Life

William, a railway coach builder, and Mary Jane nee Gibbs, were the parents of six children. They lived at 30 Cambridge Road, Smethwick, Birmingham, and later moved into No 99. The eldest child Daisy was an epileptic and spent a good deal of her life in an institution. Charles Henry was the eldest son born on the 31st December 1878 at his grandparents, Henry and Mary Gibbs's house of 22 Harrington Street, Alvaston, near Shardlow, Birmingham. Valentine Edgar was the second son, who had a very quiet voice and a most genial expressive face. Then came Ethel Maud, followed by Arthur Harold and lastly Alice Mabel.

In the time of the late 1800's these children were born in an age when it was customary for the eldest son to assume the responsibility for the welfare of his siblings throughout his life and to support his parents until their death. This was considered the natural order of things and no one questioned it, particularly if he acquired a sound financial position and was therefore able to help. There were three brothers and three sisters so each brother took a sister as his special charge as they grew to manhood. In later years, after the death of Daisy, my Father shared the help to Ethel and her family. Arthur was the youngest son. He possessed great intelligence and was a profound thinker. Some thought he was an eccentric but he followed the tradition and assisted his youngest sister Alice who was closest to him in age.

This appears to suggest that the spouses of the sisters were not able to support their families; not necessarily so. In the period before World War I men were the breadwinners and those who became more wealthy than their siblings were expected to provide luxuries and sometimes basic assistance with good grace. This attitude certainly appeared to be the norm in the background of their religious upbringing. In the years between the two World Wars my Father and his brothers were in sound financial situations and gave of their time, money and help in every way to their sisters.

William's parents lived at Kinver and all the family would have spent holidays there. Charles was entered at fifteen years to the West Bromwich School Art as a student where Joseph Pearce was the Headmaster. Charles was well acquainted with the Art Nouveau world being taught by Edward Burne-Jones and probably met with William Morris at Kelmscott House near Kinver. In the following year he entered a competition and won a prize for his designs of Gas Brackets. He was probably influenced by an article on Arthur Heygate Mackmurdo in the first issue of The Studio published in 1893, the cover designed by Charles Francis Annesley Voysey. The prize was presented by Fred Ryland, Chairman of the West Bromwich Municipal Instruction Committee. It was a book entitled 'Nature in Ornament' by Lewis F. Day, published by B.T. Batsford at a cost of 10 shillings and sixpence. It was the 2nd Edition which contained the three, 'Text Books of Ornamental Design', previously printed separately. A truly handsome and well illustrated book, beautifully bound in green leather with gilded decoration and endpapers of the repeated B.T.B. Initials.

Edward Burne-Jones had been a schoolboy in Birmingham and in his early years had trained as an architect before developing his interest in art. In later years he became acquainted with Fred Ryland. Through their friendship he introduced William Morris to the West Bromwich School of Art where Father was one of his students. Being also a friend of Charles F.A. Voysey, it can be assumed it was he who with Fred Ryland introduced Father to Mr. Voysey. At that time he was building his own house as well as being committed to other work and required a trainee in his office.

Charles left home and went to London and never returned to live in Birmingham. It is believed he lodged with Mr. Ford Madox Brown in his house, the Grange in Fulham, where he took students as lodgers. Father told me he had qualified as an architect but had never taken it up. As he would have assisted Mr. Voysey in his design work it is thought it was he who had noted Father's artistic ability and persuaded him to take up a Landseer scholarship to the Royal School of Art, Kensington Gore. He entered this school at the same time as George Kruger and they became close friends.

At the Victoria Street School of Jewellers and Silversmiths as part of the Municipal School curriculum he made a silver ribbon filigree pendant with a central green stone which he gave to Mother. He also painted a portrait in oils of an 'Italian Workman' which was exhibited. I recall seeing this picture which he gave to my younger brother but I do not know where it is now. He also received several framed pencil portraits by Father. My elder brother was given watercolours painted by Mother on her honeymoon and Father's original drawings of commissions. It is known he made a plaster bust of Lloyd George which stood on his mother's sideboard for many years and if a bronze was commissioned its whereabouts is unknown.

He married Isabel Nora Towler and they started their life in a house close to the grandparents and they had three children. When in 1916, conscription came into force he registered as a Conscientious Objector and had to leave his teaching post. He was sent as a labourer to the Burley Flour Mill but very soon was transferred into the office as a clerk. Shortly afterwards there was a fire and the mill was burnt down. Mr. James Bruce, President of Leeds Chamber of Commerce, a friend of Nora's family, took him on at his leather factory, Joppa at Beeston until the end of the War.

In May 1919 Father re-applied for the post of Head of Modelling at Leeds School of Art at £250 per annum. In Leeds Library records of meetings concerning his position state the fact although the staff, students and many others wished him to return there were two Councillors who violently objected and eventually Father was advised to seek employment elsewhere. So Leeds lost his expertise.

Father applied and secured the post of Head of Modelling at the Portsmouth Municipal School of Art. The family moved south to Thorneycroft, 4th Avenue, Denvilles, Havant where I was born. At Portsmouth he rapidly became established and a considerable number of students from the north of England and elsewhere  came to Portsmouth specifically because he was there. Later the title amalgamated three colleges to become The Southern College of Art, the other two being Southampton and Bournemouth. Many of his students became famous in their field. Amongst them were Humphrey Paget who was responsible for the design of the George V penny and Victor Voysey, the portrait painter. A competition to name a new town in Kent was announced in the newspapers and Father sent in the name of Peacehaven as did many others.

In 1932 Father was promoted to Acting Vice Principal. When Mr. Thomas T. Nelson, the Principal retired in 1938 Father was offered the post but he declined. Nearing retirement he did not wish to become involved in all the administration details to the detrimentof his teaching and he continued part-time until 1946. Mr. E. E. Pullee became the Principal and after the War he left for the Leeds College of Art!

Like his forbears he was a modest and upright man with a brilliant brain and whatever he undertook to do was done to the upmost of his capability. Indeed he was 'Capability Broughton' from laying concrete, erecting a building, painting, sculpture, pottery or just plain ' Digging for Victory'. He had an underlying sense of fun which often showed on Saturdays or on holiday.

He loved teaching and greatly enjoyed seeing his pupils tackle and achieve the success of a problem, and this has also been my enjoyment in life. If one failed to succeed in some project or he thought we had not worked hard enough, his demeanour and expressive 'Hrmph' was sufficient condemnation. His 'very good' was considered to be quite an accolade whereas 'excellent' was heard on only two occasions during my lifetime. He was punctiliously abstemious almost to the point of perfection, indeed he was often heard to state 'It is better to leave the table having had sufficient than to leave it feeling too full.' Because of his attitude of moderation he appeared to be a mild man, but there was a streak of obstinacy in certain matters. One had to be quite firm if one's own wishes were to be paramount. On the other hand provided one had a reasonable argument which could not be faulted, then he would relinquish his objection immediately and without rancour.

On retirement my parents moved to a bungalow in Godalming and after Mother's death Father moved to London where he died on 21st March 1972 aged 93 years.

## Father's Commisioned Work

Soon after becoming a Master of Art and his appointment as Head of the Modelling Department in the Leeds School of Art he undertook many commissions. He became well known for his talent in modelling and designing Bas Relief Plasterwork and Memorial Tablets. Some of the most interesting were on his work for the Wolsey Company, a memorial in Selby Abbey and a Bas Relief of the famous horse Godolphin Arabian. He also modelled war memorials for Kirkstall Wesleyan Church and a soldier of The Royal Warwickshire Regiment. These two memorials have not been located.

One of my earliest memories is of Father showing me the Lion depicted on a Tate and Lyle golden syrup tin and his comment regarding his initials hidden between the feet and tail. There is a previous drawing of the trade mark shown in 'The Tate and Lyle Story'. It is possible he drew this design for them when the two men merged in 1921. The death mask of a Mayor and Councillor of Portsmouth was observed in the making by myself and was of a much later date.

After joining the Portsmouth Municipal School of Art he was asked to design a large Bas Relief plaque of many children. This was erected above the doorway to the Teacher's Training College in Milton Road, which was opened in 1931 by the Lord Mayor. One day driving along with Father in our car he suddenly stopped. He drew my attention to this lintel and I saw the Bas Relief plaque. In recent years this entrance was closed andturned into a room. The plaque seems to have been removed, perhaps destroyed or put into store? Enquiries have not brought it to light.

# Cardinal Wolsey

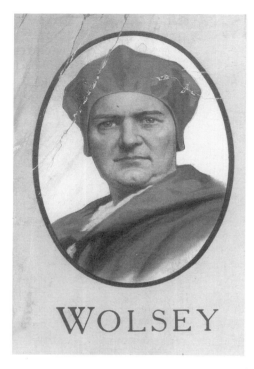

WOLSEY

One Sunday just before luncheon I noticed two pictures of Cardinal Thomas Wolsey on a Compliment Slip/Address Label and a Trade Card on Father's desk. Seeing my interest he questioned me as to what was the difference between them. Looking at them carefully I saw on the paper slip the Cardinal's cap did not cover his ears. This I knew was incorrect and the eyes were brown whereas those on the card were blue. Father then told me in 1926 he had been commissioned to paint the Cardinal's picture again because the Wolsey Company felt the previous artist's picture, possibly by Septimus E. Scott, was not authentic. Father's version continued to be in use until 1940. The originals of these are stored in the Leicestershire Archives.

One Saturday, in the autumn of 1939, Father came home from a visit to Portsmouth in a very excitable mood. He had gone to buy some underwear from J. Baker & Company Limited in Commercial Road near to McIlroys. Whilst waiting to be served he walked to the rear of the shop and to his surprise he thought he recognised the modelling of the hands on a 4ft statue of Cardinal Wolsey. This was in plaster and painted red. On examining the plinth he saw his own initials!! He had quite forgotten his work on this promotional statue commissioned by the Wolsey Company for their 180th anniversary in 1921.

The next week Mother and I went to see this statue for ourselves and a week later Portsmouth was heavily bombed and many properties in Commercial Road were extensively damaged. McIlroy's, Mr. Bakers shop and the Landport Drapery Bazaar were all completely demolished. The statue is presumed to have been destroyed in this raid. 'Smitten City, the Story of Portsmouth under Blitz' published by the Portsmouth Evening News shows photographs of this destruction. On researching for records of Father's work for the Wolsey Company I found there had been many changes of ownership and virtually all records had been lost. On visiting the Leicestershire Record

Office I established that no photograph showed Father's promotional statue in any of the Display Window Albums which had survived and concluded it was too tall to be displayed in any window.

Speaking of this statue to a friend some time ago, he exclaimed stating that when he was six years old he went on weekly shopping visits to Preston with his mother. Whilst waiting for her outside the Town Hall and Library he saw a large hoarding of a picture of Cardinal Wolsey in red robes above a shop in the Market Place.

The life-sized stone statue of Cardinal Wolsey which used to stand in the foyer of the Wolsey offices in King Street now stands in the Public Gardens in Leicester. A remodelled head is now in place after vandals had attacked and damaged the original and my friend was adamant this statue was NOT the one shown on the hoarding.

## Selby Abbey

Father designed a Memorial Tablet which hangs in Selby Abbey. This is in memory of Maurice Parkin. The specification drawings of the frame mouldings, full sized, dated September 1913, of rich wood backed in oak are in our family's possession. The inscription reads:

> To the Glory of God and in memory, of Maurice Parkin, Priest.
> During whose Vicariate this Abbey Church was restored after the fire of 1906 and rededicated by the Archbishop of York October 19th 1909
>
> Born March 15th 1857      At Rest February 7th 1912
>
> This Tablet is dedicated by his parishioners and friends.
> Rest eternal grant him O Lord & let perpetual light shine upon him
> (signed) C.H. Broughton

## Kirkstall Wesleyan Church

Another sketch by Father shows a bronze Memorial Tablet for Kirkstall Wesleyan Church. The Role of Honour lists the names of George Brown, Arthur Simpson, Harold Pearson and Henry Timpson and space for three more names. Underneath the drawing are the words, 'Sketch design for bronze tablet one-third full size = about 18 inches by 24'.

Does any reader know where the church or this tablet is today?

## Godolphin Arabian

Whilst helping Father with the plaster cast of Councillor F.J. Privett he informed me of the fact that many years before I was born, he had sculpted the head of a very famous horse on a similar sized plaque whose eye was prominent and distinctive. He mentioned its name but all I can recall is that it had three syllables and gave me the impression of being allied to the mystique of fairies, elves and medieval legend. Enquiring of my elder brother regarding this plaque he told me when he was about seven years old he watched Father working on it, but he did not know its name. All he could remember was, Father told him he was sculpting the horse for a 'Prince'. Assuming this to be a famous race horse I researched names but could not find any name of three syllables of that time.

On reading the book 'Thoroughbred Racing Stock and its Ancestors' by Lady Wentworth, I noticed on page 131 a print of the head of this horse which I had not seen anywhere else. It was exactly the same print which I remembered seeing on my Father's desk as a child with no indication of its name. He and members of our families had no interest in horses, so it convinced me that this was the one he sculpted. But who commissioned it? Could it have been Lady Wentworth perhaps on behalf of a Prince?

Having consulted with her grandson I am informed that on her demise her possessions were auctioned and although he has inherited what his parents acquired, this plaque has not yet appeared. Whoever obtained this bronze or plaster plaque is not known.

On a coach trip with a local society some time afterwards, visiting the property known as Wandlebury Ring, Gog Magog Hill, Babraham on the road to Cambridge, I found the house was demolished but the stable block still existed. Walking through the covered way of the stables I noted the grave of the famous Arab stallion named Godolphin. This was the name I felt Father had spoken of. But how to prove it?

Contacting the present owners of this property, The Cambridge Preservation Society, I was given the history of this horse and its various owners. Then discovering there was a place in Cornwall called Godolphin House I took the opportunity to call and met the owner, Mrs L.M.P.Schofield. She very kindly showed me her picture of the full portrait of the Godolphin Arabian by John Wooton and on close examination felt convinced I was on the right track.

## Lloyd George

My cousin told me a plaster bust of Lloyd George modelled by my Father stood on her mother's dresser throughout her young life. It was much treasured being created by her brother and is believed to have been modelled during a visit by Lloyd George to Birmingham in his first years of being Prime Minister. It is possible a bronze bust survives to this day amongst archives of a Mining Company or similar business corporation.

## The Royal Warwickshire Regiment

During the first World War Father drew up three designs for a Memorial Tablet for a soldier in The Royal Warwickshire Regiment who had died.

The first design showed the number 1951670 superimposed on a cross in the style of the Victorian period. The second design used the Regimental Emblem of an antelope within an elaborate wreathed frame which would have been expensive to make. The third design was again of an antelope but with a simple border – less expensive. This had the word 'SELECTED' written at the bottom of the drawing.

It has not been possible to discover the whereabouts of this Memorial. If any reader has knowledge of its existence I would be grateful for the information.

## Death Mask of Councillor F.J. Privett, J.P.

When I was nearly thirteen years old Father heard of the demise of Councillor F.J. Privett, the late Lord Mayor of Portsmouth, whom he had known very well. He received an urgent call to take the death mask at Crookley Park in Horndean before the coffin was transferred to his house in Portsmouth. Early on Wednesday Father drove to Horndean and on his return I helped to mix the Plaster of Paris to produce the reverse bas relief of the death mask. As the eyes had been closed he had the task of carving the plaster to open them. It was fascinating to watch the skill with which this was done.

On the day of the funeral, Thursday April 1st 1937, Mother asked if he was going to the funeral service at St Thomas's Cathedral in Portsmouth. He said his remembrance of the man he had known and admired was in his work on the memorial plaque, therefore his name is not included in the list of mourners in the newspaper.

When Portsmouth Guildhall was bombed on 10th June 1941 Father went to view the damage. On his return I heard him say to Mother 'The inside of the Guildhall is in ruins. There is nothing left. It's gone altogether.' Mother then made some enquiry and I heard his reply which was 'There are a few things in the Muniment Room which might have been saved, but until it cools down they cannot open the doors and I doubt very much if it was put there.' He was very disappointed to think all his time and effort had been lost, but he accepted this loss with his usual equanimity.

I remember meeting Councillor Privett with Father one day in the Guildhall and was impressed with his geniality. I feel sure he must have advised my parents and, in his role as Head of Education at the time of my traumatic experience, probably arranged my transference from Bedhampton Council School to Purbrook Park School. I recall my amazement at his likeness to the famous comedian Charlie Chaplin and exactly the same comment was made to me recently by his grandson.

## Arthur Harold Broughton    *A Tribute - by his son - D. John Broughton*

'Ejected from his living, thrown into Ipswich gaol by Oliver Cromwell, such was the fate in 1642 of the Reverend Thomas Broughton, BA. M.A. One cannot pretend that the life of A.H. Broughton was as eventful as that of his ancestor, nor as exciting as that of the pugilist John Broughton, 'Champion of England' buried in Westminster Abbey 1789. Father would care little for his antecedents, believing that one respected a person for his worth and not his parentage. Nevertheless he bore the same characteristics of learning and fortitude of the one, and determination and fearlessness of the other.'

I am indebted to my cousin for details of his father's life given in the above tribute.

Charles was 14 years old when his youngest brother Arthur was born on 26th October 1892. In his childhood he learnt to converse with his mother in French and German. He was highly intelligent, a studious and painstaking boy. In later life he learnt by self-effort, Old Testament Hebrew, New Testament Greek and Esperanto. Three of his uncles are reputed to have been inventors. One most likely having improved the original design of the safety pin but unable to obtain a Patent being employed in the trade. Another is known to have been instrumental in designing the countersunk screw but again, as he worked as an employee he was unable to secure a Patent. Lastly another uncle developed new ideas for children's toys.

Not being given the chance to go to Grammar school he left at 13 years and attended evening classes at Matthew Boulton College which became part of Birmingham University. He gained employment with C. E. Smith and Bateman, Chartered Accountants in Corporation Street. The principal of his firm sent him to examine a typewriter in a shop at Dale End in his lunchtime. On his return he reported it would not be difficult to learn to type. Consequently it was bought and Arthur became an expert typist. They were the first firm of Chartered Accountants to send out typed letters! During World War I a female was employed. She was instructed to pin her hair up, wear long sleeves and sit with her back to the other employees so as not to distract them. She proved to be unexpectedly bright and as good as any male.

His sister Alice worked at the Stuart's Crystal Glass Factory with her friend Cissie May Sutton whose job was etching glass. She invited Cissie to her brother's 21st birthday party, Cissie having celebrated hers the day before. Two years later Cissie and Arthur were married. They went to live in Wiggin Street where they had three children. The eldest boy, tragically died of pneumonia at the age of ten. Their second child was a girl and lastly another boy, the cousin referred to above. As the house in Wiggin Street suffered from bombing in 1940 Cissie and the children went to stay with friends in Wales.

The prime motivation of his life was in his religious beliefs; practising Christianity by being thrifty and exceedingly generous to others in need. In the street on one occasion he actually gave a man the coat off his back! He was a profound thinker, full of original ideas with an inventive mind; to some a fount of knowledge and wisdom, to others a reclusive eccentric. He became a member of the Christadelphian Sect and in this intellectual atmosphere gained extensive and comprehensive knowledge of the Scriptures. He and his wife were attracted to the growing Pentecostal Movement. In leaving one he found little welcome in the other. They realised he had not abandoned all his former beliefs.

He succeeded in combining the two and adding some refinements of his own thus devising a completely new theological system and gained followers from around the world. Many times he wrote leaflets on various topics having discovered a mis-translation of an original text. He would make a detailed analysis of the precise Greek or Hebrew terminology. Such was his enthusiasm his writings were sent around the world. Had he the status of degrees his ideas would have been claimed as worthy contributions to contemporary Christian thought. Instead, as an outsider, they could be dismissed as the product of an amateur theologian.

One day he climbed the hill to the church and sat in a pew to rest. A woman was busy arranging flowers and when she left she locked the doors. With dusk approaching and unable to get out of the church he was forced to summon help by pulling on the bell ropes. In response to the discordant tolling an angry Rector arrived with two very large dogs saying 'You could have been killed pulling those ropes.'

On his retirement they bought a bungalow in Rhoose which was near to their daughter's and her daughter's homes. Cissie did not wish to leave the bungalow for an eventide home. She died in August 1988 and Arthur went into hospital following a mild heart attack. His eyesight was always poor and he supplemented glasses with a magnifying glass until he was registered blind in his nineties. By then he had learned to both read and type Braille with enthusiasm. He then went into a Nursing Home where he remained alert remembering birthdays and family matters until he passed away in May 1991, aged 98 years.

# TOWLER
# TREATISE

# John Knox and the Stewart Line

I was seven years old when Mother bought the Stewart material from McIlroy's to make me a kilt. This was the first time I learned of the Stewart connection. It was another seven years before she revealed any further information.

Both brothers were leaving home and Mother was sorting photographs from her bureau drawer which she intended to give them. Standing at her side whilst she was doing this I saw, poking out from under the family photographs, a portrait print of John Knox! This had been painted by Adrian Vaensoun after his death and published in Beza's Icones in 1580. Of course I knew whom he was from history at school so I was very curious to know what his portrait was doing

*John Knox*

in what Mother considered to be our 'family drawer'. Pulling it forward I asked her 'What is this doing with our family photographs?' She gently pushed it back and did not reply. I drew it out again and repeated the question. Seeing I was not to be put off she whispered 'Well you see, he's family' and pushed it underneath again. I was astounded at her remark and begged for an explanation. Grudgingly she said 'My father traced our family tree prior to John Knox and that is why my name and yours is Isabel. It is a family name from a very long way back' and she would not say anything else.

In recent years, having done some considerable research I found the following in the Dictionary of National Biography now repeated in the Oxford edition.

'Knox now surprised both friends and foes by marrying for a second time, Margaret Stewart, daughter of Lord Ochiltree.' (Randolph to Cecil, January 1564) 'A very near kinswoman of the Duke's, a Lord's daughter, a young lass not above sixteen years of age. The Queen stormed wonderfully for the bride was of the blood and name. If Mary keeps promise' Randolph proceeded, 'he shall not long abide in Scotland. If I be not much deceived, there will be much ado before he leaves it.'

Grandfather Towler had obviously researched from John Knox to the marriage of Isabel Lennox in 1391 to Andrew Murdoch Stewart. He, in the continuance of the family name, named Mother Isabel at her birth. At my birth I was also given the name Isabel.

The National Biography states, 'of John Knox's three daughters two lines are noted as being extinct but the third line was likely to be still in existence' probably because Grandfather's papers had not been recorded and they were disposed of at the time of his early death.

When the Third Lord Avondale, son of Andrew Lord Avondale who died at Flodden in 1513, had a disagreement with his neighbours he decided to exchange with Sir James Hamilton of Finnart, the Barony of Avondale with the castle at Strathaven, for the Barony of Ochiltree and the castle in Ayrshire. Lord Andrew of Avondale became the first Lord Ochiltree. John Knox, his esteemed friend, was married in March 1564 to Margaret Stewart in Ochiltree Castle, Ayrshire.

During my researches I discovered Lord Ochiltree had supported John Knox on several of his attendances to Queen Mary. A curious fact was he had obtained a considerable loan of finance of £80 from John Knox which had not been repaid at the time of his death.

To my delight I discovered the site of the original Castle of Ochiltree! It is reported the castle had been struck by 'a thunderbolt from heaven'. It was then reconstructed into a house with secret passages and dungeons! For several centuries it passed through many different owners each of whom probably made alterations until this substantial house was eventually pulled down and a new house was built using the same foundations. The main walls of the present house, as well as the previous, appear to have been built on top of the outer north wall of the original castle. Odd stones from the castle have been used in various places. It is certainly on the same alignment as can be seen from the remains of the south east corner in situ, located in the grounds.

## Marriage of Isabel Nora Towler

Isabel Nora Towler was the eldest child of Arthur and Amy Mary Towler (nee Onions). On leaving school Nora attended classes at the Leeds of School of Art and after five years Charles Henry Broughton was appointed Head of Modelling. Their friendship soon became courtship and they became engaged. In those days a marriage was preceded by an engagement of between two to four years. This gave the couple and their respective families time to become better acquainted. During this time Nora's father moved the family from Hyde Park Road opposite Woodhouse Moor to the other side of Leeds. In Harehills he bought a detached house called 'Oak Bank' situated on a corner facing Avenue Crescent. Oak trees lined one side of the property and even now some of those trees are still there!

In this prestigious house Charles modelled a deep plaster frieze for both the drawing room and the morning room. The house having changed occupation several times from a private house to a hotel and thence to studio flats I was allowed to take photographs of his work.

Grandpapa died suddenly at the age of 62 years and with the cessation of income Grandmama was left with no alternative but to sell 'Oak Bank' and take a smaller house in Royal Park Avenue near their previous residence by Woodhouse Moor. Their sons had already left home and daughter Jessie lived most of the year in Berne in Switzerland teaching in a school near to Mont Blanc.

The chosen house was near enough to Lawnswood School for the youngest daughter to cycle there every day. It was at this juncture when it was decided to forward the marriage of Nora and Charles. This took place on 8th August 1908 at Queen Street Chapel in Leeds. Grandmama refused to be included in the wedding photographs because she was wearing black and was in deep mourning. Among their witnesses were Charles's brother Valentine, Charles's employer James Bruce, two friends of Nora and a relative of Nora's mother, Rupert Philip Dodgson. When I enquired as to who was the Best Man, Mother said it was George, Father's friend from London. This I believe to be George Kruger who was a student for four years at the same time as Father in the School of Art, Westminster Gore. They both qualified on 8th July 1904 as 'Master of Art'.

George took his wife's name on marriage and became George Kruger Gray and he was employed by The Royal Mint and his initials may be seen on coins of the realm. Mr. Graham Dyer, Librarian and Curator of The Royal Mint whom I met at the Royal Academy on 19th March 1996, very kindly gave me copies of articles which included photographs, on George Kruger Gray. Having traced Mrs. Mary Kruger Gray, his son's widow, we were able to meet and agreed that the similarity between the two photographs prove George was Father's Best Man. All George's documents are stored in her son's possession and perhaps in years to come correspondence between Father and George may come to light.

When in my early teens Mother was sorting family photographs she mentioned her mother's maiden name was Onions. She was a cousin of Rupert Philip Dodgson and Lewis Carroll was a cousin by marriage. No wonder with such an association of literary talent Mother aspired to write letters every day!!

Nora and Charles's first home was in Hilton Road but they soon moved to Hamilton View (the next road to 'Oak Bank'). At 5 years old my elder brother could walk the short distance to Cowper Street School. In the First World War when men were conscripted for service in the Forces Father registered as a Conscientious Objector and he had to leave his teaching post.

## Two Years at 'Nethersprings'

It was at this time they left Hamilton View and moved into a cottage on farmland off Scotland Lane near Horsforth. The family of Ingham were tenants of Dean Grange Farm, and as one family member had vacated the cottage when he went to War, they were very glad to have it occupied for the duration. Nethersprings cottage lay on the right hand side of the lane past the farmhouse. As the land sloped down from Scotland Lane to the valley below, it was possible to enter the cottage from the lane via the basement, or by steps up to the ground floor on the level of the garden. Another cottage flanked the upper slope and sheltered the garden and cottage from the south west winds.

Just above the cottages, a footpath led through three fields to the village of Horsforth. Both boys now went to Horsforth School and they took this path being the shortest route. I was surprised to find it still in existence and signposted with my Father's family emblem, an owl! Father had been conscripted to work for Harold Nichols in his flour mill at Kirkstall near the river and he would have also used this path to catch a train from Horsforth. As a child when I heard the name 'Joppa' mentioned in conversation between my parents, it intrigued me, so I was delighted to discover it was the name of this flour mill! Father first worked there as a labourer but the owner quickly recognised his literary skills and placed him in the office. One afternoon all the pupils at Horsforth School were taken across the road to the field above the bend in the River Aire From there they were able to have a grandstand view to see the Burley Mill on fire!

A friend, James Anderson Bruce, stepped in at this time and commandeered Father to be employed at his leather factory, Crow Nest Tannery, at Beeston. I visited this factory with Mother in 1937 and met Mr. Bruce who was not at all well. He instructed his Foreman to give us a tour of the works and I was most interested to see the whole process from the delivery of the cattle hides, through the 'baths' – horrible smell – to the final production of leather goods for sale. I was interested to meet him for he sent Mother a most handsome box of chocolates every Christmas from the time of her marriage to his demise just before World War II.

Mother, on her rare shopping trips would, I presume, push my sister in her pram and take the much longer walk via Scotland Lane. The farm was able to supply her with meat, potatoes and firewood. All other dry goods were bought in quantity and delivered. There was ample cool storage in the basement and bearing in mind the likelihood of being snowed-in Mother would stock up with supplies for several months ahead. The garden was large enough for Father to grow all their own vegetables and chickens supplied eggs. The only other item required was milk – the solution was goats! She tethered five goats above the Bramhope Railway Tunnel and every day would walk down the lane to milk them.

The lane went down towards the 'Bay Horse Bridge' over the railway line which disappeared into the Bramhope Tunnel on the left. The lane then climbed the other side of Moseley Beck Valley up to the village of Cookridge. Bramhope Tunnel was opened in 1848 and was over two miles long. This length was exceeded a year later when the Saddleworth tunnel was built. Some hundreds of navvies were employed to build this railway line and the tunnel and they lived along the valley in makeshift quarters.

Robert Ingham opened part of the farmhouse as a 'Beer House' and called it the 'Bay Horse'. He also promoted prize boxing fights on the land outside. This was a subtle move not only to increase income but to keep the farm and land free from vandalisation by the navvies.

'Nethersprings' had originally been built for Matthew and Hannah Ingham in the 1860s. As the supply of fresh water which came from the spring in the garden was vital for bleaching flax they established the 'Nethersprings Bleach Works' in the field on the other side of the lane. A photograph of that time shows the cottage and the flax hung along lines blowing in the wind.

Father tried to return to teach at the Leeds School of Art at the end of World War I. Former pupils – ex-soldiers – and some members of the Leeds Education Committee were in favour of his re-appointment but after five months he lost to a majority of the Committee. All his efforts were in vain and Father was advised to try elsewhere so they left Horsforth and went to live with the Grandparents in the family home at Kinver.

## 'The Burgesses' at Kinver, Birmingham

Traces of an ancient British Camp have been found along Kinver Edge in the soft Triassic sandstone. The Domesday Book names the Parish of Kinver as Chenevare. The church of St. Peters at Kinver is very old. Prior to the Dissolution it was serviced by monks from Tewksbury Abbey. They lived under the cliff on the site now called 'The Burgesses'. Two short tunnels were cut into the sandstone to keep food cool and for storage. In later years this gave rise to the rumour that access led up to the church. This is highly unlikely due to the height. At the Dissolution the monks left and it is logical, after a century had passed, 'The Burgesses of the Town' met in the building situated on this site, hence the name.

In 1908 our grandparents, William and Mary Jane Broughton bought the large Tudor-style house and grounds called 'The Burgesses' along the main road through the town of Kinver. The house was occupied by them and their six children. From my visit as a child of two and three-quarter years I remember the drawing room and dining room were on either side of the main door. The staircase rose on one side of the hall and opposite was the side door leading to the garden. The rear of the ground floor was taken up by an enormous kitchen and lots of store rooms. Above on two floors there were many bedrooms. In the rear of the garden and yard was a coach-house, stable, dairy and many outbuildings

Auntie Jessie, Mother's sister, would often accompany my parents on holiday visits and she would keep my brothers, aged five and three, out of mischief. One evening having put them to bed she overheard this conversation between them, which she wrote down as follows:

| Voice of three-year old: | 'I don't like Auntie Jessie.' |
| Five-year old replied: | *'Why? She's n-i-i-i-c-e!'* |
| | 'She not know what I |
| | say when I speak.' |

A pause – then came the five-year old's explanation:

*'Well, you see it's like this… If a lion came, and a tiger came, the lion not know what the tiger say. He's not the same family you see.'*
'Oh!'

There was silence until solemnly came the next thought:
*'Jesus not like you to say you not like Auntie Jessie.'*
'Oh!'

Then silence prevailed…

One night when they were sleeping in one of the attic rooms a bat flew down the chimney which gave them such a fright they never forgot it. In another of the attic rooms was a beautiful, large rocking horse. Auntie Jessie lifted me up for a ride. It was very high and the floor seemed a long way down. It was a great favourite with all the children. Auntie Jessie was instrumental in instilling in my elder brother a lifetime's interest in biology and astronomy. In his teens, he in turn passed this interest on to me in our Sunday walks on the hill behind Portsmouth.

My brothers on their way home from school one winter's day, after a heavy storm, noticed the tram terminus had become waterlogged. They watched passengers, charged at one penny a trip, being ferried across the flood in a horse and cart!

As Grandpapa reached retirement it was necessary to augment his income to support his extended family and the upkeep of the house. The Holy Austin Rock was a well known beauty spot to view the various formations of the worn sandstone rocks and was popular with day-trippers. It was decided to erect a wooden building in the garden as a 'Tea Room'. The coachhouse, stables and dairy were converted into kitchens and storerooms. Papa's eldest sister would get up at 5am to make sandwiches for eighty or more people who came in the charabancs from Birmingham and other industrial towns to visit 'The Edge'. A stall was set up against the front garden wall and lemonade, sweets and fruit were sold to passers-by. Then people began to come to Kinver for their holidays. Most of the large bedrooms were divided into two and let as Bed and Breakfast accommodation. All the family helped in these ventures. On our yearly visits Mama and I had our morning snack seated in the green-painted, wooden, latticed shelter which was against the wall dividing the garden and Tea Room from the back yard.

During the year 1918 Father undertook several commissions during his enforced free time whilst making attempts to secure another teaching post. On one of his trips to attend an interview for a position, Father took Mother and my sister to London. I believe it was probably there they met the portrait artist Charles Trevor Garland or it may have in when he was in Birmingham.

My grandparents celebrated their Golden Wedding on 28th June 1926. On that day all the Broughton family assembled in the garden for a group photograph. Young children had to sit on the ground in front of the group. Grandpapa and Grandmama were flanked on either side by their children and husbands and wives stood behind. I would not sit in the front, as the grass which had not been cut closely, poked my skin so Mama asked Papa to sit me on his knee.

As youngsters my brothers and their cousins often made forays along Kinver Edge to view the various rock formations. During one holiday coming home from camping out, they walked along the track by the church wall. One of them dropped a kit bag and it went tumbling down the cliff to land in the yard of 'The Burgesses'.

Some years later, on another visit I was taken in charge by my cousins. They took me into the back yard to show me the outside staircase which went up to the door on the first floor at the corner. The bedroom door of this room was locked separating it from the rest of the house. It was occupied by Uncle Arthur and was his sanctuary. Then we climbed the grassy bank to view the 'tunnels' in the cliff.

The historical Rock Houses which were carved into the sandstone cliffs at Holy Austin Rock are most interesting. In the early 1900s a photograph was published of my Aunt Alice and her husband, Frank Sidaway, in the doorway of their rock house. She described how they lived there and mentioned they had a fire in the living room! The distinctive chimney to this fire rises up the cliff face outside. On the opposite side of the doorway is a small recess where clothes were washed and it also had small fire.

The 'The Burgesses' was demolished in the 1950s and a group of old people's dwellings and a car park were erected on this site which is still named 'The Burgesses'. On a recent visit to Kinver I discovered behind the new buildings the large paving slabs of the original back yard in situ and in the cliff one of the tunnels can still be seen.


## To Denvilles, near Havant

In September 1920 Father was appointed as Assistant Master in Modelling, Sculpture and Allied Crafts to the Portsmouth Municipal School of Art where Thomas T. Nelson was the Principal. The family moved from Kinver to a house called 'Thorneycroft' in 4th Avenue, Denvilles, near Havant. From there Father would be able to catch a train to Portsmouth and my younger brother and sister could attend Havant Primary School. After three years I was born and Nanny joined our household.

My elder brother entered Churchers' College, Petersfield as a weekly boarder to further his education, only to be withdrawn some years later, in circumstances described in Father's letter as follows.


6th May 1925

Dear Sir,

Your note on my son's (Douglas) report for the Spring Term together with your remarks in a letter, caused me to think seriously of removing him from Churchers' College. But last night I was more amazed to learn quite casually, from an outside source, your attitude to the boy on account of his absence on the 'Sports Day' especially as a letter was sent in explanation. How could a boy be happy under such treatment?

To crush a boy of a studious nature because he is not so keen on sports as you would wish is, in my opinion, very serious. But when boys are encouraged to 'nag' him because he did not attend the sports, and you say he is to be punished by not being allowed to sit for the General School Exam, surely it is time he was removed to more congenial surroundings, where sport is not the main object of training. So please note he has now ceased to be a scholar of Churchers'.

Yours truly,

Chas. H. Broughton

From then he joined his brother and sister at Purbrook Park County High School.

On Sundays the family could attend the Congregational Church in Havant where they made life-long friends with Mr. and Mrs. T. Johnson who lived at 'Tanjong' in 1st Avenue, Denvilles. The Nichols family were also close friends. Their son, Clifford, was a school friend of my elder brother and his sister Gertrude went to Havant School with my sister.

At our Christmas parties I remember Gertrude Nichols was like an older sister. I understood I was to be her bridesmaid when she married as she had no other young girl in her family. When she married in a Registry Office I was very disappointed. A blessing on their marriage was held at St. Thomas's Church in Bedhampton and Mother and I went, although we were not invited. I was really hurt because she did not say goodbye and I never saw or heard from her again.

# STELLA'S SCENARIO

# My Early Years

My parents moved from Yorkshire to Hampshire. Father, having been appointed to the Portsmouth School of Art, bought a house named 'Thorneycroft' in Fourth Avenue, Denvilles, Havant, where I was born on the 15th September 1923 at 9.15am. A photograph taken by Papa of me in Nurse's arms at a week old shows lots of black hair and a screwed up expression, probably resenting being taken out into the sunshine. Shortly afterwards I was christened at the Congregational Church in Havant as Joyce Isabel Stella, the fourth child of Charles Henry and Isabel Nora Broughton. In my early years I answered to the name of Joyce but changed to being called Stella on entering Purbrook Park County High School.

My birthday of 15th September is memorable and significant because it was the date of the Battle of Britain. From early years it had some influence on my life, for instance, my interest in flight (Spitfire) and involvement in the Forces. Also born that year were personalities who became famous in the field of theatre and film, namely Sir Richard Attenborough, Charlton Heston and Marcel Marceau. Is it any wonder I have had a great interest in drama? On the same date the Nazi Party held it's first rally in Munich eventually bringing Adolf Hitler into power throughout the next two decades. Lenin lost his leadership of the Russian people when he had a stroke. The first public showing of a 'sound on film' picture took place in New York so that by the time I was allowed to visit the cinema in my teens all films had sound.

For my first three years Mama was a remote person as I was put in charge of Nanny who regulated my life. Of our sojourn at 'Thorneycroft' I have the memory of Nanny putting me into my pram and sitting me upright. She fastened a harness about me and there was Papa taking a photograph! For the first time I saw tree trunks, instead of watching leaves in the tree tops swaying in the breeze. One morning after breakfast Nanny left me at the table. Mama came in, pulled my high chair back against the wall and sat down beside me. Papa was setting up his camera in the doorway and I was surprised to hear him say 'Nora, tap your fingers on the tray so Joyce looks down.' Of course she did so and he took the photograph. On showing this to my elder brother recently he said 'Oh that was at Thorneycroft and you were just eleven months old!'

On Wednesday, Nanny's half day, after lunch she would dress me in my second best dress and take me down to the Dining Room. Placing me on the rug in front of the fire with my doll, bid me play quietly until Mama had finished writing letters at her desk in the alcove. Then Mama took me out to walk to the post box. On our return we had tea and then she put me to bed.

It was at this time Mama took me with her to visit Grandmama Towler who was living with Mama's sister Jessie. I remember it clearly because Jessie was to look after me whilst Grandmama and Mama had afternoon tea served in the garden. To keep me amused Jessie took me to another lawn to play with a ball. Between the two lawns a man was taking photographs of them so I trotted over to Mama to gain her attention but Grandmama sternly ordered Jessie to take me away. Then I noticed why Mama had ignored me, because she was crying! When I was older I could understand it was probably because she was telling Grandmama my sister was epileptic.

In February 1925 we moved to a house on the south side of Bedhampton Hill as a temporary measure. One Monday morning I had been put into my box swing in the garden. From there I could watch our maid washing clothes and Mama cooking at the stove. Suddenly through the hedge came a barking bundle of bristling fury. It was a Scotty dog and he thought it a great game to jump up at my swing. I screamed and screamed for nobody had thought to tell me it lived next door. Mama came running down the steps and picked the dog up. He had given me such a scare I could not be persuaded to make friends with that black furry animal.

I never really trusted any dog until some 27 years later, when working in a garden whose owner had a massive Great Dane. Suddenly the dog charged the fence which collapsed and he disappeared into the garden next door where the elderly gentleman was quietly working on his vegetable patch. He was very frightened and was endeavouring the keep the dog at bay, with a rake thus infuriating it further. There was no help at hand, the owner was out and no one else was around. As the dog's attention was focussed on the man I was able to scramble through the fence and from the rear, grabbed the dog by his collar forcing him back and sat down on his haunches. Now he was held fast and could not move. Fortunately, wearing very thick leather gloves I seized his nostrils to stop him barking and calm him down. With complete control he had to obey me. Dragging him back through the fence I managed to push him into the house. Feeling rather shaken I mended the fence as best I could and waited for the owner to return. Never would I fear any dog again after that confrontation.

It was usual in the childhood of my Parents for family prayers to be held before breakfast with family and retainers present. This was continued throughout their marriage until 1928 when the family moved to 'Speedfield'. One day my brothers lifted me into a toy hay cart and they pushed it up and down the gravel path edged with blue tiles. But not for long! Suddenly it stopped and I remember looking over the side to see why, before I tumbled out on to the points of the tiles! To this day I still have the scar between my eyes. The hay cart soon disappeared as did the tiles – never to be seen again!

Mama had made me two bibs. One for daily use was decorated with yellow chickens running along the bottom edge but the other one was very different. Mama designed an owl made of very white smooth woven material embroidered in black stitches. Tapes were sewn to the tops of two enormous red eyes, and peeping out of the bottom were red claws. This bib was special and only used on Sundays. The design was chosen because I understand the owl was my Father's family emblem.

Mama had very strict precepts. She had been brought up in the late 1880s where, if one's family was of consequence, it was considered ill-mannered to talk about money or family members. So I learnt to listen (without appearing to do so) to conversations between my Parents thereby gleaning items of information which were stored in my memory until I began to write this book. The degree of Mama's reticence did not become apparent to me until at a family party in 1936 I was introduced to Aunts, Uncles and Cousins of whose existence I had only vaguely been aware.

Nanny and I had our meals at the kitchen table but at three years old I was expected to sit in the dining room for lunch on Sundays. Sunday luncheon was a formal occasion with the best china and silver-plate cutlery. On the lace tablecloth a three-vase epergne took centre place with flowers from the garden.. Nanny, as befitted her station, was precise about manners at the table and using a knife, fork and spoon correctly. I had my own silver set of cutlery which was designed for small fingers. On the first Sunday in the dining room I tried to use the knife and fork to eat the meal but my fingers were too small to grasp the handles. Mama was horrified and Nanny was summoned to be upbraided as to why I could not behave and eat my dinner. Nanny explained I had always used my own silver knife and fork which were smaller than the dining room cutlery. Mama was very displeased and banished me from the table until I had learned to use the adult cutlery. I was very upset that Nanny, who had always taught me how to behave in adult society, was reprimanded in front of the family for something which I could not do. To my mind this was unfair and was the first time I witnessed Mama's autocratic attitude to her servants. Shortly afterwards I was allowed back in the dining room for Sunday lunch having been permitted to use my own cutlery. I think Papa must have had a quiet word, because he made a point of cutting up meat on my plate before passing it to Mama for vegetables. Mama had very little grasp of other people's problems and was quick to anger. This was a facet of her nature which made me very wary of displeasing her.

From a very young age if I expressed an interest in something which Mother did not wish to be disclosed she would ignore the question or stare me into silence. She was very punctilious regarding right and wrong – there were no grey areas – so I learnt to be utterly truthful. Therefore, from her character, I had no hesitation in believing her statement that Grandpapa Towler had researched their family history and ascertained they were directly descended from the second marriage of John Knox the Reformer to Margaret Stewart. When Grandpapa died his library was disposed of and it is assumed all his papers concerning the family history were destroyed before Mama was married. I am told her family and Papa's relatives all knew of this history at the time of their marriage. Certainly all those relations I have spoken to have imparted the same information.

Both my Parents were staunch supporters of the Congregational Church. On Sundays Mama and I would go to Morning Service. In the evening Mama would look after Beryl so that Papa could attend the Evening Service. Mama would then play hymns on the piano and I would have to sing. On weekdays Mama would play the last piece from Mendelssohn's album and The Bee's Wedding. She would also play from the book of Regina Music such as Robin's Return, Maiden's Prayer, Narcissus and Mendelsohn's

Lebenstraum until her hands were crippled with arthritis.

For several years Papa was instrumental in creating designs in the Church Hall for the Autumn Fairs of goods held to raise funds for Missionary work. The Minister, Mr. Solomon, was not married and Mama often took on the duties usually expected of the Minister's wife. One of these was to arrange the work of the Sewing Circle which she performed with consummate ease. Her artistic abilities of design and expert needlecraft were put to good use. She was very accomplished and achieved a Bronze Medal in a competition for a tablecloth design by the Royal School of Needlework when only nineteen years of age! She also designed other items, a fire screen of repoussé leatherwork, a cabinet and chair in marquetry and her crochet work was very fine. A church requested her to make a new cover for their Reading Desk using red cloth and gold raised embroidery. Before her marriage she decorated two different designs on white china. These were for her future husband and all were fired with the owl emblem on the base.

Mama was anxious for me to learn poems by heart. Just before starting school she told me I was to recite the poem, 'The Littlest One' by Marion St. John Webb to the Sewing Circle before tea. On the day Mama sat me on the edge of the stage in the hall. I insisted on having a crust to eat and sat there pretending to cry until all the ladies were sitting quietly. Then I began:

I'm sittin' on the doorstep,
And I'm eating bread an' jam,
And I aren't a-crying really,
Though I speks you think I am.

I'm feelin' rather lonely,
And I don't know what to do,
'Cos there's no one here to play with,
And I've broke my hoop in two.

I can hear the children playing,
But they sez they don't want me
'Cos my legs are rather little,
An' I run so slow, you see.

So I'm sittin' on the doorstep,
And I'm eating bread an' jam
And I aren't a crying really,
Though it feels as if I am.

My acting of this poem was extremely well received to Mama's embarrassment. From that time on I was hooked on the stage and took the opportunity to see pantomimes every Christmas.

In 1936 Mother went to see a film in a Southsea Cinema called 'Rose Marie' with Jeanette MacDonald and Nelson Eddy. She persuaded Father to see it and to take me with him! She considered it a perfect film for me to see and for my Father to appreciate the singing, which I must admit was very agreeable. This was my first visit to a cinema since my childhood. From then on in my teens I saw no less than six Operettas of Gilbert and Sullivan presented by the First Company of D'Oyly Carte in Southsea. I was mesmerised with the ability of Jack Green to speak with such clarity and at such speed. The contrast of the slow tempo solos and the thunder of the rhythmic chorus enchanted me and that pleasure has never faded. This with all the various colourful costumes and stage sets really intrigued me. For years I wished I had been able to see all the other shows of that fortnight. In the years before World War II Ice Shows became popular and Father took the family on two occasions to Olympia.

During the War in my first year in Winchester I rehearsed a group of under-21s to put on a two hour show including a one-act play to raise funds for the Congregational Church. We called ourselves the Good Companions.

When my children were at senior school I set up a drama and musical group of mature people at our local church in Tonbridge. Every year we produced a programme of items including a one act play. It was great fun and our company was successful with complimentary newspaper reports.

## General Tom Thumb and the Cat's Whiskers

When the American showman P.T. Barnum came to London, Queen Victoria invited him to bring General Tom Thumb to the Palace. It is recorded in the Court Circular that he visited the Queen on several occasions and photographs have recorded the events. In the book 'Queen Victoria Was Amused' by Alan Hardy, he writes:

'The General toddled in, looking like a wax-doll gifted with the power of locomotion. Surprise and pleasure were depicted on the countenance of the royal circle, at beholding this mite of humanity so much smaller than they had evidently expected to find him… The Queen then took him by the hand and led him about the gallery and asked him many questions the answers to which kept the party in an uninterrupted strain of merriment.'

Bearing in mind that Her Majesty was very much a 'mother figure' it is not surprising in view of the stature of Tom Thumb that she requested my Great Grandmother, Rebecca, to lift him on to a chair beside her so that she could converse with him face-to-face. On her marriage certificate Rebecca is described as 'Palace Maid'.

I was three and a half years old when Papa drove us from Havant to Birmingham, as we were to stay at Grandpa's house 'The Burgesses' in Kinver. I woke up in a darkened room. It was scary – it was not my bedroom! I must have called out for the door opened and Mama came in carrying a candle! I had probably been carried in from the car fast asleep and put down for the night. Mama picked me up and showed me the bed on the other side of the room saying she would be sleeping there herself. Now that I could see, I was happy to be put down once again into the cot which was behind the door and go to sleep. But I wanted the door left open so that I could see the flickering light of the candle which Mama had left on the landing.

A few days later Mama and I went to stay with Great Grandmama Broughton. The next morning after breakfast Great Aunt Emily said I could go with her to feed the chickens. We looked out of the front door to see if the rain had stopped. The sun was shining through the apple trees making the grass look as though it had been sprinkled with stars. She held me firmly. 'Wait, you need thicker shoes because the grass is very wet.' That seemed sensible so I was quite patient to wait while she searched for my outdoor shoes, but none were to be found. Great Grandmama clapped her hands and said, 'Emily, Tom Thumb's boots, which he gave me, will fit her!' Emily disappeared up the stairs and came down a few minutes later with a pair of black leather ankle boots with pointed toes and – no buttons!

I put my feet into them, but Oooh! they were so, so cold. Great Grandmama decreed they were too big for me to wear. Then, taking me by the hand we went into the drawing room to speak to Mama who was listening to the 'Cat's Whiskers' she said. Mama was sitting in the alcove by the fireplace with big black round things on her ears. We had to wait because she could not hear us speak. Taking the earphones off she put them on my head. There was a funny crackling sound and Mama turned some knobs on the shelf and I could hear music! I was amazed! Why was she listening to this music when I wanted to go out and run in the star-studded grass?

The problem about my shoes was quickly explained. Mama said there was no way I could go out on the grass it was too wet. I could go out in my summer sandals if I walked only on the paths. How pleased I was. At least I GOT OUT. Yes, I can see now that I was not a child to be easily persuaded from a course of action, unless there was a logical and reasoned explanation which I could accept. Since then other relatives have told me how Tom Thumb's boots came into Grandmama's possession.

# Film Star?

Mr and Mrs Johnson moved to Denvilles about the same time as our family moved to Hampshire from Yorkshire. He was a retired rubber plantation owner from Malaya. They had no children but attending the Congregational Church in Havant soon became friends with my parents and we were often invited to their house for tea on special occasions.

They had built their house on the corner of First Avenue of red brick with stone cornices, to a very fine modern style. A paved terrace overlooked a large, perfectly kept lawn surrounded by wide herbaceous borders. No flowers were ever picked from these borders. There was a large vegetable and flower garden at the rear from which flowers could be used for decoration in the house. The front door was set back under a pillared porch and led into a large square hall. Here, to my great delight, was an octagonal table of ebony extensively inlaid with pieces of mother of pearl and also a very large armchair similarly inlaid. At Christmas a small tree stood on the table and the light from the fairy lights reflected all the colours of the rainbow in the mother of pearl inlays. It was magical.

One Wednesday morning in the summer of 1925 Nanny told me I was going out with Mama that afternoon to visit Mrs Johnson, presumably for tea. After lunch I was put into my 'best dress' of crocheted peach silk, my best socks and patent shoes. Going into Mama's bedroom to be inspected, she took a coral necklace from her jewellery box and fastened it around my neck. She told me it was very precious and belonged to my sister but, I was to wear it today and take great care of it. As I had previously only been allowed to wear my best dress on Sundays, the fact that it was a Wednesday was very confusing.

Taking the bus into Havant, Mama and I walked up North Street over the railway crossing, now closed to pedestrians, along the path which bordered East Leigh Road, where lime trees gave a welcome shade in the hot afternoon sun. Turning into Eastern Road we crossed New Road and down a path to another railway crossing. We emerged into Third Avenue, Denvilles. We did not pass where I had been born at 'Thorneycroft', but walked on to First Avenue.

At the front door Mrs Johnson was waiting for us to arrive. Mama ushered me into the downstairs cloakroom for 'a lick and a promise' before joining Mrs Johnson in the dining room. Funny, I thought, there were no chairs and no food on the table! Mrs Johnson took us out on to the terrace where lots of people were standing about holding glasses. This was a very funny tea party. A gentleman came forward and was introduced to Mama. He was in shirt sleeves and carrying a small trug. He gave this to me to carry and we all went down on to the lawn. There, he asked me to go across to the other side and pick some of the flowers. I was horrified! No one was allowed to pick flowers from Mr Johnson's borders! But Mrs Johnson hurried forward and assured me that it was quite all right for me to pick two or three flowers. The man in shirt sleeves, whom I now presume was the film producer, explained that when I had picked the flowers and put them in the trug, I was to go back across the lawn to where everyone was standing and give them to my Mama. So, of course, I did exactly that and carried them to Mama who was standing on the terrace!

Stupid man! Why didn't he tell me it was all a pretend? Then I saw the man with a camera and by his side was a pretty young lady. She knelt down and told me she was pretending to be my Mama so, would I please do it all again? Off I went, picked three more flowers, put them carefully into the trug and trotted back across the lawn, and gave the trug to the young lady.

Everyone cheered and clapped their hands because the cameraman said it was a perfect take. When were we going to have tea? Surely it was time to go into the house? Yes, up the steps again but no one else was coming with us, they were walking across the lawn following a man dressed for tennis and carrying a racquet. But why? There was no tennis court in the garden. Then I found out. There was to be no tea – we were just visiting. And me in my best dress with a pretty necklace and my best shoes, and we were just going home. Oh, I did feel cheated. Seeing my disappointment Mrs Johnson sent her maid for some milk and biscuits, and I was allowed to take two biscuits.

Could this have been another way of increasing the family income? I seemed to remember it was about this time I became aware that Papa held a savings account book with my name on it in his bureau with the then enormous sum of £5. During my childhood I was persuaded to put nearly all money given to me as presents into this book. When eventually I asked Mother many years later what it had all been about, she was very evasive. Is there a piece of film, gathering dust, in someone's archives I wonder?

## A Japanese Fair

From the age of three Nanny used to take me down to the drawing room for tea on Mama's 'At Home' days. The ladies who came were mostly those who worked on the embroidering of goods which were made for sale at the Church Autumn Fair, held every year to raise funds for missionary work abroad. In 1926 Papa was asked to think of a suitable theme for the interior decoration of the church hall for the Autumn Fair. As the current fashion was for everything Japanese, he chose to follow this trend.

On the day before this event Papa left early in the morning to supervise the building of the stalls whilst Mama baked cakes and biscuits for refreshments. After lunch Mama and I went to give all the people who were working there some tea. When we arrived everyone was very busy. In the kitchen several ladies were washing up cups, saucers and plates which had been stored in cupboards and were stacking them on shelves ready for use. A huge metal urn was bubbling on the gas stove and I could see the steam puffing out of the top. The tea was soon made and we all went into the hall through an unusual door. This was covered in red paper and looked like a temple doorway from one of the pictures in my brother's book. To my amazement the hall had been transformed from a high-ceilinged bare space into one of those pictures. Papa and his team of helpers had created enclosures for the stalls with wooden supports and beams fixed back to the walls. Linking the fronts of the tables were wooden rails covered in green crepe paper. The table tops were covered in white crepe paper. Huge paper chrysanthemums were being made and these were entwined around the supports. A lattice work of strings of these flowers and leaves covered the tops of the stalls and created the feeling of being outdoors. On the rear wall a roof of red paper sloped down from the high window ledges over the stage. Hanging from the eaves were gold paper bells twinkling in the afternoon sun. Even the porch door had a red paper roof and a tall man would have set the bells ringing.

The great day dawned fine and sunny and after an early lunch Nanny and I dressed to go to the Fair. Inside, I was surprised to see all the stewards, Papa included, wearing blue-grey kimonos and the ladies behind the stalls were in colourful Japanese dress. I was flabbergasted to see the bright red pompom on the top of Minister Solomon's round black hat. It had been taken off my old slippers! No wonder they had vanished and new slippers appeared in their place!

The ladies were all wearing wigs which they had made from black wool and stabbed through with knitting needles in Japanese style. Going over to the needlework stall I was astonished to see that one of those ladies was Mama! She explained that I had been chosen to present the bouquet to the Opener. Of course I had to be dressed as a little Japanese girl. Mama produced a beautiful peach silk kimono decorated with coloured flowers and a wide blue obi was tied round my waist. My shiny patent leather shoes were well concealed under the edge of the robe and as I had naturally dark bobbed hair, and a fringe, I did not require a wig. From an old photograph it could be seen that I looked the part.

The bouquet was of real chrysanthemums and it was quite heavy. The fact that my obi was so stiff, permitting only a formal bow instead of the usual curtsey, caused considerable amusement and gratification to everyone. Mama was clever to get the 'right' effect without rehearsal from such a young child.

At Christmas I was so happy to be given a china doll dressed in a kimono of peach flowered material and wearing a blue obi just like the one I had worn. I treasured this doll and took great care to see she did not get broken.


## Roman Bedhampton

Hampshire in the seventh century was in the diocese of Dorchester. In 676 Bishop Haeddc moved the seat of Bishop from Dorchester to Winchester. In 705 the diocese was divided into Winchester and Sherborne. In 709 Winchester was divided into Winchester and Selby.

From the Winchester Diocese Episcopal Registers I quote: 'The custom of granting indulgences for various corporal works of mercy was considerably extended during this episcopate. They were granted in aid of one intending to make a pilgrimage to the Holy Land for the relief of Sir Robert Molineux, captured by the Saracens for one whose goods were burnt, and for the repair of the important Hampshire bridges of Bedhampton and Stockbridge.' In the Doomsday survey New Minster, Winchester or the Abbey of Hyde held Bedhampton. Portsmouth, Southwick and Hayling area was called Drokinsford, as a Rural Dean had charge of this area. The area around Bedhampton is full of Roman history. The earliest name for the village was Betametone. In the ninth century King Egbert granted the manor of Betametone to the Cathedral Church of Winchester.

On examining old maps and tracing the known Roman routes the road from Portchester runs through Cosham to Fir Corner and continues along what is now called Lower Lane, Bedhampton to Chichester. Another Roman track-way diverts from this road between Havant and Bedhampton and skirts the rear of Portsdown Hill to join the Portchester to Winchester road. Known Roman villas are marked along this route.

The spring just south of the site of an unknown villa probably supplied the water for their bath house before the present main road was built. This spring emerged in the field which in the nineteen hundreds was cultivated with watercress beds. It continues through a metal grill to run as an open river beside Brookside where it flows under a bridge to Langstone Harbour and out to sea. This bridge at the junction of Brookside and Lower Lane Bedhampton was originally built by the Romans. It was certainly an ideal stopping place being about five miles from Portchester and half way to Fishbourne Palace near Chichester. In later centuries it was kept in condition by monks and obviously had been widened and repaired many times in every century since.

After World War II ended, Mayland Road was built north to Scratchface Lane opposite Belmont Corner. During the building of the new housing complex a Roman mosaic floor was uncovered but never excavated. This villa is unknown but it is assumed to have been part of the Belmont Estate of recent years. I heard that it had been situated under someone's dining room, probably in Roman Way. Has it ever been disclosed since?

Before the modern Bedhampton road was built it is probable the source of the brook rose in the hill of the Belmont Estate to flow down Bidbury Meadow from which the present Brookside runs.


## To 'Speedfield', Bedhampton

During the time I was delving into my Father's activities I began to recall many incidents and events, either overheard or remembered from my childhood, which had lain dormant in my mind. Now came the realisation I possessed not only a photographic memory but I could also recall exactly what was said.

As you may have already noted, I was brought up in a strict Edwardian atmosphere where young children under the age of five were in the care of Nanny and taught to be seen and not heard in adult company. As a result of this upbringing I was able to cope at a very early age with social situations and intricacies of etiquette. Older children, up to the age of twenty-one, were expected to defer to their parent's wishes regardless of their own inclinations.

A naturally obedient child I had an inquisitive disposition, an enquiring mind and wanted to know how this, or that, was done – and why! I must have driven Mother to distraction in my quest for knowledge. Any snippets of family news, overheard whilst pretending not to hear, were stored in my memory especially those which appeared to be fraught with unexplained meanings. Sometimes when asked what was being spoken about I would be told to be quiet, not to be forward, or worst of all, stared at and frozen into silence. What a set down for an enquiring mind, but good training to keep my mouth shut and my ears open in order to learn matters of which I was not supposed to know anything. Little did my parents know what a service they did me, or how useful this trait was to be in my future life.

In July 1925 we moved from our temporary accommodation to number 14 Bedhampton Hill, named 'Speedfield' on the north side of Bedhampton Hill. I saw very little of Father as a general rule but every Saturday morning he would roll up his sleeves and slip on the 'metal bracelets' to keep them up above his elbows, sit down on the shoebox and whilst tying his shoelaces would sing musical ditties to amuse me. One of his favourites was:

> 'She was a sweet little dicky bird, Tweet, tweet, tweet she went
> Sweetly she sang to me 'Til all my money was spent.
> Then she went off song, We parted on fighting terms.
> She was one of the early birds, And I was one of the worms.'
> and another was:
> 'Down the road went Polly with a step so jolly that I knew she'd win.
> The pace was killing tho' the mare was willing for a lightening spin
> All the rest were licked and might as well n'er been born,
> Whoa mare, whoa mare, you've earnt your little bit of corn'

at which Mother would call from the kitchen with the admonition – 'Charles!' He would stop in mid-stream but with a wink continued in a whisper. It was only on these occasions I saw his eyes twinkle, otherwise his demeanour was always unruffled. His maxim was 'Everything in Moderation'. Adding a soft cap and a jacket he would be ready for work. The plan for each Saturday had been decided beforehand and he always arranged the delivery of whatever was required well in advance, which meant that no time was wasted.

When I was six years old Mother decreed I was to help Father and my brothers by being a 'go for'. This was one way of getting me out from under her feet. At 11 o'clock she would call me to carry the 'elevenses' out to them. My portion, the top of a cottage loaf buttered, a chunk of cheese with a cup of cocoa, in the open air during all the months of the year was memorable.

At every opportunity during these sessions I listened and watched Father explaining to my brothers the right way to hang wallpaper, the use of brushes, paint, repair casements and windows with putty. Father was particular about handling tools and I was very privileged to be allowed to use his chisels when only eight years old. Outside I absorbed the information of proportions required for cement laying, the way to build brick walls and erect the timber construction for a roof. In the garden potatoes and vegetables were planted and fruit trees pruned. Against the south wall loganberries grew in profusion. In front of them Mother planted Leucojums and the short species of Crocosmia, known as Montbretia, believed to be the flower symbol of her family.

One morning Father was preparing to plant some early potatoes when his spade suddenly took him off balance by nearly disappearing into the ground. Carefully stepping back he raked the soil away and found the spade had broken through the wooden top of a well!! He had a lucky escape from plunging down some 60 feet. This well must have been dug at the time when the two sets of semidetached buildings were built around 1820. Both gardens on either side had a well with overhead covers, whereas in our garden the cover had disappeared and the wooden top had become covered with a foot of soil. Obviously the previous owners were unaware of this well.

'Speedfield' was a semi-detached mid 19th century house which had a communal driveway to the rear of the property between the two semi-detached houses. Inside, the front rooms were separated from the domestic quarters by an inner hall and stairwell. A huge bookcase with carved edges, six foot high and six foot wide, stood on the main landing before the door which separated the rear bedrooms from the front of the house. A massive mirror, gilt framed, hung from floor to ceiling between this door and the three steps up to the main corridor. In the rear corridor there were two large cupboards and these held Mother's stock of Christmas puddings, jars of preserves, tins and other dry goods for which there was no room in the kitchen. A perfect layout for an Edwardian family.

We moved on the first day of the summer holidays, everyone helped and it took all day. During the next six weeks Father and my brothers worked very hard, methodically removing old gas fittings and two main fireplaces. By the beginning of September the drawing room and dining room had been painted, wallpapered and electric light installed. The drawing room fireplace surround was in mahogany and the dining room surround in oak because there was an oak sideboard of generous proportions, seven foot wide by six foot in height, which had been made by  Grandpapa Broughton.

Outside the back door was a brick washhouse. Dark leaved periwinkle bordered the three steps which led to the level of the garden. At the rear of the washhouse facing the garden was the outside privy screened by green painted lattice to conceal the wooden seat.

In the summer a pleasant enough place, but in the winter it was very cold and dark in spite of a small lamp. The privy was removed and Father built upwards to create an 'upstairs' loft, accessed by a ladder. A tiled roof and a sky light was inserted and a large window facing the garden swung open to give access for timber and goods to be stored. This loft extended to the house wall and on to the outside wall of the drive. Between this wall and the washhouse a flush toilet was installed. In the remaining open space behind the toilet my box swing was hung from a hook so I could watch Mother hanging out the washing out of the wind and it became my secret place.

One of the first jobs to be tackled was the very necessary washing lines. Somewhere, I think it may have been from a naval source, Father managed to buy a couple of ship's masts. These were set in concrete three feet deep along the garden path. Pulleys were attached at three levels on the masts and on the wash house. The very best woven rope was purchased and threaded through the pulleys. A short piece left over was bound at each end and became my skipping rope. When all three lines were full of sheets it took on the aspect of a ship in full sail. Mother could wash blankets in the morning, turn them at lunchtime and they would be aired enough to be put back on the beds by the evening. Quite a feat in those days. During the next five years every Saturday and most of the holidays were devoted to decorating and installing electric light in the rest of the house. Special paint was used to cover the outside concrete facing of the house. Our bicycles were stored under cover when the veranda was glassed-in.

An immense pile of rubbish deposited across the garden at the end during the previous century had to be removed by horse and cart! This left a hole two foot six deep which was made into a sunken garden. The horse and cart had to be summoned again to remove the remains of a dilapidated shed which used to house a pony and trap. The sixty foot high bank which formed the edge of the property to the Portsdown Hill Road had to be shored up, strengthened with mesh and faced with a thick layer of concrete. On this wall the foundation of a large garage and workshop was built with a concrete forecourt on to the driveway. Father then continued our garden wall with a gate, leaving the communal access to next door.

In the scullery a corner unit housed the copper boiler underneath which a small fire heated the water. It was my job on Monday mornings to light this fire. This was how laundry was boiled in those days. After boiling it was rinsed in the brown sink under a water pump and put through rollers of a large hand-turned mangle outside. In the refurbishment of the scullery the copper boiler and the fireplace were removed. The water pump was taken out and a deep white Bedford sink was plumbed with piped running water. Mother bought a modern mangle with rubber rollers which was clamped on to the edge allowing the water to drain straight into the sink. A labour and time saving in scooping water from the copper and draining water from the mangle outside. A full sized bath with a wooden cover was installed against the party wall. My parents were very modern in their outlook.

Being on the main coastal road we often had tramps who knocked on our side door requesting boiling water for their billy cans. Mother often gave them a spoonful of tea and a buttered crust of bread. Gypsies would call once a year selling lace and bunches of heather. Sometimes a knife grinder would call and sharpen knives seated on a tricycle which operated as a grinding machine. Milk was delivered from the local farm to the side door by a farmhand with a milk churn on his tricycle. At the door he would use a long handled ladle to measure the milk into our jugs.

We were very lucky to have a corner shop at the bottom of the hill owned by Mr. Coleman where he sold bread, cakes, groceries and locally grown fruit and vegetables. He had a bakery behind the shop in Brookside Lane. When he bought the adjoining house he opened it as a butchers. All his meat came from the local farmer and was kept in a large refrigerator at the rear. A hole in the shop wall was made into the butcher's shop so that customers could pay for their goods directly to the cashier. This business went from strength to strength and by 1939 it sold everything apart from milk, fish or clothes.One night as I was being put to bed Nanny told me she was leaving the next day to look after another little girl. Yes, I realised I was to go to school and therefore Nanny would not have to look after me during the day, and yes, I could also see she had to look after someone else. But why couldn't she still stay with us – she was MY Nanny. 'No', she said sadly, she had to go too far away. Then I asked if she would come to visit me, or, could I go to see her. She replied in a very quiet voice 'No, it would not be possible.'

I was heartbroken. What made it worse, was I had no warning this might happen. Nanny was my anchor and having her torn from me left me utterly distraught for I did not even see her the next morning to say goodbye. In fact, I do not think she even stayed the night for her bed did not look as though it had been slept in. I felt bereft of all security. The next morning Mother came to get me up and I could not eat any breakfast and she found me inconsolable at Nanny's sudden disappearance. This state of affairs lasted a long time and I became introspective and very wary of adults.

Shortly after Nanny left I started school and Mother bought a puppy for me to look after but it was ill and soon taken away. Then it was thought a kitten would be more suitable. I was taken to choose one from four pure white half-Persian kittens which were for sale. As I sat down on the floor one kitten with a blue ribbon made straight for me and climbed on my lap. I was enchanted. Mother wanted me to choose one with a pink ribbon but 'No – this one is mine' and I called him Jinky. He was my constant companion for twelve years.

I presume that the cost of medical care for my sister coupled with the costs of maintaining two boys through University and College at the same time, had to be offset by relinquishing the services of Nanny in addition to the living-in maid. A daily maid was employed from the village and the weekly washer-woman came for a whole day on Mondays instead of half a day. My sister and I were each given daily tasks to assist in carrying out the household chores.

Now came the upheaval of the change-over of bedrooms. My two brothers who had shared the second bedroom were to move into the two separate back bedrooms. My sister and I would have to share the second bedroom. Being so much older my sister was allowed to choose new wallpaper, paint and furnishings. She chose the colours from the painting called 'Greetings' by Charles Trevor Garland, a picture which always hung by her bed and was the only 'chocolate box' picture in the house.

In a cupboard in our bedroom my sister kept a beautiful doll with real hair and eyelashes which I was not allowed to touch. It was very precious and was dressed in a pure cream silk dress with a blue sash. Cream silk slippers with rosettes which were far too large for the doll were the same as those in the picture. When I had attained a standard of sewing Mother showed me how my sister's dress had been shortened by a deep tuck under the pleats to fit this doll.

It was at this emotional moment Mother suddenly divulged to me that when taking my sister out as a young child, people would stop and admire her extraordinary beauty. So, naturally, when the opportunity arose I asked 'Mother. Is that a picture of Beryl?' and was not unduly surprised at her refusal to answer. Furthermore within a week that picture and even the nail from which it had been suspended, vanished, never to be seen again. Nor was it ever referred to by anyone else. Obviously, it was hoped that being out of sight it would be out of mind. Not so. It was quite clear to me it was something important. I doubted my parents would have been able to afford my sister's pure silk dress, slippers and this doll, being such expensive items. It is most likely this was the result of the fee given for posing for the picture! Therefore, in my Mother's eyes this would be deemed as 'trade' and as such not acknowledged by her. When questioned my elder brother said he was at school and knew nothing about it, except he did remember his sister appearing with this doll after having been away with his parents. He thought it almost certain she had been the model for the picture.

Many years ago I bought a birthday card and took a photograph of a framed print which depicted the very same picture but with the slippers cropped. This picture was produced under the title 'For You' which I knew was incorrect. On a visit to Arundel just before completing this book, by sheer chance I acquired a framed print of the original picture, complete, entitled 'Greetings'.

Downstairs in the dining room I overheard Mother requesting Father to remove the large print of Adam and Eve to their bedroom. Also, the full length print of David was moved to an alcove behind a large armchair. Obviously, being nude statues, she did not think them suitable subjects to be in my sight. She could not have been so wrong, for, having seen them all my life up to the tender age of five, nude statues were simply Art. Large prints of the 'Seasons' and another of Dante and Beatrice, which had previously hung in Grandpapa's drawing room, were hung in their place.

My brothers were detailed to look after me during Sunday afternoons, giving Mother and Father time to themselves in the drawing room. My elder brother, Douglas, took over this duty every Sunday for I remember walking up the hill and on to the open ground where we would look at the flowers and grasses and he would tell me their names. Sometimes we lay down on the grass to watch ants scurrying about and he would explain their lifestyle. He talked about all kinds of things, his ideas and theories about life in general. Although a lot of what he spoke of was not within my comprehension, he did his best to make it simple enough for me to understand the principles involved. The views he expressed appeared to me to make a lot of sense.

On rainy days I was allowed to choose a volume of his Children's Encyclopaedia and we would read about mountains, rivers, places and countries throughout the world. Pictures of animals and maps of places were all duly examined. I was fascinated. These Sunday afternoons were the delight of my life and I learnt a very great deal which helped me in geography classes at Senior School.

In the holidays after the first term at University, Mother was drying his clothes on the rack above the kitchen range. She had placed a large bowl of dough on the hearth to rise and one of his socks fell on to the edge of the bowl which set fire to the clothes horse. In the bedroom above, ill with mumps, I heard a lot of shouting and things being moved about and could not understand what was happening. Eventually Mother came upstairs and said we had been very lucky. Father and my brothers had managed to prevent the fire burning the woodwork which could have endangered the whole house. The dough was well cooked with bits of wool like currants and it was given away to be eaten by chickens.

Later that year having developed scarlet fever I had a very dull birthday being much older than the other children in an Isolation Hospital. On coming home after six weeks I found everyone, including an uncle and cousin, had completely repainted and decorated the fire-damaged kitchen. The kitchen range had gone and been replaced by a new fireplace with a surround and hearth of green mottled tiles. The drying rack had been thrown out and the dresser had all new hooks and drawer handles of brass. Mother had made curtains, cushion covers, tablecloth and napkins in green/white chequered cotton. Very spring-like against cream walls and green paintwork. A new MAINS gas cooker was installed in the scullery and this was upgraded to a kitchen. The former being designated as the Breakfast Room.

On Sundays my job was pick fresh mint from the garden, chop it very fine, mix it with sugar and vinegar and put it into the sauce boat. As I grew older other cooking tasks were given me until, at the age of twelve I cooked the Christmas dinner, apart from the turkey which Father supervised. He carved the meat and Mother served vegetables from tureens. After lunch the parents would retire to the drawing room leaving my sister and myself to clear the table, wash the dishes and put them away.

The afternoon stretched ahead in peace and quiet. In summer I would climb into the loft of the outside extension with a book and Jinky who would curl up for his afternoon snooze. What bliss!

# Holidays

After moving to Denvilles Father bought a car – a Singer Tourer. The roof was of canvas and when it was in place side windows of celluloid, framed in canvas, were not entirely waterproof and rain often trickled inside. Father made a long deep box which hung behind the front bench seat. This held our picnic items, tea, milk etc. and food for our journeys.

One of my earliest memories is of travelling up the A1 and told by Father to 'Watch out for the Black Cat!' At the junction of the Bedford and Sandy crossroads a model of a large black cat sat above the eaves of a house on the corner. This could be seen from a long way off. Hence the continuance of this name on the map as the building has since been demolished.

Holidays were always taken during August and we visited grandparents and other relatives in the north until my two brothers were in their late teens. Once we stayed at a farm where we had to stuff straw into big sacks for our beds in a barn. The next year Father bought a large bell tent and a small tent for the boys. Lots of camping gear was purchased, chairs, table, basin, camp beds, and other items, all in waterproof green canvas. The bell tent pole was strapped along the outside of the car so Father had to get in and out on the other side. When all the equipment was loaded the bedding was piled on the back seat and I sat on top of it!

Annual camping holidays were taken at many other places but the most memorable was when we went to Ilfracombe. On that occasion the boys left on their bicycles about 6am. They were to secure our campsite and purchase milk and bread before our arrival late in the afternoon. We found them trying to break open a tin of corned beef with sharp stones as they had forgotten to bring a can opener! The camping site overlooked the town of Ilfracombe and was very popular.

Everyone set-to and soon the bell tent was erected. Beds for my sister and myself were ground sheets laid along each side with pillows and eiderdowns. In the middle our parents had the camp beds and the boys slept on ground sheets in their own tent. Father soon got the camp stove going and Mother cooked our evening meal.

In the middle of the night there was a violent thunderstorm and it teemed with rain. Father was changing from his pyjamas into his swim suit and Mother asked 'What on earth are you doing? He replied 'I am not going to get dressed to go outside. The stays have loosened and I must go and secure them. If I am going to get wet I might as well be in my swim suit.' Next morning the boys were missing, only to be found curled up in the car as the rain had flooded their tent!

On the last evening everyone wanted to go to the cinematograph but the problem was, as I was only six, someone had to stay with me. In the end as it was a Charlie Chaplin film, they decided I could go with them – if I was very good. This of course was the time of silent films where a pianist supplied dramatic music. First of all there was a short film of the Keystone Cops; a typically fast moving comedy film. The Charlie Chaplin film which followed I found absolutely enthralling and it encouraged my interest in drama. On the way back to camp Father bought fish and chips from a shop! What an exciting evening! Although I was allowed to visit theatres in my youth I did not see another film until I was in senior school.

When my brothers left home there were no more camping holidays. Instead I was invited to stay at my eldest brother's lodgings in London. Mother travelled with me to Waterloo Station where we were met by Douglas. He took charge of me for the next two days. His landlady was very motherly and tucked me into bed which was so lovely, soft and warm. It was a feather bed! No such luxury for me at home. The next day we went to Chessington Zoo. On the second day we visited the Victoria and Albert Museum. At the end of the holiday he took me to Waterloo Station and put me in the charge of the guard for the train to Havant where I was met by Mother.

As this proved to be a successful visit I was allowed to join him when our school holidays coincided. For some years he took me to visit interesting places such as London Zoo, Hyde Park, Tower of London, The Crystal Palace at Sydenham and the Tropical Houses at Kew. Another time we went to Whipsnade Zoo where we saw polar bears amongst many other animals. At the Guildhall the statues of Gog and Magog instilled in me a real interest in history.

In the Summer of 1940 before London and the Docks were targeted, my other brother took me to visit St. Paul's Cathedral. As he was an architect he was commandeered with other architects to take turns in guarding the Cathedral from fire bombs. If a bomb had pierced the outer dome it was imperative to be on hand immediately to prevent the timber catching fire.

To enter the space between the two domes was fascinating. One had to clamber over and under the timber framework which supported the structure of both domes. Space was very restricted so they could only sleep on mattresses laid between the baulks. Fire buckets were stationed every few yards and torches were the only lights allowed. Fortunately their services were only lightly tested.

## Hayling Island

Soon after moving into Speedfield my parents decided to rent a beach hut on the south shore of Hayling Island. The steam train of two carriages, nicknamed Hayling Billy, took us from Havant to South Hayling. There we walked down Staunton Avenue to the coastal road. On the other side was an expanse of gorse covered sand. Paths meandered through this before we could reach the beach huts which were arranged in two rows. They were all the same size, but each one had a name board and some were in different colours. Apparently I was sent ahead and on calling out 'Here it is!' our hut's name board became 'Hereitis'.

The hut was of six foot by eight foot timber construction with a tarred felt roof. A single window faced the sea and being in the rear line it was sheltered to some degree from the ravages of the wind. Inside Father had made some ingenious fixtures. The rear roof space was made into a cupboard and a timber plank which rested on batons fixed to the walls was our table. This plank could be slid into a groove between the cupboard and the floor and divided the rear space into two compartments with curtains as changing rooms. In early summer painting and repairs were undertaken and in September all equipment was removed and stored at home.

During the summer of 1932 my younger brother had acquired a motor bike. He had to go on an errand for Mother to our beach hut and was allowed to take me with him provided he promised not go too fast and I was to hold on tightly to his belt. How exciting! We set off and negotiated the many twists and turns of the main road through the island. After spending a little time on the beach we set off for home and as there was a lot of traffic about so he decided to take an alternative route. This was along West Lane, a parallel road. Near the end where West Lane joins the main road there is a tight right handed 90° turn. Whether he was not used to the extra weight of having me on the pillion, he did not make this turn but slid sideways into the hedge. Fortunately there was no ditch and his speed was such that we did not come to any harm. A few twigs and leaves were quickly removed from the bike and after he had admonished my silence concerning the incident we continued our journey. This is a particularly tricky corner but now there is a wide gap in the hedge which allows flat access into the field beyond for anyone missing the bend to slide off without incident.

When World War II began all huts had to be removed from the shore. Father bought our hut and put it up on our allotment for the 'Grow Your Own' campaign. In the brick-lined pit underneath we stored our apples and vegetables, a perfect place to keep them throughout the coldest winter and a very necessary addition to our pantry.

## Sunday School

I could not go to the Havant Sunday School as Mother was unable to take me there every week. Instead she arranged to take me to a school friend's house nearby where joining them, I could go to their local Sunday School. We were each given a card to record our attendance with a picture stamp. If we had a full card we would be taken for an outing in the summer. It would be a day out by myself and I looked forward to this event the whole year.

Mother could not leave the house one Sunday so I had to miss the class. On the following Sunday I explained to my teacher why I could not get there and she promised I would be allowed to go despite one blank space, as it was not my fault. When the day arrived I handed my card to the teacher who was supervising the trip. She refused to accept it because of the one missing picture and said I could not go on the outing.

71

I explained that my teacher, who was standing behind her, had agreed I could go even though there was one missing picture. Looking for confirmation and, in spite of my pleading, she refused to admit her previous assurances to me. The other teacher was adamant and accused me of lying!

That did it! I was FURIOUS. In front of the other girls and their mothers I protested to both teachers 'You have lied and cheated me. You should be ashamed. You cannot be trusted as teachers of the Christian principle of right and wrong. I will never come to your Sunday School again.' I stalked out in great dudgeon with my head held high.

At school I told my two friends in no uncertain terms of my disgust at the conduct of those Sunday School teachers. I believe after the outing they, amongst others left the Sunday afternoon sessions. I wonder what happened when out of the dozen or so children no less than five stopped attending. In hindsight it may have been they knew Father had a car, whereas other children were not so fortunate. But was this any reason to treat me in such a manner? I remember they were somewhat taken aback at my tirade and well they might be. After all – righteous anger is not easy to combat.

Little did anyone know what grief I experienced for this outing would have been a unique treat. I had looked forward to it all winter and spring.

## My Battle for the Annual

There were always books around our house. Father had his personal library in the glass-fronted cabinet above his bureau in the drawing room. Mother kept her embroidery books and weekly magazines in her bureau in the dining room. Cookery books were delegated to a drawer in the kitchen/breakfast room. On the upstairs landing a seven foot high bookcase held books on all sorts of subjects and those deemed not suitable for a child were removed and banished to her bedroom. My sister had a set of the Waverley Novels by Sir Walter Scott in a special glass cabinet. She was very proud of these having received them as prizes at Purbrook. I was not even allowed to touch, let alone read them. In my elder brother's room was his bed and wardrobe and it also housed his chemistry, zoology and biology books and encyclopaedias. In my younger brother's room in addition to his bed and wardrobe were his drawing board and a chest containing all his architectural papers and other books. Aunty Jessie would arrive from Switzerland to stay with us over the Christmas holidays. Every year she would place a 'Pixie' book under my pillow for me to find on Christmas morning. These were very precious to me and were kept in small bookcase by my bed. My favourite was 'The Kittie-Poosies'.

On Sunday afternoons, before I went to school and learnt to read, my parents wished to keep me quiet while they were reading. So, I was allowed to look at a special book from Father's collection. It was called 'Lalla Rookh' by Thomas Moore and contained many colourful illustrations of Persian Art. I became quite immersed in the intricate designs – a complete contrast to the full length studies of statuary that hung in our dining room.

Like most children I loved to have stories read to me and after Nanny left Mother found this was one sure way to get me to bed. A favourite was a typical Victorian story about a boy who 'loved' gingerbreads. Mother approved of the moral which was, you do not LOVE food, only people. You may LIKE food, or for that matter any inanimate object. I wonder if Mother included animals in this category of things as she did not care for pets.

One Sunday just before lunch my sister tried to get me to read 'letters' from an alphabet book. I was hungry and not in a mood to be taught. Scorning her attempts I said 'I will learn to read but not before I go to school next week.'

For some reason I was not allowed to join the Children's Library in Havant probably because Mother could not spare the time as it was more than a mile away. Instead from the age of seven till nine I was given 'The Children's Newspaper' by Arthur Mee every week. At Purbrook we had our own library and there I was in seventh heaven becoming a voracious reader.

All our newspapers were delivered by a newsagent who had a small hut on a grassy plot next door to Bedhampton School. On each side of the door were small window displays. Inside a wooden shelf fixed across the hut served as a counter. On either side of a door behind him were shelves stacked with tobacco, cigarettes and matches. If a customer wished to buy something he would disappear into the room beyond returning immediately with the item requested! Some of the older boys at school were employed by him to deliver newspapers etc. These jobs were much prized for the wages would go a long way to fund their first days at work. Every month on collecting me from school Mother would call to pay her bill.

A few weeks after starting school I saw in his window a Daily Mail Annual. It was opened at a page where a paper cut-out figure of a fairy rose up from the centre. I fell in love with this apparition. Finding I could read many of the words which ran in a narrow column down the side of the page I determined to have this book for my very own knowing with absolute certainty I would be able to read everything in it – even though I was only on Book 3 at school.

It seemed perfectly reasonable to me to go into the shop, examine it carefully making sure it contained lots of stories, puzzles etc. and check the price was that which I could afford. Then, ask the shopkeeper to take it out of the window for Mother to collect at the end of the month. At home I told Mother I was going to buy this book. I knew I had at least £5.00 in my own bank account, which Father kept in his bureau, so that the expenditure of five shillings to own this book was not excessive in my opinion.

I expected my Annual when she returned from the newsagents but it was not in her basket! On asking Mother where it was, she laughed and said it was too expensive. I was very annoyed because I had said I would pay for it. The following Monday morning I saw my book back in the window. Of course I went in and asked 'why?' He told me

Mother had not ordered it. Once again I asked him to take it out as I would be paying for it myself, but I could not get the money from my savings until the weekend when Father would be at home.

On Sunday after lunch, I was summonded to the drawing room and had to stand on the carpet between my parents who were seated on either side of the fireplace. I was subjected to a long interrogation as to the reasons for my audacity in asking the shopkeeper to charge Mother for something which she had not ordered. Further – 'Who was going to pay for it?' Replying 'I am going to pay for it with my OWN money' I was told 'Money is not for frivolous spending.' I did not consider it frivolous for I knew I would learn to read with that book. They formed a united front and I was not allowed to have the Annual. Going outdoors to my swing – my private corner – I wept with frustration.

Over the next few weeks seeing the Annual still in the window kept my determination at boiling point. Every Sunday – I was on the carpet – but I stuck doggedly to my belief – if that book was mine I would be able to read anything. I was not to be shaken from my decision. My parents used every possible argument. It was too expensive, except as a Christmas present and that was many weeks away and I had already been given my birthday present. Throughout the month of October I persisted in asking Father every week for MY MONEY and by the middle of November I was getting desperate. Other children at school were talking about what they were going to have for Christmas. Their parents were paying out pence each week for some special present, annuals included, and I could see the probability of one of them buying my Annual.

Finally one Saturday morning Father gave me the five shillings which was handed to me with the awful warning that once gone no more would be forthcoming. My delight and relief at achieving my goal despite all obstacles can be imagined. I had evaluated all sides of the matter and had come to the conclusion that this was right for me. Against all prejudice I had overcome 'authority' with reasoned argument. It gave me confidence in my ability to reason, to deduce facts, weigh the pros and cons and make logical decisions for the rest of my life. By Christmas I had read many of the stories and learnt lots of new words. From then on if I was missing Mother could be sure to find me with my nose in a book.

## Bedhampton Council School

The school was built of brick with stone mullioned windows set high on three sides above a large tar macadam playground. Spike topped railings followed the perimeter of the site and continued along Cow Lane to a jumble of bushes where the railway line closed the end of Bidbury Lane. Miss Sparrow, the Headmistress, had her living quarters at the rear of the school and in her garden she instructed the senior boys in growing vegetables and the care of beehives.

In one of the cottages opposite the school gates an elderly lady had turned her front room into a shop selling all manner of things and on opening the door a little bell tinkled one's arrival. She sold knitting wool, needles and patterns, birthday cards, paper and envelopes, skipping ropes, yoyos, cricket bats, balls, buckets and spades, sandals and stuffed toys hung from the ceiling beams. Along one wall up to the ceiling shelves held glass jars filled with sweets. On the counter open boxes were filled with jelly babies, liquorice whirls, sherbet dabs, gob stoppers and chews amongst many others, all priced from one farthing to one penny each – a veritable Aladdin's cave.

My elder brother was in teacher training and happened to be taking the infants' class when I joined the school. Used to him giving me instruction at home it was a comfortable start to school life. We had to do our lessons on slates for the first year and then we were given pencils and paper. We did not work in ink until we were nine years old. After one term he left for another school and another teacher arrived who was a very kind and gentle-voiced lady. For the next two years in her class I remember little of any importance, apart from the tussle with my parents about the Annual. At morning breaktime in Goodwood Racing Week everyone clung on to the railings to watch the stream of motor cars slowly cruising along the road, filled with top-hatted gentlemen and ladies in colourful gowns and parasols who acknowledged our cheers with aplomb. It was a glimpse of an entirely different lifestyle.

At the age of seven I moved up into Miss Randall's class. This was not a happy experience as during this time I encountered bullying, both mental and physical. From the age of five I suffered nearly all the childhood diseases, thereby losing valuable school time. She expected me to know what had already been taught in class. Although I did my best I could never please her, consequently she considered me a tiresome pupil. We had no lessons on Friday afternoons as everyone brought toys and games to exchange. For the last hour the whole school met together to learn the words and sing songs from The National Song Book. My favourite songs were The Vicar of Bray and The Ash Grove. In the Summer term we had to learn Richmond Hill and we had to sing this every Friday – how dull! At morning assembly we sang All Things Bright And Beautiful. It became the norm to close the day with Now The Day Is Over.

For some years a much older girl, named Cynthia, came on Saturday mornings to play with me in our veranda. As she had not been for many weeks I brought my Japanese doll downstairs and placed her securely in the corner of my doll's pram. She appeared unexpectedly and immediately on seeing this doll went to pick her up. I begged her to leave the doll where it was because it was fragile. She took no notice, picked it up and deliberately threw it on to the stone floor, smashing the china head. I could not pick her up – for to me, she was dead.

I was devastated. Screaming with rage I ran into the house and strived to explain to Mother through my anguished sobs what had happened. Cynthia had disappeared and even now I can see Mother holding the pitiful remains in her hands saying, 'Never mind. We can stick the pieces together.' For all her care there was one small piece

75

missing leaving a gap behind one ear. It made me feel sick and I could not take her in my arms again. Mother put the doll out of sight for I did not wish to be reminded of the traumatic ending to what I thought was friendship. Needless to say Cynthia was never invited to the house again and I could not forgive her for her act of calculated vandalism and cruelty.

## McIlroys of Portsmouth and the Stewart Line

At the age of seven I went with Mother to visit McIlroy's Store in Commercial Road, we were greeted at the door by the Shop Walker who escorted us to the lift. Mother was wearing a black coat with a long fur collar, fastened at her waist with one large button. A black hat with a wide flat brim sat full-square on her head, typical of a lady's outdoor attire of those times.

On the way I watched the assistants put money and bills into canisters which were propelled upwards along wires which looked like a spider's web to stop at a window on the first floor. Someone quickly detached the canister and a few moments later it was quickly twisted back on to the wire. A pull on a cord sent it flying back to the ground floor. Later a hydraulic system was installed and the 'thunk thrum' of the canisters as they were projected through the pipes sounded very mysterious.

In the linen department Mother was seated on one of the gilt chairs by the counter when Mrs McIlroy appeared, having been informed of our arrival. She was a tall, slim lady with snow-white hair done up in a top-knot wearing an elegant black gown. Her regal appearance was accentuated by her long string of pearls.

As a very thrifty housewife Mother was buying sheets, pillow-cases, towels, tea-towels and all other necessary linen for our household for the year ahead. She believed in buying when items were in a sale. On this particular occasion, having finished her list of purchases, Mrs McIlroy remarked 'We have just received our new stock of woollen materials. Would you be needing any for a new winter skirt for Joyce?' She indicated the two nearby stands, one of tartans and the other of checked materials. Mother thought for a moment then, turning to me said, 'Yes. You could do with a new skirt for the winter. You may choose the material.' I was astonished! This was the first time I had ever been allowed to choose something for myself!

Looking at each roll of cloth carefully I quickly decided that the usual tweeds were very dull. Being fond of the colour I chose one of a green mixture. Although it was a little on the dark side, there were other coloured threads running through it. Returning to stand by Mother's chair I waited for her attention and indicated the tartan I had finally chosen – six down from the top of the pile. She took one look, placed both her hands on the knob of her umbrella and banged it on the floor. Drawing herself up, ramrod straight, she spoke with icy hauteur, 'You may chose a tartan if you wish but you will chose the one you are entitled to wear.'

I had no idea what she was talking about and obviously neither had Mrs McIlroy, for she leaned forward and, in a gentle voice enquired 'Which one would that be Mrs Broughton?' 'The Stewart.' came the taut reply.

Gesturing to the assistants Mrs McIlroy supervised the display of the three Stewart tartans on the counter. The colourful tartan with the white background was pleasing to my eye but Mother quietly pointed out that it was not suitable for everyday wear. It was the Dress Tartan and meant to be for best. The green Hunting Tartan looked a bit dull so I had to chose the red which, of course, is the usual Day Tartan.

Mother made this material into a kilt and pinned it with a proper kilt pin. I was very pleased for it was warm and cosy to wear. For two years I wore it attached to a white bodice top. As I began to grow taller it was altered into a skirt with a waist-band. This was the first intimation I had that Mother was descended from the Stewart Clan. It was to be another seven years before I was able to get her to speak about the subject again.

## Farlington Redoubt Accident near Fort Purbrook

In later years this incident taught me how to make the best use of what is available in an emergency when quick thought and action was needed.

'Joyce, hurry up and put on your cardigan. You are to go with your Father to fetch the apples.' called Mother one Saturday morning. We had just had our cocoa, bread and cheese, and it was while this was being eaten that the subject of fetching the promised apples was discussed. The decision that I was to go by myself with Father was momentous. What an event it turned out to be.

Our Singer climbed the Portsdown Hill Road which was a one-in-six gradient, easily and we purred along merrily. The view was magnificent. The morning mist had completely disappeared and it was possible to see the ships sailing in the Solent. I hugged myself, glorying in the unexpected treat of being allowed out with Father by myself.

He had his Saturday smile on his face. It was though he had been let out of school. It seemed our excursion was a welcome reprieve for he was always working in the garden or garage on Saturdays. In fact he was actually singing one of his tunes. Ahead of us in the middle of the road a boy was waving his arms like mad. 'Hello - now what's up with that boy?' Father said as we drew to a stop. He got out and moments later came back calling 'Pick up the first aid box and come with me.' We followed the boy through the wire fence behind the bushes and up the grassy slope to the Redoubt. As we climbed I was told that this boy's friend had fallen into the moat and been injured.

At the Redoubt Father left me at the top edge whilst he followed the boy down, some sixty feet, into the moat. Peering downwards I saw several boys gathered round one who was lying very still. Father soon called up to me to ask if I could see any pieces of wood lying about. Pointing to where some piles of scattered rubbish lay round the corner he sent three boys off to rummage. They soon came back with some wood and pieces of rope to find Father had removed his tie and with two belts from other boys was strapping the injured boy's legs together. Then he called up 'Can you see anything which could make a stretcher?' At first there seemed to be nothing. Suddenly I remembered there were pieces of corrugated iron lying loose in the fort and he sent two older boys to get one. On asking if there was a better way up out of the moat they showed him where there was a landslide at the corner. Telling me he would bring the boy up this slope he instructed me to go back to the road and run to the house, Sunspan, where they had a telephone and ask them to send for an ambulance. My previous runs with my brother stood me in good stead for it was half a mile away.

At the house the owner, Mr. Light, quickly telephoned and he and his wife took me back in their car to where ours was parked. Soon we heard the ambulance bell ringing and it drew up beside us followed by a police car. Explaining to them what had happened, a stretcher, blankets and first-aid boxes were brought out and everyone helped to carry these. The two ambulance men, two policemen and Mr. and Mrs. Light all followed me through the fence. Father had organised the boys, according to height, to carry the stretcher up the slippery chalk slope. He had given his gloves to two of them and wrapped his own hands with handkerchiefs. His pullover, which I had made, was supporting the boy's head. When we arrived at the slope it was to find the makeshift stretcher nearly at the top.

The exhausted boys and our support team were spread out on the grassy down where everyone was examined for cuts and scratches. It was decided that tetanus injections had to be given to all the boys involved. Discussion took place as to how to transport them? The police could take two boys and Father could take the others in his car but there would be no room for me. Mr. and Mrs. Light suggested they would take me back to their home until his return, as having had a tetanus injection he did not anticipate being away too long. So we all clambered down to the road. It took all six men to manhandle the stretcher over the wire fence, through the bushes and into the ambulance which quickly sped away.

Sunspan was a modern house specially designed by Welles Coates which had been shown at the Ideal Home Exhibition in 1934. As this house was built on the hillside, the lower floor to my amazement was an indoor swimming pool! The entrance hall and living room were fitted with parquet. Being very tired after all the climbing and running about, I was glad to sit down in the middle of the huge semi-circular window which overlooked the Solent. Mrs. Light gave me hot milky cocoa and some delicious sandwiches while they had their own lunch.

Back at home Father remarked to Mother that I had been a great help. Not only in remembering about the corrugated iron but in getting the ambulance there so quickly. It meant the boy had been rescued out of the moat and into the ambulance without any delay. Father considered the loss of a good pair of gloves, handkerchiefs, tie and a nearly new pullover a small price to pay for such a successful result.

# Vengeance in the Nettles

It was two years before I relented and this gave Cynthia the opportunity to once again cause me great distress. At lunchtime on a Tuesday during the first week of June, Cynthia insisted on giving me a 'piggy-back'. I wasn't keen but in order to keep the peace I agreed but only as far as the end of the ribbon development of houses set well back from the road. Just after the last house the path went over a hill and I requested to be put down. Instead she ignored me and turned into the narrow path edged with nettles to the electric building. Here, out of sight of the road, she calmly tipped me off backwards on to the enormous bed of 4 foot high nettles. To prevent me getting up she knelt on me pressing down on every limb. I screamed for help but no one came to my rescue as we could not be seen due to the height of the nettles and eventually she ran off.

The nettles had stung me through my dress and my arms, back and legs were numb with pain which was indescribable. It took me ages before I could master the effort to raise myself off the crushed stems and roll over to crawl along the gravel to the grass-edged path and stand up. Instinctively my feet carried me home going past our neighbour, whom I called Aunty Scragg, without stopping. When I reached our kitchen she was but a couple of steps behind me and I heard her say, 'Mrs Broughton, I do apologise for walking in without knocking but Joyce went by my gate and did not recognise me! What has happened?' Between them they gently removed my clothing and Mother threw a newly washed sheet over the kitchen table so that I could lie face down with my arms over the edge. Mother picked up her purse and leaving me with Aunty went across the road to telephone the doctor. She quite forgot to take off her pinafore!

Dr. Dewhurst arrived in just ten minutes having driven from the Havant surgery a mile away. As he came through our hall I heard him say 'Now Mrs. Broughton what IS the matter?' Entering the kitchen I heard him exclaim 'OH MY GOD!' And then there was silence. He was too professional to have sworn in that manner without extreme provocation. Apologising for his outburst, he asked Mother if she had any Calamine Lotion but she only had Dettol. Diluting it with cool boiled water and using cotton wool, he swabbed my body from neck to toes. Whilst doing so he spoke to me in a consoling manner both to distract me from the pain and endeavouring to discover who had attacked me and why. He tried to be gentle but as there was no space between the blisters it was a painful procedure and being in such pain I had no embarrassment at my nudity. He then gave me a tetanus injection and I think a sedative as I can only remember being helped to lie face down on a soft bank of cushions and left without even a sheet over me, it was too painful. Dr. Dewhurst took Mother with him in his car to Havant to buy Calamine Lotion and Aunty was left to stay with me until she came back.

It was very late in the evening when I woke to find Father applying Calamine

Lotion all over me. I knew he had been a First-Aider in World War I and accepted his unusual attention with equanimity. Mother told me that evening that whilst I had been asleep there had been a meeting between Miss Sparrow, my parents and Dr. Dewhurst. Cynthia was to be expelled the next morning.

The next day the blisters had subsided but my skin was very tight. Mother had to keep using the Calamine Lotion which was lovely and cool and I could sit on a soft down cushion to eat my meals. In hindsight this nettle poisoning probably caused me to develop hay fever and allergic reactions which I experienced in my adult life for so many years.

Mother told me I would have to go to school the next day. I was adamant. If I was sent back I would run away. I would not return to that school to be subjected to Miss Randall's spite, for Cynthia had been her favourite pupil. Mother knew I meant what I said and asked 'Where do you think you can continue your education?' I replied 'Can't I go to Purbrook? And I want to be called Stella, not Joyce.' My parents consulted Dr. Dewhurst and he advised them it was in my best interests, psychologically, to accede to my requests. Mr. Stedman, Headmaster of Purbrook and Councillor Privett were invited to a meeting with my parents, Miss Sparrow and Dr. Dewhurst. Everyone agreed that I might attend Purbrook for the last six weeks of term, starting the following Monday, with the proviso I was to return to Bedhampton school for one day – Friday. I agreed, but only if Mother would go with me and explain to Miss Randall that I MUST take our cushion to sit on as my skin was still very tender and sore.

Our school desks were in doubles and racked so that everyone could see the blackboard. I shared mine with Bubbles, my best friend. On Friday morning, barely ten minutes into the arithmetic lesson someone at the front of the class laughed. Miss Randall turned round and immediately challenged me to admit being the person who dared to laugh in her class. Taking absolutely no notice of my denials she not only gave me six strokes of the ruler on the palm of my right hand but put the Dunce's hat on my head. She ordered me to stand in the angle of the chimney behind the blackboard where Miss Sparrow would not have been able to see me when she overlooked our class through the dividing glass screen. I gritted my teeth thinking it would only be till breaktime and listened to the lesson in order to write it down later. It came as no surprise when Miss Randall decreed I was not allowed out to play during the break.

But there was more to come. After break I had to stand behind the blackboard yet again until lunchtime. Now I was positive she would make me work on arithmetic all afternoon instead of joining the rest of the class in exchanging toys and games. As you will imagine I was feeling not only very tired, having stood in one place for two and a half hours, but angry at her unwarranted attitude. I was determined she would not succeed in her revengeful treatment so I thought about how to prevent it. In my desk the pencil box was my only possession and I was not going to leave it behind. So, undercover of clearing my desk, I would secrete it under my jumper. When changing into my outdoor shoes I could put it and my plimsolls into my shoe-bag and conceal that under my coat. Then she would not realise I was not going to come back that afternoon. It was only after everyone had left the cloakroom that she released me to go home. With my back to Miss Randall who was watching from the classroom door, I managed to do all that I had planned.

At home I delayed eating my pudding until Mother suddenly realised it was too late for me to get back to school. It was then I told her I was not going back. Mother was shocked, asked why, and sat down and made me tell her all that had happened that morning. Poor Mother what was she to do? In half an hour she was expected to chair a meeting at the Church. There was only one thing to do – leave me in my room with my cat Jinky and a book, lock up the house and get back home as quickly as possible. That evening Father visited Miss Sparrow again and he came back with my cushion! I had forgotten it! Now I could forget Bedhampton School and all the unhappiness connected with it.

Miss Fountaine, Headmistress of Purbrook, informed Mother I would not be permitted to wear Purbrook School uniform for the next six weeks as technically I was still on the Bedhampton Council School register. Mother decided I was to have new cotton dresses as my uniform. On Saturday we went to McIlroys and bought three lengths of Horrock's flower pattern cotton in green, blue and yellow – enough for three dresses and matching knickers. I was even allowed to have full gathered skirts and puffed sleeves! We also bought a Panama hat and blazer, new plimsolls and socks. No badges could be added until the new year began in September. On joining Purbrook I insisted from then on I would be known as Stella, which was my third name. I made a vow I would never willingly speak to anyone with the name of Cynthia for the rest of my life.

## Visit of the Hindenburg – July 5th 1936

What an extraordinary thing! I feel as though I am watching a play and yet I am one of players. Not two minutes ago my usually placid Father burst into the kitchen calling for Mother to come and see. Being curious I followed her down the hall and out of the front door. They were both looking up into the sky. There hovering as any galleon of old was an enormous silver grey airship, not more than 100 feet above the houses opposite. 'What is it?' I gasped. 'It's a dirigible' said Father. A droning noise came from it penetrating our senses and drowning all other sounds. I could see a swastika in red and black on the tail plane and the name HINDENBURG was on the side. The faces of officers and passengers could be seen looking down at us through the windows and it was weird and very frightening. Slowly it pivoted to follow the coastal road and disappeared towards Cosham.

Father turned and looking at me with such sad eyes said quietly 'We are seeing the beginning of a new era. It means that anyone can fly over land or sea.' Being an astute man he further commented forcefully 'The Channel is no longer a barrier. Now, no one is safe' and went in to the house. Shocked I turned to Mother for some explanation but she brushed passed me as though I was invisible calling out 'Charles what do you mean?' and followed him into the drawing room closing the door behind her. Never had I known such isolation. It was unheard for me to be left unattended outside the front door! Closing the front door, hearing no sound not even talking, I crept back indoors. Eventually when Mother returned to the kitchen the look on her face caused me to refrain from making any reference to such unusual behaviour. The sound lingered in the air like a magic spell but something remained – an elusive yearning for the unknown. My parents would never understand my fascination with the wish to experience the feel of speed in space.

The following year, May 1937, it left Berlin on a flight to the U.S.A. It was delayed by headwinds and as it approached Lakehurst it was forced to circle the aerodrome and wait for a thunderstorm to clear. As it neared the mooring mast the airship suddenly burst into flames. This horrific accident was viewed by the relatives and friends of the passengers and a live broadcast by a reporter relayed the tragic event to the world.

Years later I realised that Father having experienced raids by Zeppelins in World War I had seen that this flight of the Hindenburg showed the probability of the German Air Force being able to bomb cities throughout the British Isles. The English Channel was no longer our first line of defence. How right he was.

In Bedford one day in May 1990 I heard this same droning noise. Looking out of my window saw the dirigible from Cardington floating serenely past and the above story came flooding back into my mind.

In World War I some German aircraft were called Gotha. Because of this nomenclature, George V changed his name from Saxe Coburg-Gotha to Windsor.


# A Family Party

Throughout my early years I only had brief glimpses of paternal family relations during our short visits in the summer holidays. Apart from Mother's sister Jessie who stayed with us for Christmas holidays, I knew of no other relation of hers.

Mother's brother, wife and their two sons, Esmond and Russell, were to visit Vancouver and there was a possibility of emigration. Before they left my parents decided to hold a family party and invited them to stay with us overnight. Mother's youngest sister, husband and daughter, Father's sister and daughter were also invited. With our family we were a party of seventeen.

As with every event in our household everything had to be planned well in advance and this was no exception. Such excitement for weeks beforehand. The planning of extra beds to be brought down from the attic, mattresses, bed linen etc. to be placed in the bedrooms. In the dining room china, cutlery and table linen, was washed, counted and stored in the commodious sideboard. Breakfast would have to be in two sessions as only eight people could sit round the dining table. One Aunt and Uncle would stay at a Trust House Hotel and another Aunt and Uncle could be accommodated in the spare bedroom in Mr. and Mrs. Price's house across the road. In our four bedrooms, with the extra beds and camp beds, we could sleep twelve!

On the day we were all kept busy with one thing or another. By tea time everyone had arrived and there were conversations going on in all the rooms. Early next morning Mother and I served breakfast in two relays and when everything had been cleared into the kitchen, we all went outside to have our photograph taken. A short time afterwards most of our guests went on their various journeys. The rest helped to put our house to rights. That was the only time I saw some of these relatives.

## John Russell and Bird's Foot Trefoil

Mother was a very thrifty person and one summer's day she asked me to collect some blackberries which grew in profusion along the top of Portsdown Hill. As I walked by the fence bordering the last house, I became aware of a rustling in the undergrowth by someone who was keeping pace with me. 'I can hear you. Who's there?' I challenged. A young boy's face appeared over the fence asking 'What are you doing?' 'I'm going to pick some blackberries, just over there,' I replied. 'Why?' came the next question. 'Mother is going to make some blackberry and apple jam,' and the next second he disappeared from sight.

Picking some flowers which grew along the edge of the path, I was startled when he appeared once again with another question, 'What is that little yellow flower?' 'Oh. That is Birds Foot Trefoil.' I said, 'Haven't you seen it before?' 'No,' he said, 'It doesn't grow where I come from!' And once again he ran off.

A few days later, about the same time in the afternoon, I was not surprised when he appeared again saying 'I saw you climbing up the hill.' 'Oh. How could you? You can't see the path past this wall.' Grinning, he chortled, 'I was on the wall watching the tennis next door.' I thought – so that's how you saw me. The wall was very high and divided The Towers from Admiral Luard's tennis court and garden.

Then he asked my name and I gave it as Joyce Broughton saying I lived on the main road at the bottom of the hill. I wanted to know his name and his reply was 'Russell' which caused me to refer to my cousin whose Christian name was also Russell. On asking his surname I still got the answer 'Russell'.

Suddenly another boy appeared and Russell scurried like quicksilver, dashing away through the trees. They were obviously playing some kind of game so I started to walk on. But the other boy came to the fence and said, as though to excuse his friend's behaviour 'Take no notice, he's funny like that. I'm his cousin'. Which I thought most strange.

On Saturday afternoon I encountered him once again and he wanted to show me the talking bird. 'Was it a parrot?' I asked. And he said 'No'. So I assumed it was a Mynah. 'Come to tea on Wednesday. SHE won't be here.' I understood this to mean it was the person who looked after him when his grandparents were away.

At home I asked Mother if I could go to tea on Wednesday, but she would not let me go. The locals thought those who lived at The Towers were eccentric as they were only there during the summer months.

My persistence I had been invited to tea eventually caused Mother to relent and on the following Wednesday, dressed in my best dress and shoes, I rang the bell at The Towers. The door was opened by the butler and I stated my name and I had been invited to tea with Master Russell. 'I will enquire,' he said, and left me on the doorstep to return a few moments later to say 'Master Russell is not at home,' and shut the door. I was devastated at such discourtesy and went home. Shortly afterwards he was sent to school.

I did not meet up with him again until after 31 years when I visited Woburn Abbey with my husband and daughters. In the souvenir shop I took the opportunity to speak to John Russell, the Thirteenth Duke of Bedford. I asked him if he had any memory of our encounters over the fence of his grandparent's house – 'The Towers' – at Bedhampton. Although he did not recall all of the above he did remember talking to me about the Birds Foot Trefoil. We had a most pleasant conversation and in a side room he arranged a quick cup of tea for us whilst recalling those days before he went to school.

## Sir Matthew Hale to His Son

The following letter written in the 17th Century, was given to me in my teen years. It inspired me as to its truths and enabled me to cope with various experiences throughout my life.

N E V E R speak anything for a truth which you know, or believe to be false. Lying is a great sin against GOD, who gave us a tongue to speak the truth and not falsehood. It is a great offence against humanity itself; for where there is no regard to truth, there can be no safe society between man and man. And it is an injury to the speaker; for, besides the disgrace which it brings upon him, it occasions so much basement of mind, that he can scarcely tell truth, or avoid lying even when he had no colour of necessity for it; and in time, he comes to such a pass, that as other people cannot believe he speaks truth, so he, himself scarcely knows when he tells a falsehood. As you must be careful not to lie, so you must avoid coming near it. You must not equivocate, nor speak anything positively for which you have no authority but report, or conjecture, or opinion.

B E  N O T  too earnest, loud, or violent in your conversation. Silence your opponent with reason, not with noise. Be careful not to interrupt another when he is speaking; hear him out and you will understand him the better, and be able to give him the better answer. Consider before you speak, especially when the business is of moment; weigh the sense of what you mean to utter, and the expressions you intend to use, that they may be significant, pertinent, and inoffensive. Inconsiderate persons do not think till they speak, or they speak and then think.

S O M E  men excel in husbandry, some in gardening, some in mathematics. In conversation, learn, as near as you can, where the skill or excellence of any person lies; put him upon talking on that subject, observe what he says, keep it in your memory, or commit it to writing. By this means you will glean the worth and knowledge of everybody you converse with; and at an easy rate, acquire what may be of use to you on many occasions.

W H E N  you are in company with light, vain, impertinent persons, let the observing of their failings make you the more cautious both in your conversations with them and in your general behaviour, that you may avoid their errors.

I F  A  M A N  whose integrity you do not very well know, makes you great and extraordinary professions, do not give much credit to him. Probably you will find that he aims at something besides kindness to you, and that when he has served his turn, or been disappointed, his regard for you will grow cool.

B E W A R E  also of him who flatters you, and commends you to your face, or to one who he thinks will tell you of it; most probably he has either deceived and abused you, or means to do so. Remember the fable of the fox commending the singing of the crow, who had something in her mouth which the fox wanted.

B E  C A R E F U L  that you do not commend yourselves. It is a sign that your reputation is small and sinking, if your own tongue must praise you; and it is fulsome and unpleasing to others to hear such commendations.

S P E A K  well of the absent whenever you have a suitable opportunity. Never speak ill of them, or of anybody, unless you are sure they deserve it, and unless it is necessary for their amendment, or for the safety and benefit of others.

A V O I D  in your ordinary communications, not only oaths, but all imprecations and earnest protestations. Forbear scoffing and jesting at the condition or natural defects of any person. Such offences leave a deep impression; and they often cost a man dear.

## Purbrook Park County High School

From records I have collated the following historical information. The school began in 1906 as a Baptist Chapel Schoolroom in Cosham. By 1913 numbers had increased so they moved to a large house. In 1921 the school moved into a large hut at Farlington on Portsdown Hill. Now it was recognised as a Secondary School and was called 'Waterlooville and District County School'. As we lived outside the Portsmouth area my younger brother and sister on leaving Havant School had to attend this County School. There was an extensive school programme of English, French, History,

Geography, Mathematics, Art and Science. and senior pupils took the Oxford Certificate Examination. They did not have a sports field but facilities were found nearby. The provision of hot dinners at three shillings and three pence per week, eaten in the school, was an unusual precedent and I remember it caused great excitement.

In 1924 the Hampshire Education Committee purchased Purbrook Park, a Georgian mansion. It had a large shrubbery of rhododendrons and four acres of land. With 78 pupils and Dr. P.T.Freeman as Headmaster, Purbrook Park County High School was established. Within a year Mr H.E.Dalton-Morris became the first assistant master and a few months later when Dr. Freeman left, Mr Ernest Stedman succeeded him as Headmaster. Miss Gray, who was the senior mistress, resigned and Miss Fountaine was appointed Headmistress. The school motto was VINCENT VERITAS – Truth Conquers. The school badge with this motto was of a Lion Rampant in yellow on a circular blue background. This was sewn on every pupil's cap, blazer and hatband. My elder brother, having left Churchers College, settled into the Fifth Form where senior pupils were expected to take the Oxford School Certificate. In the Upper V Form he won the London University Certificate and in Form VI he achieved the Inter B.Sc examination. About this time he won a Bronze Medal for his achievements in sports before going on to attend Reading University.

My younger brother was keen on running and he trained for the mile coming in first with his brother in second place. On Sunday afternoons, when he was charged to look after me, we would go down to the shore. Between the sea and the land was a raised embankment with a path along the top just over a mile long. He would challenge me to run to the style at half-way and when I got there he would start to run and try to catch me up before the end of the mile. We did this many times during that summer. On the last occasion he was surprised to find we ended the run together! These runs, although exhausting, gave me a sense of competition and a great feeling of achievement. They may well have been responsible to some degree for my physical strength and endurance in future years. On leaving Purbrook he went on to study architecture at college and became an Architect and later was a Town Planner for London

When the school increased in pupil numbers and teaching staff a large Hall, equipped as a gymnasium, was built. It also had a stage and two small dressing rooms at the rear which doubled as classrooms The Georgian kitchen was refurbished and extended to cope with lunches served in the Hall. The grounds were laid out for sports, one area for football and cricket and the lower field for hockey and rounders. The hard tennis court in the shrubbery was also used for netball matches. An ancient tree separated the sports field from the four grass tennis courts constructed close to the house. It was venerated by everyone and became quite a landmark. Sadly it was cut down when alterations were made after World War II.

I never forgot the kindness of Miss Lawson to me during the six weeks of July before I started my first year in Form I in September 1932 wearing the official uniform. Reporting to the school office I was escorted upstairs to the Ladies' Staff Room to meet

Miss Fountaine, the Headmistress. She took me into the small room which overlooked the main entrance and left me in Miss Lawson's charge. I held Miss Fountaine in great respect for she always listened to what I had to say and this made my traumatic experience fade into oblivion.

The school day started with Assembly in the Hall. The youngest boys and girls were the first to enter from opposite sides and were to line up on two markers leaving a gap down the centre. Miss Lawson was getting agitated because none of the girls in my class were willing to lead and this was holding up the rest of the school. I had no qualms at being first into the Hall and got annoyed at their reticence so I calmly strode in front and said 'follow me!'. Lining up on the marker I looked up to see Mr Stedman smiling down at me from the reading desk in front of the stage, approving my action. So began my years at Purbrook.

The school bus collected pupils from as far away as Emsworth, the furthest point from the school. The final stop was at Bedhampton where, being the last one to board, I had to sit on a box next to the driver, there being no other seat. This 'privilege' enabled the elderly driver the opportunity to give me an occasional treat – an apple from his garden, big and juicy. A fatherly gesture never forgotten.

That autumn we collected sweet chestnuts from the shrubbery and Miss Lawson allowed us to cook them on the hot plate of the stove. I think this room must have been the day nursery of the Georgian house. Many times I collected pocketfuls of beech nuts, which were fiddling to open but delicious to eat.

School events such as the Choir Festival and Sports Day took place in Winchester annually. For several years we entered our Choir and often came second in the County. One year we came first and this shield was proudly displayed in the foyer beneath the boards displaying all the names of the successful entrants of the Matriculation and the Inter B.Sc since 1925. Every summer the school would travel in several coaches to the Annual Sports Day. This was held in grounds to the south of the town. It was a packed and exciting day. A running track was laid down and each school was assigned to one section of the grounds. All the schools competed in athletics and Cups for the winners were presented at the end of the day. Pupils had to wear uniform and carry packed lunch and tea. Drinks could be bought from various side stands. There were no loos on site but each school was allocated one of the cottages alongside the road, and lines of pupils formed at their gates. The trek through the cottage gave one an insight into people's living rooms on the way through to the outside loo down the yard.

Unfortunately, due to children's illnesses in the Junior School, causing much loss of schooling, no one realised how much basic work in mathematics I had missed. Therefore when I was 15 years old it was obvious I could not hope to gain a pass in mathematics, one of the four subjects necessary to obtain the School Certificate. As the cost of both school and College was the same (viz. £5.00 per term) Father offered me the choice – a year at Art College or a year in Form VI. I opted for the former which actually gave me a far better grounding for my future.

To celebrate George V and Queen Mary's Silver Jubilee in 1935 all school children were to receive a china mug. In our school instead of a china mug I was privileged to receive an unusual green glass one. I understand other glass mugs in different colours were produced but I have never seen them.

The School Magazine was produced every term. Here is an amusing anecdote from 'The Purbrookian' of 1934:

'The wayfarer, while about to cross the road was knocked down by a large dog. Before he could get on his feet properly he was knocked down again by a baby car. A policeman arriving on the scene asked the man if he was hurt. 'Well,' he said dazedly, 'the dog didn't hurt me. It was the confounded tin on his tail that did the damage'.'

In the 1928 issue there was the first Chapter of 'The Book of Haj'. The author is unknown. Here is the first verse:

'Now in the land of Pur which lyeth next unto that of Pompey there is a great centre of knowledge where divers tribes collect to absorb the words of wisdom which floweth from the lips of the Great Es and his attendant priests.'

This was followed some years later by the 'Book Of Hex' which I assume may have been written by Mr. Dalton-Morris and/or Form VI.

At the end of lessons at 4 o'clock until the buses left at 5 o'clock, there were many clubs available to us during that hour. Such as, any sport activity, photography, including developing and printing, chess and stamp collecting. All of these were very popular. If I missed my bus it meant a three mile walk home over the Downs. On one of these walks I found a very rare Bee Orchid!

Mr. Morris was one of my form masters and he was instrumental in instilling my fascination for research and my love of history. Miss Fountaine was my geography teacher and in this subject I found great interest in cartography. These two people were the most influential teachers in my life, and to whom I am most indebted. I count myself extremely fortunate to have been educated at Purbrook for all the teachers had good academic qualifications and were adept at passing on knowledge

In 1939 as the school was in a 'neutral' area not affected by evacuation, pupils numbers had increased to nearly 300 as neighbouring schools were evacuated. Extensions to the school buildings had been started in early 1939 and consequently the premises were large enough to accommodate the new intake. Air raid shelters were built and the school became a rendezvous for the Fire Services. In March 1941, in the space of three days, 1,750 Auxiliary Fire Servicemen were fed and slept in the school. Up to a hundred lived at the school for weeks at a time. Police, A.R.P. men and Demolition Squads were also given food and shelter and a Squadron of the Air Training Corps established its headquarters there. School classes continued throughout as though nothing was happening!

Even in my day the first step of the main staircase built in Georgian times had been worn to a thin shell. So it was not surprising to find the stair treads had been resurfaced when I visited the school some thirty years later when I was invited by the Headmaster to be the first person to ascend after its refurbishment. A photograph records this momentous occasion.

# Embroidery and Design

At the age of nineteen Mother won a Bronze Medal for a competition at the Royal School of Needlework. She embroidered a six-inch border of a flower design in peach filoselle silk on a sage green cloth. I drew a coloured copy of her design, as I remembered it, and sent it to the School for their records.

From an early age Mother encouraged handmade Christmas presents for the family as these would be less costly to make. I learnt to knit scarves, pullovers, embroidered needlecases in felt and crochet mats. Cards of buttons and bookmarkers were decorated in script writing for birthdays.

At Infant School we were taught plain knitting and made dishcloths. In the Junior School we had to sew by hand the obligatory pinafore. This took a long time and was boring, so when at Senior School we progressed to items of underwear and thence to summer dresses I was delighted. Being already adept at hand sewing and using a sewing machine these were quickly completed.

In 1930 I vividly remember helping Father to reupholster our settee and two chairs. He showed me what he called 'a trick of the trade!' He took a strip of cardboard and deftly hammered tacks through the card and cloth at the top edge of the back. The material was then pulled over and tacked underneath the bottom rail. Using a special needle and thread I was given the job of sewing both sides and this gave a tight finish to the back area. Now I was given the job of pleating and sewing the roundels on the front arms! His teaching of the skill upholstering was never forgotten.

At Purbrook in our Art Classes we explored many difference styles. Exercises in designing repeat patterns were a favourite, especially when allied to a practical application. For example, pelmets, cushions, wallpaper and endpapers for books. Metal work also intrigued me and I designed a decorative metal grill of a bird in a tree. Sometimes I found my designs could be transposed into projects in needlework and embroidery.

In 1937 Father started to take an interest in my art work and it was then I found him as a friend. To develop my talent he gave me his book prize, 'Nature In Ornament' which influenced my school work to a considerable degree. At the same time he gave me a book called 'The Art of Illuminating as Practised in Europe from the Earliest Times' by W.R.Tymms and M.D.Wyatt, Architect, being the Second Edition in Octavo published in December 1859 by Day & Son Ltd. It had originally belonged to my maternal grandfather who purchased it sometime before 1866.

In the late 1900's I was fortunate to obtain the services of George D. Davidson, a Fine Art Book Restorer who was intrigued to discover the First Edition had been in Quarto! The book was full of beautiful illuminated pages and every page was loose! They had only been stuck, never sewn together. Furthermore to my amazement all the text and the coloured plates were present – not a single page was missing! Inside the cover was a Bookplate of a shield, crossbanded with the name, Arthur Towler.

Then I discovered a talent for design following the Art Nouveau trend of simplistic flowing format. Needing a new pair of slippers I designed a peacock's head in green silk lined with peach. Using different stitches embroidered and outlined the quilted peacock extending the wings to form the sides. Attaching the fabric to the flanges of a pair of soles, these made warm comfortable slippers which were worn for many years.

During the last two years at Purbrook the Art Mistress allowed me, after completing whatever was on the curriculum, to sew and embroider my own projects. One afternoon, having finished my prep. and being anxious to finish stitching a cushion cover as a present for Mother, I was quietly working away when Miss Fountaine, who was taking the homework class, appeared at my side. She enquired in a whisper, 'What are you doing?' Explaining my wish to use every available minute to finish before the end of term I showed her what was involved. It was a Spanish design of brilliant colours, worked in wool and gold silk cross-stitch. It was part of the collection of embroideries and silks left to Father by a previous Art Mistress of the College. One quarter had been completed and the rest was a blank canvas. No chart or pattern was supplied. One had to count every stitch and transpose them in reverse on each of the remaining quarters to complete the cushion. She was most surprised at the intricate detail and amazed at the degree of concentration and skill required. She urged me to be sure to show it to the Art Mistress at my next class.

Many times in my life I have used my designs in other ways; for instance, stylised trees painted on silk panels for lampshades and a wide border of fruits for a large fire-screen. When Mrs. Wyldbore-Smith needed a circular window to be put in her private dining rooms she approved of my design as described under 'The White House School' at Husborne Crawley, Bedfordshire.

For my parent's three tiered Golden Wedding cake I made a vase of gold roses and fern for the top. Along the sides of each tier I painted oval water-colour pictures. These were edged with gold balls and bows of gold ribbon to complete the Regency style. The top tier depicted two churches and two of their houses. The middle tier had eight ovals and these contained symbols of their crafts e.g. Modelling, Technical Drawing, Plasterwork, Pottery, Needlework, Cookery, Painting and Gardening. The bottom tier had 12 ovals and these contained pictures of incidents in their lives with both Singer and Vauxhall cars. The cake when finished weighed some 24lbs and my daughters and I conveyed it, very carefully by car, to my parent's celebration at their bungalow in Goldalming.

## Charles Francis Annesley Voysey

At the end of each summer term at Purbrook there was a great milling about, everyone trying to buy second hand or third hand copies of books on the form list from pupils who had finished with them that year. This could be quite a financial saving.

One book on my list was 'Prester John' by John Buchan who had just been appointed as Governor General of Canada. Because of this connection it was not easy to find a copy it being so popular amongst the boys. But I was lucky to find one copy being sold by Eric N. Voysey who was entering the Sixth Form. It had already been used by three pupils before him and was well thumbed. We negotiated a price and during the summer holidays I read it more than once. It was an enthralling story and stimulated my imagination to the extent I still have it on my bookshelf today.

On writing the above paragraph I am reminded of an unusual incident which happened in the 1930s. One morning Father entered the breakfast room in great excitement clutching a letter he had just received. Showing it to Mother I heard him say 'I have just received this letter from MR. VOYSEY! He says he is sending me, not his son but another relative to see me. I shall invite him to lunch next Sunday.'

To have a guest for Sunday lunch was so unusual I knew it had to be important. When the young man, Victor Voysey, was introduced I thought he was about the same age as my brothers because he had a boyish appearance but it seems he was much older. After lunch he and Father had a long conversation in the drawing room before he left to catch the ferry to the Isle of Wight. Father's comment on this visit was 'That boy will be a famous portrait painter!' I was surprised at this statement because for Father to make such a positive forecast was very rare.

Recently I discovered Victor did become a well known portrait painter and understand he was possibly Charles Voysey's second cousin. No wonder Father was excited to receive a letter from his previous employer. In addition I have been fortunate to find Victor's family still living on the Isle of Wight. His father's papers are with his son and maybe, sometime in the future, my Father's letter may come to light.


## 1938. School Trip to Dinard, Brittany

Excited at the prospect of my first visit abroad, travelling with my school instead of members of my family, I looked forward to it with great anticipation. As I was the youngest pupil in the group Mother made one condition. She arranged for me to share a bedroom with an older girl.

We left school in a coach and at Portsmouth harbour boarded the ship for the port of St. Malo. The day was sunny, the sea was smooth and I enjoyed the trip. From St. Malo we travelled in another coach to our hotel in Dinard, a seaside town. Apparently we were late in arriving so the teacher who was allocating the bedrooms was under pressure to be quick as the hotel staff were waiting to serve our meal. The girl Mother had asked to look after me decided to room with another, which left me at the end with the last single room! I must admit I felt left out but determined to make the best of it. Consequently, until I decided to go off on my own, I was thrown into the company of two boy classmates most of the time, there being no other girl of my age.

At the supper table we were served with a cup of tea and a slice of a large omelette.

We only had sandwiches for lunch on board ship and we were all very hungry. Eventually some slices of bread and butter appeared and I managed to get two slices! Breakfast I knew would be the French croissant and jam – not really enough for my appetite and lunch seemed a long time coming, but the following supper was more substantial.

One day we had a coach trip to a market where we watched Breton ladies making lace. Being careful of the little pocket money I had, I bought a small lace butterfly and a very small bottle of Chanel No.5 perfume as a present for Mother. Another day we had a coach trip to Dinan. There, everyone went to the shops to buy cakes and mementoes. Seeing a guide collecting a group of French and German people to be guided around the local castle, I joined them. I was most interested to see the strength of the castle's defences and surprised at the thickness of the walls. Although I only partly understood the guide's graphic descriptions of the interesting features as I was not very proficient in the French language at that time.

Our return journey was overnight and because of fog we had to anchor in the middle of the Channel for several hours. Many people felt seasick with the rolling at anchor, but I loved it! That night I developed neuralgia due to a bad tooth and the headmistress allowed me to sleep on a bench in the open air tucked up with a blanket, as I found the heat in the saloon made it worse. We eventually disembarked at Portsmouth at about 6am and were taken to a café where we were given a large English breakfast which was appreciated by everyone!

On arriving home I found my cat, Jinky, sitting on the gatepost waiting for me! Mother said he had pined for me while I was away but half a hour before I arrived had got up from his basket, gone outside and down the drive to sit on the gatepost. This had always been his favourite place to wait to greet me when due home from school. How did he know I was on my way home just half an hour before? Animal instinct is incredible.

This was my first taste of foreign travel and I loved it in spite of being left to my own devices. The possibility of a job with travel intrigued me. I would have loved to be a King's Messenger but of course this was 'pie in the sky'. I was female and did not have the languages which would be required. But nowadays who knows what I could have accomplished? I believe this experience formulated my interest in history and research. Since then, apart from my visit to Paris the following year, I have only been abroad for one week to Majorca.

## 1939 – Visit To Paris

Travelling with Maud, another schoolgirl, both on exchange visits to Paris in 1939 I was met by Nicole Chabanel and her mother at the Gare du Nord. They lived in an apartment on the Left Bank and I was to stay until September 2nd when Nicole would accompany me back to England for a month.

During the first two weeks we visited the Louvre Museum where I was impressed with the vigour of the Winged Victory. I thought the Venus de Milo was very dark and was surprised to find it not as large as pictures had indicated. Other visits were to the Tomb of Napoleon and Notre Dame. My memory of the Sacré Coeur was of a very long flight of steps which led up to the entrance. From there the Agrandissement of Montmartre appeared as an interesting collection of small jumbled buildings nestling under the shadow of this famous church.

Another memorable visit was to the Palace of Versailles. The circular bedroom of Marie Antoinette with its mirrored walls, gilded pillars and blue ceiling dotted with stars, was fantastic. Such a contrast to the almost bare bedroom of King Louis. The long gallery with its fabulous mirrors was very impressive. There were eleven octagonal lampshades in the main gallery and entrance hall and I was told the twelfth hung in the staircase hall of the Petit Maison, the little house which had been built in the garden for her amusement.

During my visit Maud and her French exchange girl invited us to tea. When we arrived we were ushered into the best room where the table was laid with cups and saucers, a jug of milk, sugar bowl and a plate of biscuits. Two other French girls were introduced and we all sat down. It was obviously an occasion for the teapot was brought in and ceremoniously placed in the centre of the table. The tea, when served, looked very weak but this did not bother me. What did, was the fact it was COLD!! Amongst embarrassed giggles it transpired the tea had been made with cold water. What could I do but offer to show them how to make 'English Tea'.

During my third week there was a sense of urgency as troops began arriving by road and rail every day. The Tuilerie Gardens became a massive camp with tents everywhere.

Listening to the early morning overseas radio on Thursday 24th August we heard someone recommending all Americans to leave Europe immediately. Turning to Nicole I said 'If it's good enough for them Maud and I should get back to England this weekend, as it appears the outbreak of war is imminent.'

By lunch time we had contacted Maud and agreed to leave Paris as quickly as possible. Our tickets were checked and we were told to travel to Calais where ferries were sailing to Dover continuously. Pooling our money we went to the Post Office and sent a cablegram to my Father saying as we were leaving Paris on the midday train would he meet us off the ferry at Dover on Saturday about 4pm.

To my amazement, when arriving at the Gare du Nord, I found not only Maud, but also her French exchange girl. Her parents were quite insistent that she was to travel with us otherwise she would not be able to have her month's holiday in England. So we were bundled on to the train, luckily securing seats, and arrived at Calais about 2pm. Following the crowds to the quays we were shepherded, four-abreast, into a queue which went to and fro in an 'S' formation. At first we could not see the ferries or even the end of the queue, for the hundreds of people with luggage. Moving slowly snake-wise we saw one ferry pulling away from the distant quay and within a matter of minutes another one appeared alongside and the queue started to move again. We saw at least five ferries pull in and depart fully loaded before we got within distance of seeing one of the gangways. When we were within the last 30 people from the nearest gangway – off went the ferry to our left. On our right another one was nearing the quay and yet another was steaming along about six miles out. At last we got on board and eventually landed at Dover harbour about 7pm.

Maud and I were through Customs quickly and we waited for her girlfriend who being French had, of course, to go through the foreign side. As she did not appear after 10 minutes I left my case with Maud and went through to the other side. No other foreigner was there and I found this 13 year old girl, with limited English, being questioned by three Customs Officials. I had to explain what had happened and reassure the Immigration Officer that she was on a School Exchange visit. After giving them the name and address of Maud's parents and accepting the fact that she might have to go back to France they allowed her come with me. Her suitcase had been taken on to London and it was several days before it arrived back at Havant.

Now where was Father? And the car? After looking around the area where cars were parked, Father suddenly appeared! He said they, Mother, my sister and Maud's Mother, had watched the arrival of all the ferries from Calais since early afternoon. They were so relieved to see us safe and sound but oh dear – what about the seating in the car? There were too many of us with the luggage! After some discussion I suggested that Maud and I take the train to Havant and we could catch a bus or walk the short distance home. Then there would be room for everyone and our luggage in the car.

At first Mother was very apprehensive about us going all that way by ourselves. But I said, if we could arrange to travel from Paris through all the hassle of troop movements in a foreign country, we could surely manage a train journey from Dover to Havant. In the end this was what was decided. Father gave me some money and we walked to the station and bought our tickets. At that time of the evening we had to change at Brighton with an hour's delay.

On this train we were joined by another French girl who was much older. She was travelling to stay with relatives at 'Ov'. She had booked to Brighton but did not know what to do when she got there! Although her English was good she found it difficult to communicate. At Brighton we offered to help her find the bus. Before leaving the station we made sure of our return to catch the connection to Havant. The man on the gate was very helpful and told us where to catch the bus. There it was to discover buses had stopped running earlier in the evening. As it was now late and she was very tired, I suggested she stay at one of the numerous Bed and Breakfast houses overnight and continue her journey in the morning. Selecting one which proved to be clean and comfortable at 5 shillings per night, we left her with a pleasant landlady who undertook to see her on the bus for Hove the next morning.

At Havant we were very glad to see Father waiting to take us home. He had been able to take Maud's mother and the French girl to their house in Lower Lane and then leave my sister and Mother at our house with plenty of time to collect us. What a day!

## World War II

During World War II as a civilian I was privileged to play a small part in all three sections of our Armed Forces. To have worked alongside many men who gave of their energy and expertise in many fields, to succeed in setting free the peoples of Europe in the Nazi programme and the dictatorship of Adolf Hitler.

As a broadcast by Neville Chamberlain the Prime Minister was expected on Sunday Mother and I joined Father in the drawing room instead of going to church. At 11 o'clock he announced in a sombre tone that a state of war now existed between Germany and Britain. Father turned off the radio and there were a few moments of quiet thought until he turned to Mother and said 'We must plan for 25 years ahead. Examination results must be downgraded immediately otherwise there will be insufficient qualified teachers available for when the war is over. You must stock up on suitable clothing and shoes for the next five years.' Leaving them to discuss what needed to be done I crept out of the room feeling very apprehensive of what might happen and a little excited at the prospect of a very different life which might be opening up for me. My entry to the College of Art was but a few days away – would I be able to go?

That night the air-raid sirens went off for the first time. We hurried down into our cellar and sat in deck-chairs wrapped in eiderdowns for it was bitterly cold. How poor our preparations had been. This was soon improved by putting down some carpet, better chairs and camping facilities to make a hot drink. We each had a small suitcase to hold emergency clothing and any precious item. At night, even if the mobile guns were firing and travelling up and down the back road, we found we could sleep as the sound was muted through the ground. My cat soon made himself snug in his bed under a shelf in the corner.

Being only a short distance from the shore it was important that no chink of light could be seen at night. Father conformed to the black-out regulations by fitting plywood shutters to the inside of windows in the downstairs rooms behind our heavily lined curtains. Upstairs, blackout curtains were hung underneath pelmets and only 40 watt bulbs were fitted. Many times on hearing raiders approaching before a warning siren went off we would drop everything and run for our cellar. One day when dog fights were leaving sky trails Father and I were standing in our front porch when something landed on the tiles with a clink! It was a piece of shrapnel about 4 inches long with very jagged edges. It was wise to be under shelter when aircraft were overhead.

# Southern College of Art, Portsmouth Centre

The Southern College of Art had three colleges in Bournemouth, Portsmouth and Southampton. The Portsmouth College of Art was on the seventh floor of the two-winged building behind the Guildhall. Mr. Edward E. Pullee was the Principal and my Father was Vice-Principal. The other floors were occupied by the Technical College.

To catch a train which took half an hour to reach Portsmouth Station, Father and I walked the half mile to Bedhampton Halt. Some of our fellow travellers had known Father for many years and one of them made the following comment to me, 'You must find it awkward to have your Father as a Tutor?' 'No, not really. It is a question of discretion. It's like having two sides of a coin. One side is home and the other is college. Father trusts me not to repeat anything overheard at College or at home. He expects me not to embarrass him in either place. It's quite simple.'

The main door into the entrance hall of the two wings of the Colleges was approached by a steep flight of steps. The door-keeper knew the faces of all students and would nod his acceptance of one's entry but he was very quick to challenge a stranger. A square stairwell rose seven floors and between each floor two flights of stairs were on either side of a mezzanine landing.

As a full-time student I attended morning, afternoon and evening sessions all week. Mr. Townsend was Head of the Architectural Department and gave me – the only girl – instruction in the art of Tracing and Draughtsmanship. He also allowed me to attend his lectures on building construction with slides worldwide which I found most interesting. Father taught me Perspective, Technical Drawing, Lettering and Pottery. Other tutors gave me instruction in Millinery, Glove-making, Couture Dressmaking, Embroidery and other crafts. A full quota of learning.

At the end of my first term a fancy dress Christmas Ball was held for both Colleges. On that evening I accompanied my parents and we were met by the Principal dressed as a Chinese Mandarin. Very clever makeup, even to the fingernails!

During lunch breaks an architectural student and I had practised the London Tango. When the London Tango music started only two couples besides ourselves started to dance. After one circuit I noticed they had stopped to watch us. We used the floor like professionals forming some very intricate steps. He was dressed as a Spaniard and I was dressed in white, sprinkled with playing cards as 'Patience', so our costumes complemented each other in colour. When the music finished we were given an ovation from the 300 people assembled! My parents could not be embarrassed by my expertise, could they?

The end of term notices were given me to produce to show the various styles learnt each term. In the summer term of 1940 I was asked to paint in Roman lettering, six inches in height, on a board some five feet by three feet 'Southampton College of Art Portsmouth Centre'. This was to be hung from the banister of the stairwell so that it could be seen from the entrance hall seven floors below and it was there for many years.

One day in mid-summer, having no coat or umbrella I paused at the entrance realising the downpour was so heavy I would get soaked running to catch my bus and there was no shelter in front of the Guildhall. Dr. Peter Hey, one of the Technical Tutors, suggested I share his umbrella as he was to catch the same bus. He knew my Father and was obviously concerned at my predicament. Attending a meeting at a lady member's house of a local archaeological group some 34 years later and 150 miles distant from Portsmouth, to my utter amazement her husband was Mr. Hey. What a coincidence!

For the first few months of the War life went on more or less as usual until the first bombs fell on Portsmouth. I was glad on that autumn morning of my navy wool cardigan, school issue though it was, for new clothes could not be bought until old ones wore out.

The architectural room took up the whole of one wing of the building. The swing doors from the main stairwell gently thudded-to behind my desk and a freckled face appeared over my board. 'You're late,' I said. 'Bus was late!' came the reply. From the far end of the room the Master's voice boomed 'And what time do you call this young man? Hurry up and join us. You'll have to make up for lost time.' A grudging whisper came 'Not my fault the bus didn't run is it? Blame the War.' At the end of his lecture Mr. Townsend retired to his office and quiet once more descended on the drawing office.

Above our heads the rising wail of the Air Raid Warning siren started. Mr. Townsend emerged shouting 'Everyone out! Hurry up! This way!' holding open the small door to the spiral staircase which led down to the next level and concrete stairs to the basement. Leaping off my stool I grabbed my instrument box and handbag and jumped for the gangway. Seeing the Master urging his students through the narrow doorway it was obvious to us at the other end, it was touch and go if everyone got down in the allotted time, let alone us in the rear.

Noting their slow progress I gasped 'No way!' and Jenkins, the erstwhile latecomer, made a snap decision calling out, 'We'll take the main stairs Sir' and to me said 'It'll be quicker. Come on. Run!' I did so agree and we flew hell for leather. Speed was essential and he took the stairs two at a time, urging me to keep up for we had seven double flights to go. My feet seemed to skim each step with the merest touch and the aircraft sounds thrumming the air lent extra impetus to our flight.

Running into the basement tunnel we collided with the senior technical students. A few minutes later we heard Mr. Townsend's voice calling 'Jenkins are you there?' 'Yes sir. Here sir.' 'Where is Stella? Is she with you?' 'I'm here.' I managed to splutter, being partially crushed behind a large, hefty engineering student. Thrusting him aside he towered above me. 'Thank God you're safe. You must have flown down those stairs.' Jenkins explained 'We couldn't have made the spiral stairs Sir. We didn't have time. We just ran.' and I added 'Yes Mr. Townsend, we knew we could make it. We're both fast runners.' He was so relieved and had to agree to our sudden action. It had been a sensible decision having arrived in the basement before him and the other students!

Marking us off his register, all his students safely accounted for, he smiled benignly and said 'Join me at the other end when you've got your breath back' and he disappeared.

Panting for breath and shaking from our exertions we lent against the green tiled wall. This gave us a sense of security even though it felt chillingly cold. Suddenly the wall appeared to shudder and move! We looked at each other aghast. There was no noise. 'Did you feel that?' I asked. 'Yes. What was it?' 'Bombs I expect'. All that could be heard was the muted throbbing of aircraft which penetrated our underground refuge. Had the bombs been aimed at the Guildhall they could easily have missed and struck the building above us. Gradually the sounds faded away and the All Clear rang out.

Back upstairs we discovered that nobody else had felt the walls move. Incredible. But true. This was the first Air Raid on Portsmouth when bombs were dropped at North End.

Soon afterwards on the 5th December 1940 a bomb demolished the Carlton Cinema in Cosham. Roy S. Pearce, one of my classmates at Purbrook, was killed.

## Memorial To Battle Of Britain Pilot

It was a very hot Wednesday afternoon in 1940 when Mother and I went to visit her friends, William and Valletta Slatter in Emsworth. Mr. Slatter was a chemist and had a pharmacy in the High Street. Wednesday was his half-day closing so we were able to go out for a walk. Crossing the High Street we turned down Nile Street which ran down to the water. On our left were the ruins of some cottages. These had been bombed a few days before at the same time as the raid on Portsmouth when I was sheltering in the College basement.

There was a light breeze and it blew something into my eye. Mr. Slatter whipped out his eye-glass, turned back my eyelid and with the corner of a pristine white handkerchief removed a minute glass splinter! It was very painful so we returned to his shop where he washed out my eye. As the pain persisted he put in some eye drops which froze the eyeball. That evening my doctor confirmed that the glass splinter had scratched the eyeball and I had to keep it frozen until it healed.

Shortly after our visit they received the devastating news that their only son, Pilot Officer Dudley Malins Slatter, had been shot down over the Channel – four miles from Dover. His squadron had only just arrived at Hawkinge and were ordered to patrol 20 miles south of Folkestone. He was a Gunner with Pilot Officer J.R. Gardiner in L7016, one of the nine Defiants which took off. The squadron was suddenly attacked by Bf 109s both above and below them and within seconds the squadron was decimated. Four were shot down in flames and Gardiner was the only pilot who was rescued, wounded, from the sea.

The book 'Battle of Britain' by Francis K. Mason gives a very descriptive and comprehensive account of this combat. Dudley's body was never recovered and his name is recorded on Panel 10 of the Runnymede Memorial.

Mr. and Mrs. Slatter were understandably shattered and wanted a memorial of their own. They asked me to write the details of his life in script under a photograph and this was framed and hung on their living room wall.

## Dodging Hedgehoppers

Prior to the expected German invasion, code-named 'Sealion', their aircraft made sporadic sorties across the Channel to photograph ports, aerodromes and defences along the South Coast. The normal procedure was to fly at low level along the Channel then turn inland for a short distance and fly in a half circle to head back to France. Consequently, people who lived within two miles of the coast did not rely on air raid sirens as they were unable to give enough warning. We relied upon our ears listening for changes in the note of an engine to sense the direction of any aircraft. This would alert us to take shelter as German pilots had a tendency to fire at anything which moved. This could be difficult when houses were set back from the road but much easier in the country where hedges, trees and ditches offered instant cover.

During this time there were many occasions when one had to move swiftly to get out of sight. For instance I recall on cycling home to lunch one day having to throw my bicycle down and run some ten feet to seek shelter beneath a hedge. At the same time an Austin Seven was abandoned by its driver who leapt over a wooden fence on the opposite side of the road. It was fortunate that the belt of trees along this fence were very tall, forcing the pilot to climb steeply to avoid crashing into them. As the aircraft circled out to sea I picked up my bicycle, the driver got into his car and drove off, all as a matter of course. A delay of no more than three minutes.

The half acre of land which Father rented as an allotment lay above and behind the gardens of the houses along the main road. As it was 60ft above the back road it was virtually inaccessible. Our only access was possible by the goodwill of our neighbours who allowed us to cross their back yards.

It was open ground so, as a safety measure, we planted rows of runner beans on tripod stakes at 90o to the line of attack by raiders – east to west – instead of to the southern aspect as was the norm. This proved to be a valuable precaution. One day, when picking runner beans for lunch a German aircraft came flying in directly towards our allotment from the south. Throwing myself full length between the rows of stakes and wearing green overalls thought it unlikely I could be seen and the aircraft passed overhead having missed me completely.

Another time when I was digging I heard an aircraft approaching and decided to run for the house. As I ran past the large walnut tree at the corner of our neighbour's garden in order to cross the drive, I saw it only a few feet above the house coming directly towards me down the drive. Leaping back I pressed against the massive tree trunk thinking bullets could not possibly penetrate. Then realised I would be exposed to the rear gunner as it flew past. So, as it went overhead followed underneath to place myself out of sight against our garage. When I got into our house it was to see Mother in a state of shock for she had watched the whole incident and feared I had been killed.

A week or so later Mother's friend and her neighbour were sitting on a settee in the bay window of her bungalow drinking coffee. Hearing a low flying aircraft approaching they dropped their mugs and flew out of the room across the kitchen and into the Anderson shelter by the back door. On their return it was to find their mugs quite untouched but, there was a line of bullet holes across the settee!

The civilian staff of H.M.S. Excellent were evacuated to Bordean House which had been taken over as a naval establishment. They boarded a coach in Portsmouth which then stopped at 'The George' for Don Fry and myself. At half past seven one winter's morning there had been a heavy fall of snow on top of ice and it was very cold. I was glad to be wearing my navy velour coat and trousers. Having left my bicycle in Don's garage we set out. Walking past the last house we skirted the edge of a small quarry and climbed keeping an ear on the sound of an aircraft in the distance.

The early morning mist had cleared the top of the hill but as we neared the gap we heard the engine note change. Scanning the sky over Portsmouth Island we found everywhere was completely shrouded in dense mist. Desperately searching for a glimpse of this aircraft we were appalled to see a Junkers 88 emerge, barely half a mile away above the airport, literally on a level with our eyes. 'Quick! Under the hedge!' I shouted, leaping through the gap to throw myself into the hollow previously noted and a moment later Don fell on top of me. The shadow of the Junkers passed over us and it cleared the last house on the other side of the road by just a few feet. Firing its machine guns it disappeared out of sight and later a couple of sheep were found dead. Don scrambled out and turned to help me up. Shaking with shock and spitting out leaf debris into which my face had been pressed, I spluttered, 'Did you have to fall on top of me?' Smiling with embarrassment he said 'Sorry, but there was nowhere else to go.' Of course he was right.

My clothes were covered in mud; thorns and twigs from the hedge cuttings were embedded in my coat. Pulling these out gave us time to get over the shock of the incident. Now it was imperative to move quickly for we were late. Near the road the last two yards of turf was frozen ice and appeared to be a sheet of thick glass. We had to crawl on hands and knees to get to the surface of the road.

Don raced ahead to the cross roads and when I caught him up it was to see our coach slowing chugging up from Portsmouth in a line of traffic. On our side the traffic was nose to tail and we could not get across. Frantically jumping up and down we waved like mad at the driver so that he would wait for us. Then a lorry driver pulled up and signalled us to cross the road in front of him and thankfully we climbed aboard our coach.

My dishevelled appearance caused the senior girl clerk who was sitting in the front seat to draw her skirt aside with a grimace and a verbal exclamation of disgust. On joining our colleagues at the rear of the coach they joyfully remarked on the probable activity we had been up to, until we calmly stated we had been dodging a Junkers. Had they not seen it? They had! The driver had stopped half way up the hill as there was a petrol lorry just in front. If the Junkers had turned towards them, everyone would have had to get out and run like fury. Such were the times we lived in, with no warning sirens, just using our wits to stay alive.

## After Dunkirk – Apple Pies and Jam Crusts

Operation Dynamo took place at the end of May to early June 1940. Of the 330,000 men who were rescued from Dunkirk, those who were fit were stationed within two miles of the South Coast ready to repel the impending invasion. Several hundred were under canvas or quartered in commandeered houses, such as Leigh Park House and grounds just north of Havant. They were allowed out of Camp in the evenings for a few hours. Walking down North Street they would queue two-deep along the pavement for the NAAFI canteen opposite the Congregational Church. As they could not cope with the numbers of troops Mother organised the opening of our church hall in Elm Lane as a additional facility. Ladies attending our church and others from the Church of England volunteered to man this canteen. Extra rations were allocated for this purpose of tea, sugar, bread, butter, flour and lard.

Our canteen opened at 6pm and closed at 10pm every evening except Sunday. During these hours the ladies worked in relays serving tea and kept the kitchen ticking-over with preparation of food and washing-up. A cup of tea cost a ha'penny, a slice of bread and butter was one penny. The crusts were spread with jam, donated from private homes, and cost a ha'penny – a great favourite as troops had very little money. A variety of cakes were made by the ladies at home from these extra supplies. Mother cut the cakes into portions at a cost of one penny. If a cake could be evenly portioned e.g. 6-8 pieces, this was fine. I was roped-in to deal with the odd sizes – 5/7/9 portions.

At home we had lots of apples from the allotment so Mother bought several baking trays, each of four pans. In our kitchen she prepared large basins of sliced apples under water. Another basin held a dry mixture of flour and fat ready for pastry. With the supplies of flour, fat and a little sugar she baked apple pies.

One exceptional Friday she cooked some 36 pies during the day to take down to the canteen. They cost tuppence each and were much sought after. When I got home from work soon after 5pm, it was to find one batch of twelve in the oven nearly ready. I prepared another set of three trays whilst eating my own tea. Then, leaving my batch cooking in the oven cycled to the hall and delivered the cooked ones to the kitchen. Back home again and continuing in the same sequence all evening, by half past nine we had produced over 100 pies. That evening it was calculated just over 700 cups of tea were served!

During that evening, having delivered my first batch, a soldier in the queue called out to enquire if, when he got inside, there were going to be any. Estimating the numbers in front of him and the time it would take me to get home and back again I reckoned he would have a good chance. When I returned with the next batch it was to see him just within steps from the table, so I think he got his apple pie.

Visiting Havant in 1993 I walked up North Street to find that little had changed and I made contact with a member of the Congregational Church. She sent me a copy of a page from the Havant Congregational Recipe Book produced in June 1924. Both Mrs. McIlroy and my mother, Mrs. Broughton, donated their recipes for Gingerbread. It reminded me of finding this book inside Mother's big black recipe book when I started to learn cooking. Mother told me, in 1930, she had considered including her recipe for Parkin. in which she was an expert, but considered it not suitable being a Yorkshire delicacy. The book was prefaced with the following:

"We may live without friends, we may live without books,

But civilised man cannot live without cooks."

As Ruskin was a favourite author of my mother I believe she was responsible for the inclusion of a quotation from him shown on the leading page.

The original NAAFI building opposite the Congregational Church had been built well up off the ground and set back from the road. The metal roof construction can still be viewed inside the present-day Pet Shop, previously Connells Cycle and Toy Centre.

After some months when Eagle Day had past and the threat of invasion was over, troops were dispersed to other camps around the country. Our church canteen was no longer required and the Navy took over Leigh Park and the Estate which then became H.M.S. Dryad, the mining department of Portsmouth Dockyard.

## Saturday Outings by Bicycle

I first learnt to ride on a friend's bicycle and soon I was allowed to ride Mother's. This was an old fashioned 'sit-up-and-beg' with a large basket on the front and suitable for the weekly shopping trips to Havant. On starting work in 1940 it was necessary for me to have one of my own and I chose to buy a standard Raleigh which cost £5.00!

When I joined H.M.S. Excellent at Whale Island in Portsmouth my daily journey increased to seven miles each way instead of the mile to Havant. During this time I changed the wheels to a lighter weight and fitted dropped handlebars. This made a difference to my speed. With a large rear saddlebag, a storm cape and hat I was equipped for any weather throughout the seasons.

On Saturdays after washing up and putting away the dinner dishes I was free to amuse myself until tea at 4 o'clock. Often I would cycle along the road from Bedhampton to Horndean. The road was usually clear of traffic and I could speed along at a tremendous pace – this was exhilarating. I think these forays trained me to undertake the long cross country journeys of war-time years.

One Saturday afternoon in the summer of 1940 I thought I would try to cycle to Chichester, a total of 20 miles there and back. This I could do at a speed of at least 14 miles per hour if I left no later than 10 past 2pm. I tried to make this journey throughout June and July but kept being thwarted. Something drove me to succeed. By mid August, after many frustrating attempts and by dint of subtlety, I managed to get away just in time wearing my special light-weight cycling shoes.

The road to Chichester is more or less straight and virtually flat with hardly any traffic after Havant. It was very quiet and speeding along I noticed there were two young girls, cycling side by side, some way in front. Noting there was no oncoming traffic I reduced my speed by half, rang my bell and moved out to overtake. The older girl looked behind her, signalled right and moved over to the other side of the road. The younger girl drew into the kerb so I allowed more room to pass her than was necessary. This was extremely fortunate. As my front wheel came in line with her rear wheel I was horrified to see her turn in front of me! To prevent a head-on crash there was only one thing to do. Turning sharply right, braking alongside and putting my left shoulder under hers, nudged her off her bike without her falling. I continued to the far side of the road ending up against a hedge.

Parking my bike I looked back to see both girls were talking with two women who had been chatting outside a shop. Fuming with anger at this near accident I strode up to them and said 'Are you the mothers of these girls?' Without giving them time to reply I continued: 'That girl,' pointing to the elder, 'knows the Highway Code. She looked behind her and signalled correctly. But that young child doesn't. She is extremely lucky that I am an experienced cyclist and was able to prevent crashing into her.' Then I saw that she had been carrying a milk bottle, for this lay smashed in the middle of the road. Pointing to the glass I said, 'Had I done so she would have been badly cut with that glass and I would have catapulted over her and would probably now be lying in the road with a broken neck – dead! For goodness sake teach her properly and don't let her on the road again until she has learnt the Highway Code.' Neither of them said a word. I think they were speechless at being berated so fiercely by me. They had no defence. Picking up my bike I quickly rode off but it took a couple of miles of steady cycling before I felt in control again. I had to continue and not let this incident prevent me from achieving my object of getting to Chichester.

Circling the cross in Chichester I drew up alongside the Cathedral and sat down on one of the seats. A few minutes later a group of boys and girls came along and we got into conversation. When they left one boy stayed behind and we discussed the wall painting on the side of the building next to the Cathedral. He told me it advertised his uncle's haulage business. It was of a motor lorry with an exhaust pipe emitting smoke above the roof of the cab! The painter had made the smoke curl around the frame of a small window and disappear into the eaves. Many years ago, 120 miles away, we were to meet again and became good friends.

In the summer of 1941 Don Fry and I decided, for the sheer enjoyment of a long run, to cycle to Bordean House. After work on the way home we stopped near The Devil's Punchbowl on Butzer Hill to eat our tea. Whilst there our coach appeared chugging up the incline and our colleagues waved vigorously. It was a very pleasurable trip.

One Sunday soon after joining Supermarine I decided to take a trip through the New Forest to Bournemouth a matter of 70 miles. On the way a boy cyclist came alongside and asked if I was one of the Supermarine party going to Barton-on-Sea as he had missed them. He also worked for Supermarine so, as we were going in the same direction, I accepted his companionship. As we approached the turning for Barton he asked me to join the party and we found them on the green sward above the bay eating lunch. By mid afternoon when I had to leave, he suggested my taking an alternative route via Southampton so I could visit his house for tea. Afterwards, as the light was fading he offered to accompany me back to Winchester.

On holiday in Bournemouth later that year I wanted to visit the area south of Studland, reputed to be associated with Hengist and as there was no bus I hired a bicycle. I took the road to Compton Acres down to Poole and onwards to Wareham where I stopped to view the Saxon church. Picking up some sandwiches I continued onwards to Corfe Castle and turned left on the road to Studland. Instead of returning by the same route I took the lane past the Toll down to Southaven Point. The ferry boat was not very large but they were able to take my bicycle and me across the channel which is narrow and very deep. Then it was but a short ride back to Bournemouth.

Eric Balch was a member of the Drawing Office and had recently been the winner of a race organised by The Hampshire Cycling Association. As he lived at Fareham I thought I would see how far I could get on the way home before he passed me. One Saturday I clocked out some six people ahead of Eric and got away pretty smartly. The road is fairly straight but not very flat. At one point I was surprised when I actually passed a car! On arriving at the T-junction at Fareham, thinking he must have gone home a different way, I went into the shop to buy an ice cream. Seconds later, who should come in – but Eric! We were both surprised and he said 'Weren't you in the office this morning?' 'Yes,' I replied 'and I was just in front of you clocking out. I thought I would cycle to Fareham and see when you would pass me.' He was intrigued and remarked 'You must have come along at roughly 22 miles an hour because that's what I was doing.' Finishing my ice cream I left him and took the coastal road to Cosham and home but at a more leisurely pace.

One of the benefits of lodging in Battery Hill was the fact it was on the edge of the town with country lanes close by. Sometimes I would cycle to Hursley on the main road and at the end of the day take the track from the village, which followed the side of the hill for some four miles before emerging into Oliver's Battery. Leisurely cycling along this quiet, unfrequented track was a wonderful way to relax from the hectic pressures at work. I felt a great sense of timelessness and thought it possible this track was an ancient way from Norsebury Ring Fort down to the River Test. There a ship could sail to the sea long before the Romans came.

In the first three months of our marriage my husband bought a tandem and we spent many weekends touring the countryside of Kent. We disposed of it on moving to South London but kept our single bicycles. Some years after our children were born I heard that an old school friend was to emigrate to Canada. I wanted to say goodbye and as the journey by train over two days would be expensive, I decided to cycle from London to Cosham. Leaving the children with my husband over one weekend I set off. It was a long run and this was the last time I attempted any distance by bicycle.

# The Laws of The Navy

by

Rear Admiral Ronald A. Hopwood

1896

*Now these are the Laws of the Navy*
*Unwritten and varied they be,*
*And he that is wise will observe them,*
*Going down in his ship to the sea;*
*As naught may outrun the destroyer,*
*Even so with the law and its grip,*
*For the strength of the ship is the Service*
*And the strength of the Service, the ship.*

# Kenneth More, H.M.S. Excellent/H.M.S. Belfast

On leaving college I took a job as a clerk/storekeeper to earn some money at fifteen shillings a week, whilst I searched for a position in a drawing office. The local firm in Bedhampton had a workshop behind Woolworth's in Havant. There, they repaired engine nacelles and needed someone to dispense the stores and deal with the paperwork. After a few months I read a newspaper advertisement inviting applications from tracers to join the Experimental Drawing Office of H.M.S. Excellent on Whale Island. This was my opportunity. At the interview I was surprised to see there were 22 applicants, all much older than myself. Everyone was given a simple tracing as a test piece of our ability and when these were collected the result, we were informed, would be decided within a week. Having brought samples of my college work I approached the Chief Draughtsman and asked if he would like to see them. Looking through my portfolio of drawings, he asked me to wait and left the room. On his return he was very affable and asked how did I intend to get to the office by 8am as my home was seven miles away. Although there was a bus route to the end of Stanley Street I explained my intention to cycle all the way on to Whale Island. To my delight a couple of days later I received a letter appointing me to the job. For the next eighteen months I expanded my knowledge of engineering and expertise in tracing.

Cycling fast one morning, having been held up by traffic, I was nearly halfway past the quarterdeck when 'Taps' was sounded. A naval Sub Lieutenant stopped dead in front of me and, turning to face the flag, came to attention. Being so close I had to jump off my bike very quickly and, being a civilian, I stood still by his side as a matter of courtesy. Out of the corner of his mouth he whispered, 'I thought I could just make it to my quarters.' When 'Taps' was over, he turned and apologised for causing me to crash stop and we both walked the rest of the way to the corner where we parted, me to my office and he to his quarters. Years afterwards when I saw the film 'Genevieve' I was puzzled as to why Kenneth More's face seemed to be so familiar. On reading his book, 'More or Less' and checking the relevant dates, I realised the Sub Lieutenant mentioned above was him. No wonder his face was known to me.

Early one Monday morning the Chief Draughtsman was called out to draw up a design for protection shields for the 4 inch gun turrets on board a cruiser which was anchored in the harbour just behind the quarterdeck of H.M.S. Excellent. On his return to our office he quickly sketched the drawings and came over to my desk saying 'Clear your board. This is most urgent. These have to be made before the end of the week and it is the first ship to have them fitted.'

Drawings had to be transferred on to linen for permanent record and as these shields had unusual curvatures, I never forgot them. The minute they were completed he hurried off to start them being made – that day! Many times in my life after leaving this office I wished I knew the name of that cruiser. Imagine my excitement when, some sixty years later, I glanced across the River Thames to where H.M.S. Belfast was anchored and to my amazement recognised the curved shields around her 4 inch gun turrets. Any passing pedestrian would have thought me mad as I exclaimed 'That's it!' What a thrill!

Fired with this knowledge I got in touch with Nick Hewitt, the Exhibition Officer who, on hearing my story, invited me to visit for a closer look and a chat about the wartime history of the ship. On close inspection of the fixings and curvature of these protection shields I was able to confirm my memory of the design.

H.M.S. Belfast was commissioned with the Royal Navy on 5th August 1939 and from September operated from Scapa Flow. When leaving the Firth of Forth on 21st November she sustained major damage on contact with a magnetic mine and consequently was out of service having been taken down to Devonport for repairs. These took a very long time during which she was sent to Portsmouth to have her guns checked ready for action and that was when she was anchored off Whale Island. After many years of service she came to London to rest in the River Thames as a permanent exhibition being one of the few ships to survive the war. The Imperial War Museum, of which she is now a part, have issued a comprehensive booklet which gives a full account of her meritorious service.

Her sister ship, H.M.S. Edinburgh, was on her way back from Mumansk when she was attacked on the 30th April 1942 and she sank two days later. On board her cargo consisted of some five tons of gold bullion and forty years later in 1981, these gold bars were recovered!

## Evacuation to Bordean House

In September 1941 Portsmouth was experiencing many bombing attacks and it was decided to evacuate the Experimental Drawing Office and some civilian clerks to the country. The Navy had commandeered Bordean House, a few miles west of Petersfield, and we were allocated the drawing room as our Drawing Office. Free transport was provided by a coach which left Portsmouth at 7am, travelling along the A3 to Petersfield where we had a 15 minute stop for essential shopping. As Don Fry, who was also a member of my D.O, and I both lived some miles from the rendezvous it was decided to pick us up at 'The George' on top of Portsdown. To do this I would leave home by 6.40am, cycle to Drayton where I could park my bicycle in Don's garage, and together we would climb Portsdown to reach 'The George' by 7.30am.

Bordean House was a large country mansion set high on a ridge of dense woodland. As this was a naval establishment the civilian personnel were required to have separate cooking and dining facilities. A local lady was employed as our cook and upstairs, in what may have been a dressing room, she produced excellent meals on a Calor gas cooker. Two small rooms were converted into male and female dining rooms! At the rear of the house there was a large kitchen garden through which we had access to some fields. Discovering a profusion of blackberries in the hedgerows we collected pounds of fruit and, with apples from Father's allotment, our cook made us superb blackberry and apple puddings.

As winter approached the sailors allowed myself and three colleagues to use their table-tennis table, which was in the cellars, for our lunchtime recreation. Two cellars had been made into one space and the table just fitted between the two projecting support walls. There was only three feet on each side and no more than four feet at each end. Playing doubles we became very proficient at scooping shots from the side and lifting drop shots off the ends. Both doorways became crammed with naval personnel who applauded our expertise with enthusiasm. I had a great time that winter in spite of the disapproval of other 'ladies' because I played table-tennis with the men. Well, I had to work with them as a colleague and not as a clerk.

During that winter a naval Lieutenant was seen to take advantage of the heavy snowfall to practise his ability to ski on the slopes of the hill at the rear of the house. One evening our coach did not arrive. It had broken down and we were told another transport was on its way. This proved to be a naval lorry with a canvas cover and wooden plank seats along both sides. Everyone was helped aboard and my elderly colleague, being a tiny lady, was lifted with ease by the Chief Petty Officer – such was his strength! He advised all the girls to sit alternatively between the men, who linked their arms to prevent us being thrown about. Tarpaulins were tucked across our knees and by sitting close together most of us had a reasonable journey in spite of the cold. Some of the girls were too embarrassed to comply with the Chief's advice and I think they were sorry afterwards. Needless to say the Senior Clerk (mentioned previously) refused to travel in a lorry, and telephoned home for a car to collect her. Whose petrol ration we wondered?

## From Ships to Spitfires

During my life odd bits of information would not have come to my attention except as a result of coincidence. For instance, becoming bored with my job as a tracer in the Experimental Drawing Office at Whale Island, Portsmouth. I enquired if there was any way in which I could improve my position and the reply was, as a girl under twenty one years and with no H.N.D. qualification there was no possibility of anything else being available. Therefore I decided to look for a more challenging position.

A week later my Father, knowing of my wish to obtain an interesting job, happened to meet Gerald Gingell in the Southern College of Art at Southampton. He was looking for someone who could read plans, elevations and detail drawings, who could draw freehand and in perspective, had some engineering knowledge and could trace on to linen for the final process before being printed. Accuracy and secrecy were a priority. He also mentioned no one suitable had come forward although this job had been advertised throughout the south of England. Did Mr Broughton know

*R.J. Mitchell*

of anyone who fulfilled these requirements? Father was delighted to say, 'Yes. I do. My daughter. She is looking for a new job.'

On arriving home he spoke of this meeting with Gerald Gingell and gave me the telephone number to arrange an interview. The next day I approached the Chief Draughtsman to request permission for time off for the interview. He was very pleased to hear of the proposed job and told me to use his telephone to contact Supermarine where it was arranged for me to attend on the following Tuesday at 2pm. Instructions were given as to location and entry to meet with the Chief Draughtsman, Mr Eric Lovell-Cooper.

Consulting bus and train timetables it was discovered it would not be possible for me to get to Hursley Park before the time of the interview. This left me with only one alternative – to cycle. The prospect of some 30 odd miles was of no great hardship as I had previously undertaken other long journeys. Two days later the Chief said if Supermarine gave me the job I could leave within the week as he could find a replacement from the applicants previously interviewed. It seemed to me that someone at Supermarine had been in conversation with him and wheels were set in motion. Was I right?

Tuesday dawned bright and clear and it was a sheer delight to hear my wheels humming merrily as I traversed up and down hills in a westerly direction. Crossing the main road at Eastleigh I came at last to Hursley village. The entrance to Hursley Park was guarded by a military post and having shown my pass I was directed up the drive to another gate just before the main house. Here, having parked my bicycle, I was escorted down some steps into a hangar which was half underground and covered with camouflaged netting.

After a quick wash and brush-up I was shown into the Chief Draughtsman's office to meet Mr Lovell-Cooper exactly on time. My first impression was of a very tall, large man with a stern visage and a gruff voice. Quickly noting my name and address he introduced Gerald Gingell, Section Leader of Technical Publications. Stating I could not speak specifically about my work at H.M.S. Excellent as I had signed the Official Secrets Act, other than to say that the Chief Draughtsman was complimentary of my tracing ability.

Mr Lovell-Cooper then enquired of Mr Gingell if he considered I was competent to do the job which was required. His reply was 'Yes sir. Absolutely.' The next question was 'When can you start?' My reply was 'Immediately,' as there was no problem replacing me in the Whale Island office. In order to arrange accommodation and to have a short holiday I requested a week's delay. Lodgings would have to be found in Winchester as I could not commute from home. This was agreed and my starting date was confirmed as the following Monday week. Father suggested I lodged in the same house as that in which he had been living for four nights every week, since the evacuation of the Portsmouth College of Art to Winchester. His landlady agreed to this arrangement with the provisos mentioned in the following title 'Landladies'.

The next day I called at the Portsmouth Labour Exchange to transfer my green card Work Permit from Portsmouth to Winchester. They promised it would be ready for me to collect at the end of the next week. On Tuesday, thinking it might be advisable to check this had been done, I dialled from a telephone box. Somehow I was put directly through to the office in the Labour Exchange which dealt with the movement of labour. Incidentally eavesdropping on a conversation between two Officials and before I could speak this is what I heard: 'Oh, very well. We will send out call-up papers for all girls born in 1923 tomorrow.' I replaced the receiver very gently. This was horrendous news! My call-up papers would arrive in the week I was unemployed and before starting employment with Supermarine. There was no way I was going to let this happen and I ran for the bus home.

Not being expected before late afternoon Mother was most surprised to see me back before lunch. My explanation that I would be called-up for the Forces if I was not employed before the end of the week, gave her a shock. By that evening I had packed my case and was all set to join Father at his lodgings. Arriving in Winchester in the middle of Wednesday afternoon I went straight to the Labour Exchange to collect my green card Work Permit knowing it was extremely unlikely it was there. I prepared myself for an almighty bluff if this was so, secure in the knowledge that Supermarine had been given carte blanche to employ any person from any occupation or area. It was imperative I started at Supermarine the next morning.

The Labour Exchange was a small hut with a corrugated iron roof. Inside a wooden counter stretched across and two conscripted lady clerks were sitting behind this with a senior woman seated at a desk. At the counter I enquired for my green card explaining, when she could not find it, that Portsmouth Labour Exchange had promised to send it to them for me to start work at Supermarine. The Senior Clerk then came forward and telling the other clerks to get on with their work she dictatorially stated I could not decide to move from one job to another, let alone in another area. Jobs had to be advertised etc, etc. and I was to go back to Portsmouth and take any job in that area. She continued to reprimand me for thinking I could get whatever job I liked, much to the embarrassment of her clerks.

Fuming with anger at such rudeness from her senior position to a young girl, I reacted by striking both hands flat on the wooden counter and in a very strong but restrained voice loudly stated, 'Did you not know that this post with Supermarine HAS been advertised for the last SIX months throughout the whole of the South of England and no one has been found with all the necessary qualifications? I have been interviewed and chosen to fill this position and I am instructed to start immediately.' As she continued to bluster I calmly picked up my coat and suitcase and said firmly, 'When my card arrives you will please forward it to Supermarine' and walked out slamming the door behind me. Outside I was surprised at my temerity speaking as I did to that senior official but I was determined nothing and no one was going to stop me.

The next morning I caught the firm's bus and arrived at the gate to the Drawing Office where one of the guards escorted me to Gerry Gingell's desk. He was amazed to see me but when he heard what had happened he poured me a cup of tea and sat me down at his desk and told me to wait. He disappeared out of the hangar to see the Employment Manager in the main house. Ten minutes later he returned beaming broadly, 'That's all right. You start today!' I was so relieved that in spite of all the obstacles I had achieved my goal.


# The Unpayable Debt

by

Joyce Lucas

Willingly they answered the country's call
Gave up their peace time living to fight for us all.
From cities and hamlets, fenlands and hills
From the Empire they came offering their skills.

Ground Staff and Aircrew they each played a part
In taking the war straight to the enemy's heart.
So many died that we might live in peace
That our unpayable debt can only increase.

Some decades later and older than their years
They returned to reflect and share silent tears,
Remembering when conflict filled the sky and earth
And each of them proved to be more than his worth.

The unchanged winding lanes welcomed them back
To the nearby village church and a special plaque
Which in sombre metal on sacred stone
Acknowledges that debt for which we cannot atone.

## Technical Publications Department – Hursley

The Drawing Office comprised of some 200 draughtsmen and my appointment caused some embarrassment from the fact I would be the first female under 21 years to sit at a board!

As the Technical Publications Section under Gerald Gingell was adjacent to the all female glass-enclosed Tracing Office it was decided to place me on a drawing board there but next to the glass wall where I could be in touch with Gerry. Everyone thought I was under the Head Tracer until the Drawing Office was reorganised a year later. The tracers were of different ages and some were rather dismissive of what they called 'pretty pictures'. The Head Tracer of course, was well aware of my skills and also the fact my wages were considerably higher than those under her who were still in apprenticeship and of the same age. She is to be congratulated on her ability to pass me my pay packet every week without anyone else observing it.

The hours were from 8.30am to 5.30pm Monday to Friday and half day Saturday to twelve noon. At 11am each day we were served with a free cup of tea and a biscuit at our desks. Management did not pay for their lunches in the Dining Room. All Staff paid a shilling per day for their lunches. The staff from the House and hutments used the canteen in the basement. The Drawing Office staff were served in their own canteen hut in the grounds. The lunches were well-balanced and varied using meat, cod or herring, or one ounce of cheddar cheese dipped in batter and deep-fried, all served with potatoes and a green vegetable. The puddings were often of rice, sago or similar, a portion of sponge, or 'spotted dick', all served with custard. When our time-table changed and we were working until 7pm we were given a 4.30pm tea break of twenty minutes where a free cup of tea, a sandwich and a piece of cake were served at our desks.

One year it became necessary to cull a twelve pointed deer from a herd on the estate. It was a huge animal and it hung from the ceiling to the floor in the basement corridor of Hursley House for a week. As it was not possible to serve the cooked venison to both canteens at the same time it was arranged for the Drawing Office canteen to be closed that day. All the employees were to take their lunches in the house canteen at different times. It made quite a change, not only in our routine but in mixing with other departmental people with whom we had little contact.

On my first day I was given a huge pile of pencil drawings which had to be traced in ink on to linen for final production. This backlog referred to Spitfire Mark III and I was instructed to do my best to clean up the sometimes wobbly lines and produce clear drawings. These perspective drawings had been drawn up by artist draughts-men who had no knowledge of the intricacies of laying ink on to linen. It was up to me to finalise the masters. During the following year I steadily reduced this pile, in spite of additional work being added every day. Everyone was racing to get modifications drawn up and out to the production units.

Due to the pressure of the demand for Spitfires and Seafires to aid the war effort, the structure and personnel of the original departments throughout Supermarine had to be increased. In some of the sections family members of staff were conscripted. This decision made the security of the work a feel of 'family' within the firm. Lord Beaverbrook gave Supermarine 'Carte Blanche' to commandeer anyone who had the necessary expertise to improve the situation. One of my colleagues who had joined the Forces was seconded to Supermarine. This was an unusual example as he wore RAF uniform but was not subject to RAF discipline.

When I joined the Drawing Office I noticed that as a consequence of the influx, members of each section tended to converse and socialise within their own group. Work was rarely discussed thereby keeping the processes of development on the basis of 'the need to know'. Being in the company of young females with whom I had little in common my lunchtime breaks were spent with those who could converse on such subjects as art, gardening and geographical topics. These were usually original Supermariners such as Reginald Dickson, Gerald Gingell, Alan Clifton or Reg L. Caunter who became Chief

Draughtsman when Mr. Lovell Cooper retired. Jack Rasmussen, in his special capacity, was another with whom I spent many a break.

My first Christmas after leaving Whale Island I sent them a card which showed a Spitfire soaring above a naval ship to represent my change of occupation. When many months later two girls were added to our Section, I drew a birthday card for one of them. This depicted sketches of the heads of our team carrying tee-squares on which they all wrote their signatures. Later I was asked to design a birthday card for a typist in another department. Their team signed on the ribbon emerging from the typewriter.

## Landladies

From a civilian point of view my experiences of landladies during wartime were somewhat different from those who were billeted by their Departmental Officers, such as Irene Young in her book 'Enigma Variations'.

Due to the bombing of Portsmouth when the Guildhall next to the Technical and Art Colleges was gutted, it was decided to evacuate the Southern College of Art to Winchester. My Father had found lodgings with an elderly lady for four nights a week and so was able to continue normal life at Bedhampton.

When joining Supermarine in May 1942 it was necessary for me to find accommodation as it was impossible to commute daily from home. There was a firm's bus service from Winchester to Hursley Park so it was logical for me stay at the same house with my Father. This was quite an experience. The Landlady would only take me if I made my own breakfast and sat in the kitchen. Also, before leaving the house I was to take a glass of hot water to her in her bedroom. Having been brought up to cook and housekeep from an early age this was no problem. She would leave tea, milk, two slices of bread and marmalade on the kitchen table. Sometimes there would be a herring or a kipper, or, as a special treat, an egg!

The evening meal was served in the dining room. Every week the same menu. Monday – stew. Tuesday – cold meat and salad. Wednesday – meat pie. Thursday – sausages. Friday – fish. All meals were served with various vegetables and followed by a pudding made with milk. Evenings were spent in the drawing room with Father reading his newspaper and myself being occupied with knitting or needlework. Often we played a game of Bezique or Chess. Rather a dull life but no more than was usual at home. When Father decided to semi-retire, thereby only being in Winchester for two nights a week, our landlady informed us that she was going to take a relative to live-in as a companion and we had to find other accommodation.

This time it was with a family. The father was employed in the local Town Council whilst his wife kept house and looked after their lodgers. Meals were taken at a large table in the downstairs kitchen and timing was crucial in this household. Breakfast was served on the dot at 7.30am to their daughter and myself and half an hour later we were ushered out of the house. Then it was breakfast for the two gentlemen for they had to leave by 8.30am. At 6pm everyone sat down to the evening meal. As I was under twenty-one years of age, this Landlady was inclined to treat me in the same way as her teenage daughter. After dinner we girls were expected to clear the table and wash up the dishes before joining the adults in the lounge, until other duties such as homework or letter writing enabled us to retire to our rooms. As will be understood, mine was the smallest room having just a bed, chair and chest of drawers. Sometimes I was able to stay over the weekend which gave me the opportunity to lunch in town, do some shopping and visit the Cathedral. On Sundays at the Congregational Church I met up with a group of young people and we called ourselves the 'Good Companions'. We were all under twenty-one years and we put together a two hour show of items and a short play to raise funds for the Church Charities. I missed being in the school choir and wanted to continued training my voice. I was very fortunate to be able to study under the Choirmaster of the Cathedral, but as my job became more demanding I had to give up these activities.

One evening at the dinner table I was very embarrassed to be taken to task by the Landlady. She wanted to know what I did at work, and with whom? All I could say was that I worked on a drawing board and having signed the Official Secrets Act, I could not discuss my work. This did not satisfy her and she continued to ask for answers. Looking to Father for help I saw that he was astounded at her complete lack of concern regarding security and could not speak. It was her husband who came to my rescue, telling her in no uncertain terms to stop her questioning and the meal ended in silence. Feeling very shaken and upset by this incident which appeared to challenge my veracity and her indifference to the posters stating 'Careless Talk Costs Lives', decided me to find a more harmonious lodging elsewhere particularly as Father was to leave Winchester at the end of term.

Fortunately at work I heard that one of the cleaners had a room to let. Within a week I was safely installed at 89 Battery Hill with Mrs Ward, her mother and three boys. She was a widow dependant upon the income from several part-time jobs and letting a room was essential. She never alluded to my work or allowed her mother to ask questions as she had also signed the Official Secrets Act. The fact that she swept the office floor and cleared my wastepaper basket was never mentioned.

Grandma kept house, cooked the meals and supervised the children out of school hours. This enabled Mrs Ward to attend her different jobs. In spite of the strict rationing we were all well fed. Grandma was a dab hand at making scrambled egg from the dried powder and this was a favourite breakfast dish. Cheap cuts of meat cooked very slowly with vegetables from the back garden and potatoes from the market made sustaining meals. These were followed by puddings, either milk or sponges, baked or steamed with whatever fruit came to hand, with custard. No cream then – it was too expensive. In the autumn on Sundays I would often go out with a packed lunch and come back with pounds of blackberries. Nothing was ever wasted.

## Mistaken Identity – Deanna Durbin?

One Saturday, not having been home for several weeks I was cycling along West Street, Havant, when I became aware that people were staring at me! As I parked my bicycle on the forecourt of Woolworth's more people seemed to come from nowhere and congregated in groups whispering together. What was going on?

At the counter I asked the young assistant for the items Mother had asked me to buy and she promptly dissolved into giggles. At this the Supervisor stepped forward and took over serving me. Having paid her I left the shop, only to discover a crowd had collected. Quickly getting on my bike I made for home feeling as though I had stepped into a weird dimension.

At home I asked Mother what had caused people to turn and stare at me. Was wearing shorts considered 'fast' or was it because I was not in any kind of uniform when all my age group were in one of the forces. Very odd! She was obviously embarrassed by my questioning but I pressed her for a reply. Eventually she said 'Well. It has been rumoured that Deanna Durbin is staying somewhere nearby'. I was flabbergasted and could not speak realising of course, I did look like her.

No wonder my occasional visits home, which varied between two to four weeks on Saturdays, fuelled the rumour.

## Spiteful and Seafang

In early January 1943 the Tracing Office had to move to another building to allow the enclosed area in the Drawing Office to be allocated to the secret project – Spiteful – under the leadership of Bill Fear. This meant I had to move into the main Drawing Office. The telephone on Bill Fear's desk was just by the door and if the door was open, it usually was, conversation could be heard by whomsoever worked on the first two desks in the main Drawing Office. Reginald Dickson, who collaborated with Bill Fear in this project, sat at the first desk and obviously, being deaf, would not hear anything which was said.

As I waited for Gerry, my Section Leader, to tell me where I was to work, Mr. Cooper, the Chief Draughtsman, who was checking all the changes of staff movement, came up to Gerry and asked 'Are you going to sit behind Dickson?' Gerry's reply astonished me 'Oh. No. I am going to put Stella there. She can be trusted not to repeat anything she might hear. I will stay at the back.' It was then, I, the first female, was allowed to sit with my colleagues in the main office.

During the previous year my salary had steadily increased to the extent it superseded what was considered the norm for my age. As I was still under twentyone years my salary was increased to the same standard as a draughtsman which was an unheard of precedent. I did not realise at the time my integrity had been so recognised by my superiors. But later this was borne out by the special tasks which I was given to do, which were not part of the work of my Section. These were given to me directly by Joseph Smith, the Chief Designer.

On one occasion he asked me if I would be willing to make new tracings of several detail drawings which had been done by another office. It was clear to me that whoever had processed them had not laid down sufficient ink to allow them to be printed and this had caused considerable embarrassment. It only took a couple of days for me to redraw them.

On another occasion I was summoned to Mr. Cooper's office where Joseph Smith proceeded to give me certain instructions. To save time in reproducing a particular drawing I was to change

*Joseph Smith*

the title on a master tracing from Spitfire to Spiteful. This name was the top secret of Bill Fear's Section and I was told that Gerry had been instructed not to enquire as to the work I was given! Furthermore I was to keep my work under cover at all times and if I wished to leave my desk he was to guard it until my return. This meant we had to split our lunchtimes for the next couple of days. At a later date I had to change another master tracing from Spitfire to Seafang.

The next month Gerry asked me to draw up the control panel of the aircraft which was in the Experimental Hangar by the Hursley Gate. Transport was not required because luckily I had my bicycle. It was quite a distance, passing the house and gardens, cycling down the mile long drive through the grounds. At the Hangar, as I was wearing a skirt, the Foreman followed me closely up the steps of the scaffolding where he helped me climb in the cockpit. It was not easy to see where to put my feet and there was no seat installed so he grabbed a parachute pack for me to sit on. A bit uncomfortable but at least I could see the panel. It was covered in dials of varying sizes and I found it tricky to draw a picture.

At one of the Supermarine Reunions held in Southampton, Stanley Seve came up to me and said 'I remember you. You came into the Experimental Hangar and climbed in the cockpit of the Spiteful. I was one of the fitters and we all wondered who you were.' At the same reunion I met up with some of Bill Fear's staff and found that not one of them had any knowledge of my involvement in their work. They were astounded how well this secret had been kept. Only Joseph Smith, Alan Clifton, Eric Lovell-Cooper and Bill Fear were privy to my participation.

# Reginald Dickson

*Jeffrey Quill*

Being totally deaf he was nicknamed Deafy by all and sundry but there are many unusual stories about him. One person told me that before the War he often saw him cycling to work and reading a book at the same time!

Meeting Innes Grant at a Supermarine Reunion on the 16th November 1993, he was reminded by John McDonagh of an incident Innes had experienced with Deafy. He had picked Innes up from work and they were travelling one lunch time in his car, a Ford 8, to have a drink at a pub called The Clump before going on to Bassett Close East. Suddenly switching off the engine and flinging open his door Reginald fled into the ditch on the far side of the road leaving the car to gently roll forward. Innes, not knowing why he took this action, decided to emulate it on his side and a few moments later a bomb landed on the road ahead! Dickson's explanation was that he had felt the change in the atmospheric pressure and realised a bomb was descending just above them.

Of course, he could not have heard anything, as he was profoundly deaf. But he had obviously experienced the same pressure on previous raids in Southampton and had immediately recognised the signs. Had they continued their journey they would have been killed.

Many pupils in my class at senior school took up the craze of learning the deaf and dumb alphabet at which I quickly became adept. Deafy Dickson's desk was just in front of mine and this skill proved extremely useful early in 1943. Joseph Smith, Chief Designer and Alan Clifton, Assistant Chief Designer, accompanied by several visitors came down to Bill Fear's office for a conference. The Test Pilots, Jeffrey Quill and Alex Henshaw were also there. On their way through the Drawing Office they were joined by Eric Lovell-Cooper, Chief Draughtsman, and Jack Rasmussen, Ministry of Aircraft Production Liaison Officer. Shortly afterwards they, and others from Bill's section congregated around Deafy's desk.

Deafy could read lips extremely well and could communicate quite freely with everyone, so I was surprised to see his face appear over the edge of my board and to hear him say, 'Stella, come and tell me what he is saying please, I can't understand him.' indicating one of the visitors from the Ministry of Aircraft Production. I was glad to help, but it was an enormous challenge to deal with not only technical terms but also details on a subject of which I had no knowledge, it being the design and data of the new wing for Spiteful.

Later Bill told me how pleased and intrigued everyone had been at how I was able to keep up with the questions and answers between two and sometimes three people at a pace which allowed normal conversation to flow. This was mainly, in my opinion, because Deafy could 'read on' words after a few letters coupled with my lips, thus speeding up the process of communication. After this episode I was often called upon to 'talk' with Deafy and his colleagues as it saved time not having to write details down.

In a letter to me of 1992 Jeffrey Quill wrote: 'Deafy was a remarkable man and his contribution to the success of the Spitfire was very, very great. After the War he went to the U.S.A. and became a Technical Vice President of Lockheed.'

My own memory is of a bright cheerful countenance peering over the edge of my drawing board every day. One noticed his great energy and concentration. Time was not wasted in trivialities. The job was to find the solution to problems.


## Time Table Changes

At Supermarine we were working the usual eight hours a day and a half day on Saturdays. Every weekend leaving the office at 12 noon I cycled some 30-odd miles to arrive home before tea-time. As Mother was of advanced years she relied heavily on me to deal with the household chores of cleaning and washing as though I was still living at home. After lunch on Sundays I would have to leave by four o'clock to cycle back to my lodgings ready for work on Monday morning. This routine was not only exhausting but did not allow enough time for my own recreation nor could it be done in the approaching winter. I had to find a solution to this problem.

I went to see Mr. Cooper and told him I did not have enough time to assist Mother at the weekends. I suggested, if I could have a night's rest before cycling to work every Monday morning, thereby losing half an hour's work-time, I could make up the lost time by working one Sunday every seven weeks. This was agreed and it worked very well for the next few months.

The time table change I had adopted appeared to be successful both for myself and the work. Consequently, having noted how well it worked, Eric Cooper probably consulted Joseph Smith about the inability of his men to spend a night at home during the normal weekend. Many company employees came from far afield necessitating several hours travel on the railway. Joseph Smith decreed that a different work schedule should now be adopted especially in expectation of the increased work load. The new schedule was Monday to Friday, twelve 10-hour working days. Two complete days, Saturday and Sunday, was our free time off. This would allow the men to have at least one complete night in their own homes depending on how far they had to travel. We worked these times throughout the winter of 1943 and on through 1944.

# Station X – Bletchley Park

*Alan Clifton*

Due to the U Boat activity in the Atlantic we were experiencing severe losses of supply ships. At the time I was having a short conversation with Alan Clifton in the main corridor of Hursley House.

Joseph Smith came out of his office in a state of great excitement. He quickly checked there was no one else about. Looking directly at me and grabbing Alan's hand he burst out with the following words 'I've just been told Station X have got the German naval codes!' Without anything else being said I understood that this was an item of very secret information. He strode back into his office followed by Alan who shut the door.

Thinking about this information on my way back to the drawing office I realised I had been very privileged to hear this very secret news. It was obvious we had access to all the German naval messages and perhaps our losses in the Atlantic Ocean would now be diminished. The story of the acquisition of these code books by the Royal Navy before the captured U Boat sank only became generally known years after the war.

Some 5000 people were employed at Station X and many of these were Wrens. The staff were able to decode the messages received and deliver them to a Department where they were sent onward to those who required the knowledge – often within minutes of the messages being received and sometimes before the message had even arrived at its destination! Such was the speed and our people's determination to beat the common enemy.

It was not until the 1990s before I discovered that Station X was the wartime code name for Bletchley Park.

# Supermarine Personnel – Photographed

In the summer of 1943 photographs were taken of the outside and inside of the Experimental Workshop where the Spiteful was in progress. Also the inside and outside of the Drawing Office where my Section can just be seen.

Victor Scott Paine, who had retired from working with R. J. Mitchell, visited Hursley that day. After calling on Joseph Smith he came down to talk to Gerry Gingell who was now in charge of his old Section. Afterwards he came to my desk and made generous compliments as to the quality of my work. He then went on to tell me that one hour saved on my desk was one day saved in transport to London. Also it was one week saved in the printing process to be distributed. This gave me a great sense of purpose and the realisation of each person's contribution to the problem of increasing the production of Spitfires to fight the War.

'Stella, you're having your photograph taken,' a colleague said as I was standing by his board. Looking up I saw a flash from the far end of the hangar. This was most peculiar because we were supposed to be in a security zone!

*Part photograph of Supermarine personnel*

Soon afterwards walking along a corridor in the house I was grabbed by Alan Clifton with the message 'Stella, YOU must be in this photograph.' Protesting I had already been photographed in the Drawing Office, he brushed this aside. Taking me by the hand saying 'Come on' he escorted me past Joseph Smith out of the front door. The visiting dignitaries, Joseph Smith and Management followed. Alan placed me in front of the personnel assembled from Supermarine Headquarters to be next to Mr. Gooch who was leading the Management to stand in the front row. Mr. Gooch, who was very tall, stood in front of me so I had no option but to lean to one side holding the arm of the girl next to me. This action can clearly be seen in the resultant photograph. I.B.M., who took over Hursley House many years ago, published this group photograph in their house magazine. Photographs were also taken of the outside and inside of the Drawing Office and the Experimental Workshop near the Hursley Gate. The interior photograph of the Workshop shows the prototype of the Spiteful. These have been reproduced in 'The Spitfire Story' by Alfred Price.

# A Moth-Eaten Rag

by

Sir Edward Hamley.

A  moth-eaten rag
      On  a  worm-eaten  pole

It  doesn't  seem  much
      To  stir  a  man's  soul.

'Tis  the  deeds  that  were  done
      'Neath  the  moth-eaten  rag

When  the  pole  was  a  Staff
      And  the  rag  was  a  Flag.

## The Challenge

Making my way home midday on Saturday 27th May 1944 I by-passed the village of Southwick. By cycling down a track beside a farmhouse I turned on to the lane which led up to Fort Widley and crossing a small bridge turned sharp right to climb the hill. From the left hand side of the road two soldiers leapt out of the ditch in front of me brandishing their rifles with fixed bayonets! 'What was I doing there?' An officer was sent for because I had to be taken  into custody. He wanted to know how I had missed the road closure signs. Explaining that my usual route home across country was via the farm house track which bypassed Southwick, he immediately sent men to investigate and close the access.

On showing him my Work Pass with photograph which was evidence of my employment with Supermarine, I begged to be allowed to continue my journey. If I had to go back to Southwick, cycle through Purbrook up the hill and down to Cosham I would not arrive home for another three hours and my parents would be extremely worried and anxious. Stating further, I would not look to my left as I climbed Portsdown to pass Fort Widley and Fort Purbrook to my home in Bedhampton.

Realising I posed no threat to what was an obvious sensitive area he let me go. Then I thought about Monday saying 'I will be coming back this way about 6 o-clock on Monday morning. You will not prevent me passing through I hope because I have to cycle 30 miles back to work?' He nodded and his expression convinced me that all was well. On Monday I was rather apprehensive and very much aware of the troops concealed at that corner, but they did not challenge me again.

Apparently Field Marshal Montgomery had arrived and was in his caravan in the grounds of Broomfield House only yards from the corner. S.H.A.E.F. (The Supreme Headquarters of the Allied Expeditionary Force) was in Southwick House just beyond. No wonder those lanes had been closed and were closely guarded!

## Jack Rasmussen - His Story

Jack was the representative of the Ministry of Aircraft Production and having been appointed as the Liaison Officer to Supermarine had a desk in the newly-built Drawing Office at Hursley.

At a meeting of the Spitfire Society in the Hall of Aviation at Southampton on 15th November 1985 I met up with Jack again and Kenneth Knell was also there. In 1994 on a visit to Jack and his wife, I took the opportunity to ask him about the incident which took place on 1st June 1944. He consulted his diaries and, having checked his movements during May and June, gave me the following details:

'On the 1st May 1944 I went to Odiham to meet Group Captain Mayes of 84th Group 2nd TAC. Later I was interviewed at Hursley by an Air Vice Marshal who instructed me to hold myself in readiness for special duties. On the 1st June I was summoned to Odiham again and was put into R.A.F. uniform. Before going home I had to call at Hursley to collect my belongings.'

It was lunchtime. Gerry Gingell and I had returned early to the empty Drawing Office to listen to the news programme on his radio. As we listened a figure appeared making a bee-line for us and we were astonished to recognise Jack wearing R.A.F. uniform! How could he have been called up? In reply to Gerry's query he straightened his head and shoulders and declared with resignation, 'THEY have put me into uniform.'

Although wondering whom 'they' might be, we knew better than to enquire further. Shaking our hands, saying goodbye, we wished him good luck. We watched him disappear up the steps and out of sight not knowing if we should ever see him again.

## Overlord – D-Day

From 'Memoirs' by Field Marshall Montgomery he quotes:

*'He learnt at an early age to play a lone hand and become self-sufficient and he acquired the ability to concentrate – to sort out the essentials from a mass of detail.'*

I also noted that he called all the General Officers of the Field Armies to a two day conference on 7th April 1944 at St Paul's School, Kensington. This was their brief and he stated:

*'My object was to put all senior commanders and their staffs completely into the Overlord picture – as affecting the general plan, the naval problem and plan, and the air action. This was done on the first day. We examined certain situations which might arise during the operation – either during the approach by sea or after we had got ashore. Great energy and drive will be required from all Senior Officers and Commanders.'*

He visited all personnel who were involved in the preparation of the operation called Overlord, such as groups of factory workers, railwaymen, miners, etc. At the end of May, he made an 8-day tour of all the camps of invasion forces from Sunday 23rd May to Monday 31st May. He stated that in these visits:

*'...I was determined to address all Officers down to the Lieutenant-Colonel level, and to get over to them the main issues involved in the tremendous operation on which we were about to embark.'*

As the 50th Northumberland Division under the command of Major-General D.A.H. Graham was the nearest camp to his Headquarters, he probably left this visit to the last. Between them it was agreed that the General would host a Farewell Party for the most senior Commanding Officers, British, American and Canadian, involved on D-Day landings to meet each other in a relaxed manner. A lady would be required to act as Hostess to give a semblance of normality to the evening. The next day their Intelligence Officers visited Joe Smith at Hursley House.

The following account is written as an appreciation and tribute to the memory of a gallant and caring Commander, Major General D.A.H.Graham CBE. DSO.MC., and Joseph Smith, Chief Development Designer of Supermarine, whose faith in my integrity and discretion led him to recommend me to the former. I feel honoured to have been a small part of Operation Overlord and very conscious of the trust placed in me, by those whose aim it was to enable the Commanding Officers to order men into battle in a calm and decisive manner.

How shall I begin to describe the events of Saturday 3rd June 1944 when thousands of men were elated with the knowledge that, at last, they were going into action against

Hitler's rule of domination. Apprehensive of their personal survival and yet determined to overcome all obstacles in their way to achieve victory? How to convey the electric tension which prevailed amongst the Commanding Officers who were responsible for the first and second waves of the invasion forces and the lives of those under their commands. I can only set down what was for me a unique and memorable time and hope by so doing, future generations will understand what an individual feels on the eve of a battle.

My story begins with the following strange, and at the time inexplicable, event which occurred on Wednesday 31st May. During the afternoon my Section Leader, Gerry Gingell, was called up to Joe Smith's office in the main house. On his return he came to my desk looking very agitated and asked belligerently, 'What have YOU been up to?' Startled I said 'What are you talking about?' and he went on to say, 'I've had to answer some very searching questions about you.' He pressed me further but all I could say was, 'I have no idea what this is about.' We racked our brains and concluded the only thing to do was to wait and see what might develop. Understandably I was not convinced this was the sole reason. There had to be something else. Indeed it was not until compiling dates and data for this book that the above incident came to mind. This coupled with the briefing before the party made me realise that it had been an Army Intelligence investigation as to my ability to act as Hostess to a large number of men. This made cohesive sense of the whole episode.

At 10.15 am on Saturday 3rd June 1944, a shaft of sunlight fell across my board sending a brilliant white reflection into my eyes. Bother, I thought, now the ink will dry too quickly and these curves are so tricky to do. Moving so that the shadow of my head covered my work I became aware that Joe Smith and a Military Officer had entered the hanger and were approaching the Chief Draughtsman's office. Being used to a variety of visitors to the Drawing Office I did not take any further interest in their arrival, so when Gerry paused by my desk shortly afterwards I was very surprised to hear him say, 'Stella, you're wanted in Mr Cooper's office.'

Speeding to the cloakroom to wash the ink off my fingers I wondered what this summons could mean. Saturday morning! Oh no! It must be they wanted me to work overtime. I hadn't planned anything special for the weekend, except to visit the cinema. Making my way between the desks and along the main gangway I saw Joe Smith disappearing out of the hanger doors. Turning towards the Chief's office I felt, rather than saw, many pairs of eyes swivelling in my direction. Eyes, always watching, always curious, wondering what I am doing. Is it because I am a girl? Well be curious, you'll not find out from me. Knocking on the open door I stepped into his office, 'Good morning Sir. I understand you wanted to see me?' 'Yes Miss Broughton. Come in and close the door please.' His manner and voice was exceptionally cordial, different from his usual bark and was that really a smile? Although he commanded respect and immediate attention to his orders I had never felt intimidated by his attitude which was his way of dealing with the pressure of work and getting the best out of his staff of some 200 men. He waved a hand to the chair in front of his desk so I sat down waiting to hear why I had been summoned. Leaning forward he asked in a hesitant manner 'Are you doing anything particular this afternoon?' Here we go, I thought, what's up now? And what's HE doing there catching sight of the military officer seated on a low chair in the corner, for I had assumed he had left with Joe Smith.

'Nothing in particular Sir. I'm not going home this weekend. Do you want me to come in?' 'No, no.' he replied, 'Not to work, but we wondered,' and he turned to the Officer clearly being uncertain how to continue, 'if you would be kind enough to accept an invitation to a party tonight?' 'A party? Tonight?' I exclaimed. Thoughts flashed through my mind – why me? Surely senior staff warranted this sort of invitation?

Feeling stunned and thoroughly bemused I found I was being introduced to Major General Graham. He had drawn closer to the desk and was shaking my hand saying, 'I would be delighted if you would honour me with your company this evening as my personal guest. The party is to celebrate the opening of a new Officers' Mess in the camp and I would like you to act as my Hostess.'

Mr Cooper, having done his job of introduction, had sat back in his chair and was beaming benevolently at my obvious astonishment. To gain time I thanked him slowly, thinking, could I have heard correctly? Hostess? Its meaning in those days was rather risqué, but both Mr Smith and Mr Cooper appeared to think everything is all right otherwise they would not have introduced this Officer. Therefore, as it had been approved by the head of the firm, I could accept this unusual invitation. So I replied, 'Thank you very much I will be delighted to come.' Pausing, I was appalled to realise I had no evening dress in my limited wardrobe at my digs, although I did have my gold dancing sandals. Hastily assessing the number of clothing coupons in my book and the amount of money in my bank account I continued, 'But I have no evening dress with me. I don't know if I can get one this afternoon.' He hastened to assure me that it was not to be a formal affair, so I said, 'Oh in that case I have a yellow day dress, would that do?' He appeared to freeze. His eyes glazed over and the thought came to me that he might think it was the ghastly lime yellow currently in fashion which he absolutely abhorred. This caused me to comment further, 'It's an old gold colour.' At this his eyes refocused on mine and he said in a very quiet and controlled voice, 'That would be most suitable.' How suitable I was not to know until much later.

'Might I ask how many other ladies will be there?' and I was told he hoped there would be several, one being a lady who worked in the main house and some American ladies. Problems of access made me enquire, 'How shall I be able to get there and into the camp?' Thoughts of the almost non-existent bus service and the Notice Board which could be seen along the road stating: 'Civilians are forbidden to loiter or talk to the troops', plus the announcement that all military camps were sealed and no one was allowed in or out. Quickly he explained, 'I shall send my jeep and the driver will have a special pass for you.' I was still not completely happy. 'Yes, but will it get me out again? The camp is sealed is it not? I must be able to get back here for Monday morning.' I was thinking of the complicated and unfinished drawing on my board which a dispatch rider was due to collect by midday. He smiled and said quietly 'I am the Senior British Commanding Officer and no one goes in or out of any camp without my personal signature.'

Being confident all my queries had been resolved I asked him what time did he want me to be ready to be picked up. 'Would seven o'clock be too early? And may I have your address?' Mr Cooper handed him pen and paper and these details were quickly written down. A final handshake, a brief 'Thank you' to Mr Cooper and I left the office.

Back at my desk I was able to say to those who wanted to know what was going on, that I had been invited to a party. No need to say where, with whom or even when. Fortunately by lunchtime everyone was dashing off to their homes for the weekend break and had no time to question me further.

That afternoon whilst pressing my dress and making a gold headband from some velvet ribbon to match, I thought through the morning's conversation in Mr Cooper's office. 'That would be most suitable.' A very strange remark the General had made about the colour of my dress. Not what one would normally expect from a mature military gentleman to an unknown twenty year old girl. Very peculiar!

I wondered how I came to have been recommended to be the General's guest. It must have been Joseph Smith. Security was obviously the primary factor for the door to the Mr. Cooper's office, which was always left open, unless Joseph Smith was present or I was summonded. On previous occasions when I had been summoned to Mr Cooper's office, either with or without Mr Smith being present, the door was firmly shut whilst I was given my assignments. Mr Smith and Mr Cooper knew that I had always worked in predominately male situations and that I could cope with aplomb in the present Drawing Office of some 200 men. They were also aware that I had signed the Official Secrets Act, not once, but twice. It was possible that Jack Rasmussen, the Representative of the Ministry of Aircraft Production at Hursley, who acted as a Liaison Officer, may have been consulted as he knew me very well. I came to the conclusion that the reason for the party was not entirely correct; it was a cover for something more important.

# On The Way

**Stella,
before and after
the Party!**

'Here it comes!' cried one of the twins and all three made a beeline for the hall only to be held back with the raised finger of Mrs Ward who said firmly, 'Stay put.' So when the knock came I indicated to her that she should open the door, not me, after all it, was her house, I was just the lodger. Unknown to either of us the eldest boy, David, had quietly whisked out of the back door and when I got to the front gate, there he was courteously holding it open and wishing me 'Good Evening', much to the amusement of the driver. I did not know until some 46 years later that David had recorded all the names of the jeeps he saw. There were only two which had entered our close and apparently this one was named either Clarence or Diarrhoea! Could the latter have been indicative of the Commander in the field going through the battle zones like a dose of salts? Can anyone tell me?

I had never ridden in a jeep before and this was an American vehicle so I took notice of the driver's advice to sit in the middle of the rear seat. Even then it was not exactly a smooth ride being both noisy and chilly as the weather was distinctly cool for the time of the year. I was very glad of my yellow and brown tweed jacket.

At the gate to the estate the driver presented his credentials and the authorisation paper for my entry. The guards were not at all happy to let me through so I took out my Works Pass which included a photograph and told them as this was my place of work they could not refuse my entry. We were then allowed to proceed. Following the road past Hursley House we turned up the hill towards the edge of the woods. Here, there was an eight foot high mesh fence and a heavily guarded gate. The jeep stopped and as the driver pulled on the brakes, two hands appeared above him, grabbed him by the shoulders and heaved him out of the jeep to disappear from view into the darkness. At the same time two soldiers brandishing drawn bayonets swept close on each side – those shining blades were within inches of my face. I froze. One soldier said to the other in a strong cockney accent, 'What's she doin' 'ere? She can't come in 'ere.'

I remained glued to my seat not daring to do other than to look straight ahead. It seemed an interminable time before my driver was released and we were allowed to go on. Apparently the guards had been changed after my driver had passed on his way out and they had to send for an Officer to confirm the signature and instruction on the document signed by the General. Thinking this was the last check point I was surprised to find we were approaching yet a third gate. Here our reception was less traumatic. Even though my driver was known personally to the guards on this gate, we were still not allowed through until our passes had been checked by another Officer. Finally the jeep roared up the steep track to the top of the hill and came to a stop outside a Nissen hut tucked underneath the shade of the overhanging trees. My driver requested me to remain in the jeep whilst he went inside. A few moments later the General came out and escorted me past the two M.P's who were standing on guard at the doorway.

Saturday 3rd June 1944

SPEECHES.

# At the Party

At first the bright light dazzled me, but I was drawn to one side and introduced to some of the General's staff. Giving my jacket to one of them with the instruction to put it into his quarters, he took me down the centre of the hut. On the right hand side was a magnificent buffet where some waiters were busy putting the last minute touches to an array of such quantity and rarity in those days of rationing, that I stared in amazement and scarcely took in the arrangements of the tables and the bandsmen trying out their instruments. The buffet was made up of some five trestles covered with pristine white cloths, decorated with greenery and loaded with every conceivable culinary delight. There were whole roasted chickens, a baron of beef, a whole leg of lamb and a huge joint of pork. Bowls of fruit salad, jugs of cream, iced cakes, sausage rolls, apples, pears and wonder of all, a hand of bananas! Further along were bottles of different brands of whisky and gin, wine and liqueurs as well as fruit juices and numerous cans of beer.

It was obvious that the influx of the American sector must have supplied many items as their contribution to the party. Bananas had not been seen in the shops for a very long time and oranges only spasmodically. Along the rear wall were the stands and instruments for the band. On the left hand side, tables had been set up end on to the wall with stools on either side. The perfectly polished wood reflected the gleaming cutlery and coloured serviettes giving an atmosphere which was both stimulating and exciting. How could I ever forget this scene – for parties were but memories of childhood in my experience?

We stopped by the side of a table where a white coated waiter was laying up with his back towards us. The General said 'Would you please leave that.' The startled man turned at this request and stammered, 'I'm sorry Sir, I haven't finished yet.' The short command 'Out' and a jerk of his thumb, sent the waiter with a deferential, 'Yes Sir' scuttling rapidly for the door.

Being taken aback at this curt command I glanced back and was astonished to discover that the hut was empty of all those who had been milling around on my arrival. The doorway was completely blocked by the backs of the two Red Caps. Obviously the order had been given that when the lady guest arrived everyone was to leave. It was a weird sensation and left me in no doubt as to the seriousness of the security for no one was to know what was to be my brief.

I paid close attention as the General proceeded to outline what he wished me to do to make the evening a success. My presence as a civilian in the environment of this secluded camp was to bring an element of normal everyday life to the event. He told me his Officers were expected to spend at least ten minutes, and preferably half an hour, in my company. This had been put to them as a request but it was virtually an order. Would I please welcome each Officer, persuade them to eat something and generally talk and relax in the atmosphere of the party. He finished the five minute briefing by apologising in advance for not being able to stay by my side for much of the time as he wanted to make sure that everyone came into the Mess. He expressed the hope that I would enjoy the food, drink, music and he would make sure I was escorted home at the end of the evening. I said I had understood all his instructions and, thanking him once again for his invitation, promised to do my best to make it a memorable evening.

Leaving me in the centre of the hut he spoke to the Red Caps who moved away and in poured the 'team' who quickly finished their final preparations just in time for the first arrivals. From then onwards the General was kept very busy greeting everyone at the door and then bringing them to be introduced to me. Every Officer was from a different regiment or unit. They were introduced by their correct rank, but having little knowledge of military titles, I chose to address each as 'Mister' which enabled me to avoid a faux pas. This was instinctive on my part but with hindsight it proved to be the best thing to have done, for the evening became more of a private party irrespective of any military overtones. Just what the General wished to achieve, n'est pas.

Some time later having noted that I was coping with the continuous flow of visitors, he kept disappearing and then returning with another Officer in tow. One of them in answer to the question as to what he would like to eat, said, 'Oh I don't think I really want anything.' Expressing surprise I showed him what a variety of food was displayed and because of my attitude he took some food and sat down with me and talked. I was aware that the General was very pleased with this reaction.

Shortly afterwards he came to my side saying how pleasantly surprised he was at the unexpected arrival of some senior American Officers and would I come with him to meet them. As we crossed the room he spoke to me saying, 'This is Lt. General Omar Bradley, but his rank is the equivalent of mine.' As American names were unfamiliar to me, this name eluded me for years until I discovered that there was no other American Officer of that particular rank on that day.

I was introduced and he took my hand and was profuse in his thanks for my being present that evening. But whilst talking he would not let go but placed both hands around mine and kept them there. At first I thought he might be drunk but then I realised he was holding on to me as though it was in sheer relief at being able to be close to someone, so I did not draw away. After a few minutes he turned and introduced me to the other American Officer as Major General Clarence Huebner, who likewise expressed his thanks for my attendance. He appeared to be very calm but was keeping his feelings under tight control. The name of Huebner sounded to me like a flowing river and I never forgot it. As we now know Lt. General Omar Bradley was in command of the First US Army and Major General Clarence Huebner was in command of the 1st US Division. Shortly afterwards they took their leave as they had a long journey to get back to their ship before midnight.

As they left, the General took me over to the other side of the room to be introduced to three other Senior Officers. The first was Major General Rodney Keller, who was in command of the 3rd Canadian Division and they were to land on Juno beach. Next was Major General Thomas Rennie, who was in command of the 3rd British Division, and they were to land on Sword beach, and the third was Major General Richard Gale, who was in command of the 6th Airborne Division. Our host, Major General D.A.H. Graham, was in command of the 50th British (Northumbrian) Division, and they were to land on Gold beach. Major General Gale only stayed for a very short time as he was due back to his camp for dinner. The other two stayed for a while longer.

When I searched my memory for the names of the Officers I met that evening, many came to mind because of their association with colours, spelling or family names. Here is an example. Two Officers came in together and walked smartly up to the General to report they had arrived. The first to be introduced was Lt.Col. R.A. Phayre, Commanding Officer for the 147th Field Regiment. On shaking his hand I queried, 'F.A.I.R.' He smiled and replied 'No, P.H.A.Y.R.E.' I remarked, 'Such an unusual spelling, I shall never forget it.' The second Officer was Lt.Col. A.E. Green, Commanding Officer for the 6th Bn. The Durham Light Infantry. To him I said, 'How strange, I shall never forget your name as I have just met a Mr White and a Mr Black.' These were Lt.Col. G.W. White, Commanding Officer for the 5th Bn. East Yorkshire Regiment and Lt.Col. T.J. Black, who was A.A.&Q.M.G. on the Staff of General Graham. Colours being important in my sphere of art meant that these names were never forgotten.

Suddenly, Lt.Col. Green gave a violent shudder which caused his colleague to ask, 'Are you all right?' to which he replied, 'Yes, just a chill. I'll be all right for the next few days.' This was the start of the attack of malaria which prevented him leading his troops on D Day for he was confined in hospital. His second in command, Major G.L. Wood took over at very short notice. Other Officers I remember meeting during the evening were,

Brigadier F.Y.C. Knox, (C.O. 69th  Infantry Brigade)
Brigadier C.H. Norton, (C.O. Royal Artillery)
Brigadier R.H. Senior, (C.O.151st Infantry Brigade)
Brigadier Sir Alexander Stanier, (C.O.231st Infantry Brigade)
Lt. Col. R.H.W.S. Hastings, (C.O.6th Bn. The Green Howards)
Lt. Col. S.V. Keeling, (C.O.2nd Bn.The Cheshire Regiment)
Lt. Col. Sir William Mount, (C.O. 61st Reconnaissance Regiment)
Lt. Col. C.A.R. Nevill, (C.O. 2nd Bn.The Devonshire Regiment.)
Lt. Col. E.H.M. Norie, (C.O. 1st Bn.The Dorsetshire Regiment)
Lt. Col. P.H. Richardson, (C.O.7th Bn.The Green Howards)
Lt. Col. H.D.N. Smith, (C.O.1st Bn. The Hampshire Regiment.)

Others from the General's Staff were Lt. B. Henderson A.D.C., and Captain P.D. Crichton-Stuart, Staff Officer. As most of the Officers were in Mess uniform or in Battledress, the appearance of the latter in full Scottish dress caused many to gasp at the sight. He gazed around in astonishment at his colleagues and said, 'I thought this was to be an occasion.' which of course, it was.

Speaking to Lt. Mant who was a Liaison Officer on the Staff of General Graham in August 1985, he said, 'Although I was not at the party I heard on Sunday, when on board H.M.S.Nitch from Lt.Col. Norie – what a good do it had been.'

Another Officer brought in by the General was clearly very reluctant to stay for more than a few minutes and refused to take any refreshment. The General had to take him back to his billet. This Officer was killed shortly after landing.

Several ladies in American uniform were engaged in dancing the jitterbug but they did not stay longer than an hour or so. The General hurriedly excused himself from my side during this time to remove an American Officer who had been overcome with emotion. He rapidly escorted him and his dance partner, Joy Cooke, out of the hut. She was not to be seen until some five days afterwards, when meeting her in the corridor Joy told me she had not been allowed out into the public area until that morning! It was part of my brief to cover any such incident and ensure the continuance of the social atmosphere.

By nine o'clock all the guests had arrived and I was able to relax. One Officer asked if he could get me a drink and I asked for orangeade. Then another said, 'May I fetch you some food?' and from then on, a non stop procession of courteous young men vied with each other to keep me supplied. I quickly organised a little of this and a little of that, keeping everyone happy, making sure they fed themselves at the same time.

Although remaining at the centre table my companions changed frequently. The ensuing conversations varied from comments about places, holidays, gardens, flowers, trees, famous houses to visit, music and musical concerts – such as those I had attended in Winchester given by Dame Myra Hess and Benno Moiseiwitch. Photography was mentioned and I was handed a photograph of the wife and child of one of the Officers and I remarked, 'Oh she is a charming little girl.' His neighbour slapped his hands on the table and stood up saying, 'Excuse me,' and slipped away leaving everyone stunned into immobility. Pushing the photograph towards its owner I suggested he put it back into his wallet.

This was one of the tricky situations of which I had been forewarned could happen at any time during the evening. Somehow, I had to break the tension. So I started to talk about a visit to the National Gallery a few weeks before. By the time I had described some of the pictures they had all regained their composure. Asking, 'Has anyone visited the National Gallery or any other Exhibition?' I got a response and soon they were talking normally again. What a relief.

Knowing nothing about Regiments but recognising both Hampshire and Dorset badges, I enquired as to the Sphinx and the word, Egypt. This would be a safe subject, and I was told a little of the Regiment's history. Then indicating a white double headed cross on some of the uniforms, remarked that it looked like the sword of retribution, similar to the cross of Lorraine. This caused many amused chuckles. My instinctive thought was that it could be a recognition sign for the invasion of France. Years later I was informed it was the badge of the Tyne and Tees, representing the three rivers, Tyne, Tees and Humber. The H is shown when the badge is turned on its side.

The General having welcomed his guests began to relax and asked if I would like to dance, and what was my preference? The request to the band for a waltz was given and I think we gave a very creditable performance as at the end, applause accompanied us off the floor.

As the last guests were leaving the General said, 'I'm sorry I shall have to ask you to wait for a while before I take you home because I must see all my men in bed before I leave. I hope you don't mind.' I assured him it did not matter what time I returned as my landlady had given me a key. As everyone was scurrying about removing all the food, dishes, cloths and tables, I queried as to where I should wait as I did not want to be in the way. Finding a seat in the corner he explained they had to clear the hut by midnight. He left saying, 'I will try not to be away too long.'

Chatting to the waiter who was clearing tables I learned, that earlier that day the General had returned from SHAEF H/Q at 10am and instructed his Staff to put into immediate action all arrangements for the party. Invitations were sent out to all Commanding Officers of the D Day invasion and their Staff. A few minutes later he had left the camp on his way to meet Joe Smith at Hursley Park House. From there he was taken through the grounds to the hanger, which was covered in a camouflaged net – half underground – to the office of Eric Lovell-Cooper, Chief Draughtsman of Vickers Supermarine.

Just before midnight the General returned carrying my jacket and whilst I was putting it on, heard him say to an Officer, 'I am taking Miss Broughton home and you will be in charge while I am away. I will speak to all the guards on my way out.' Then turning to the two M.P's he said, 'When everything has been cleared, lock up and you are free to go off duty.'

## Going Home

Outside his jeep was waiting with the same driver who had brought me into camp earlier. Climbing into the rear seat, the General got in beside me. It was a bumpy ride down through the forest and I was glad of the support of his arm. At each gate he got out and spoke to the men on guard duty, giving them explicit instructions as to who was in charge whilst he was out of the camp. He reminded them to keep alert and on their toes. When we reached the main road the driver sped off in the direction of Winchester. To make conversation I remarked on how much organisation had gone into making the evening such a success. Then he said, 'I hope you were not too disturbed by the various incidents which happened.' 'Not at all.' I replied. Thank you for your instructions earlier, they helped me to cope when you were not around.'

135

In trying to reply his voice broke, so when he asked, 'Do you mind if I put my arms round you?' I said, 'If you wish.' for I realised he was desperately fighting for control and needed the close human contact. As his arms came round, his head dropped on to my shoulder. His whole body was shaking and he held me as though he was clutching for dear life on to a lifebelt in the sea and I was his anchor. I must admit that for a moment I was shattered to feel the depth of the emotional outburst from this man who had in his command the lives of thousands of men.

All throughout the evening he had kept a cheerful countenance seeing that everyone had what they needed. It was vitally necessary for him to release his internal turmoil so that he could face the coming days with confidence in his command. Being concerned that the driver should not be aware of his breakdown, even though the noise of the jeep was considerable, I pulled his head into the collar of my jacket so that his deep shuddering sobs were muffled encouraging him to cry it out, saying, 'Cry it out, hold on, hold on tight.' as one does instinctively to children to reassure them that it is all right to cry. Gradually his heaving shoulders became still. He was so embarrassed to have lost his equilibrium but I said, 'Take this comfort in the spirit in which it is given. I do understand the enormous strain you have been under. You needed to break the tension and it was best to be with me, for there is no one else to help you and I can be discreet.' During the rest of the journey we did not speak again, but I held him close to give him time to recover his composure.

As we approached Battery Hill I suggested he told the driver to stop at the junction and he could reverse ready to return while we walked the last 100 yards. I knew if the jeep drove into the close at that time of night it could wake everyone up and too much notice would be taken by the neighbours. Silently we walked down the path and as we turned into the close he put his arm round my waist and seemed reluctant to say goodbye. Suddenly I thought – I must not say goodbye – it would be too final. Clasping his hands within mine I whispered, 'I will not say goodbye but – au revoir.' I could say no more.

As I opened the gate he took a step forward. A look of query on his face gave me the feeling that it was only then he realised I knew precisely what was going on. Would I divulge anything? Should he really let me go free into the public area with all the information I had acquired during the evening? I stepped back and looking straight into his eyes said, 'Don't worry. I won't say anything. My prayers go with you and all your men.' This seemed to reassure him as he stood tall in the moonlight – a veritable leader of men. Raising a hand in farewell I walked to the door feeling his eyes still upon me but I did not look back – it would have been the wrong thing to do.

Quietly turning the key I stepped inside and bolted the door. Removing my shoes I crept up the stairs and into my room. Standing at the open window I heard the jeep start up and draw away into the distance. The General was on course to continue the campaign.

It has not been an easy task for me to write down the experience of those hours. The remembrance of that time brings a lump to my throat which threatens to overcome my composure even as I write nearly 50 years later. But I have been persuaded to record this event because it is considered unique in military history.

## Secrets Secured

As the strain which I had held in check all evening could now surface I found that sitting on my bed I had to grab hold of the metal framework whilst I shook uncontrollably to let the tension gradually ease from my body.

I memorised every detail and relived the enormity of what I had witnessed. I recalled the names of the officers, their regiments, all code words and some of the conversations. My thoughts turned into prayers for their safety in the days to come and for the man who was to lead them. He had cared for them so intensely that day with no thought for his own comfort. I hoped that my support had done all that could have been done.

It was not until having reviewed everything which had happened could I release my grip and push all knowledge into my subconscious, knowing it had to be forgotten for the time being. When writing this book I allowed the memories of this time to surface and they came flooding back as fresh as if they had just occurred.

## Sunday 4th June 1944

On waking up I was horrified to view my face in the mirror. I looked years older with shadowed eyes and pale complexion. Applying some careful makeup began to look more like myself but could not do anything about my lack of energy.

Downstairs the boys had gone out and their grandmother was busy in the kitchen. Mrs. Ward asked if I had enjoyed the evening and I suddenly realised I would have to cover remarks about the party. All I could think of to say was, there was dancing and some wonderful food.

Aware that I could not face any further questions there was only one thing to do. Pack a picnic lunch, get on my bike and disappear for the rest of the day. Crossing the main road, taking a country lane due west into the open countryside for some ten miles, to the memorial obelisk of a horse called Farley Mount. This pyramidal monument was erected by Mr. Paulet St. John in memory of his horse which, in September 1733, leapt into a chalk pit 25 feet deep when out fox hunting. In October 1734 they won the Hunter's Plate on Worthy Downs. The horse being entered in the name of 'Beware Chalk Pit'.

No one could approach without due warning. My brain felt numb and the physical effort of cycling coupled with the warmth of the sun enabled me to relax and for most of the day I dozed. Although I tried to read a book, my thoughts kept turning to the enormous undertaking of the assembly of the invasion forces.

What was likely to happen at work the next day? How was I to evade any questioning? Thinking this over the answer seemed to be, 'FOOD'. I could describe the buffet with genuine excitement, toss in the dancing and people would be satisfied. This would be my gambit for the day. After all no one else would know of the many different Units who were there. All they knew it was just a camp of British and American troops. Returning to my digs I went to bed being relatively hopeful that I had prepared myself for the next day and slept soundly.

## Invasion - Waiting for the News

Sure enough, back at work on Monday morning my colleagues were quite satisfied with my description of the food. But as is often the case, there was a snag. One man from another section, I think he was something to do with a Union, was persistent in his questions about Joy the only other English girl at the party. 'Where was she? Why wasn't she at work?' I suggested she probably had a hangover and had stayed in bed.

The next day he accosted me again saying 'She is not at work, not at home, and her parents don't know where she is.' Knowing full well why she was not around I had to stop his meddling in this matter saying 'I cannot tell you as I don't even know her or her family.' My obvious air of aloofness finally persuaded him to leave me alone. I imagine when she appeared some days later he had to drop his sleuthing.

All that day I was on tenterhooks waiting for the announcement of the landings. At lunch time I listened to the news on Gerry's radio but there was no indication of an invasion. By mid-afternoon my hands had started to shake and I could not hold my pen steady. Was it possible the landings had been aborted or, had the invasion failed? Obviously I was in shock and it was imperative no one noticed my predicament. With only two hours to go I would cope. Going to Gerry I quietly told him I could not work. His immediate reaction was to send me home but I said 'Please don't make any fuss. I will be alright after tea. Please cover me and keep anyone away who may start asking questions.' He was puzzled, but agreed to my request.

That evening there was still nothing on the nine o'clock news. A quarter of an hour later, when we were playing a game of cards, we heard the steady rumble of aircraft. Mrs. Ward exclaimed 'We didn't miss the warning did we?' Grandmother hurried into the kitchen and then called out 'Come and look! There are lights in the sky!' Everyone scrambled down from the table and out of the back door to see a magnificent sight.

Over Winchester three separate columns of aircraft were converging into one line. Group formations of layer upon layer of aircraft towing gliders followed reaching up into the night sky. Their red and green wing-tip lights were so close they appeared to touch. Wave upon wave passed by us, barely 200 feet above, to follow the valley towards the coast and France. It was a glorious and heart-stopping vision. The invasion was ON!

Indoors I allowed Mrs. Ward to know that what we had just witnessed was the reason why I had to get away from everyone on Sunday. She was so relieved because she had been keeping a wary eye on me as my appetite had suddenly lessened. I was confident of her discretion because I knew she had signed the Official Secrets Act.

My memory of that evening is best described in the first paragraph of an article written by me which was published by Southern Tourist Board and Normandy Tourist Board in November 1993 in the Travel Trade and Veterans Newsletter.

'The relief felt on seeing the aircraft and gliders forming up a few hundred feet above Winchester, all navigation lights on, wing tip to wing tip and stacked in columns reaching high into the night sky.'

Anyone who saw the film 'Close Encounters of the Third Kind' will have experienced a similar sound at the approach of the space craft. The pulsating rhythm of their engines was thunderous. David, Mrs. Ward's eldest son, who was 12 years old at the time, recollected witnessing that evening's unique activity when I met him recently.

## Farewell Party, Proven by Brigadier Robert A. Phayre

My searches to contact any of the Commanding Officers who attended the Farewell Party on Saturday 3rd June 1944, hosted by Major General D. A. H. Graham, took several years. Eventually finding a person of the same unusual surname in Scotland I was given the telephone number of his cousin. To my delight he proved to be Lieutenant Colonel R. A. Phayre, Commanding Officer of the 147th Field Regiment R.A. who had been present at the party. Now retired as Brigadier he lived in Camberley, Surrey. His letter to me of November 1992 recalled his memory of that occasion and our conversation regarding the spelling of his name. He also noted I was the only lady present and he remembered other officers were Lt. Col. 'Cosmo' Nevill of the 2nd Devonshires, and Brigadier Sir Alex Stanier, Commanding Officer of the 231st Brigade. He continued with his recollections of D-Day as follows:

On Sunday June 4th 1944 I joined Brigadier Stanier with a small staff to embark in H.M.S. Nitch at Southampton for our one-way trip to Normandy. We changed into a landing craft from H.M.S. Nitch some ten miles from the beach. Close to the shore we were sunk by a mine and had to wade, waist high in rough water. We established a temporary H/Q by the sea wall and I was responsible for controlling the Artillery Fire in support of the units of 231st Brigade Group. These harrowing memories are very painful. Some months later before the crossing of the Rhine, when 8th Armoured Brigade of which the Essex Yeomanry were part, were in support of 31st Highland Division, General Rennie, the G.O.C. invited Commanding Officers to the 'last supper', which was sadly very appropriate as he and his C.R.A. Brigadier Shiel were killed the next day.

I am extremely sorry not to have been able to visit and accept his invitation to lunch as he developed bronchitis and died shortly after writing to me. The Brigadier's cousin and wife kindly invited me to spend a week with them to research places and buildings relating to my family. They were most helpful and I particularly appreciated his criticism of my first attempts at writing episodes for my book.

## Colonel Philip H.A. Brownrigg's Testimony

In 1995 Colonel Brownrigg sent me his thoughts relating to the time when he was a Major and Second in Command of the 61st Reconnaissance Regiment for inclusion in this book. I am indebted to him for his insight into the character of his Divisional Commander.

'Lieutenant Colonel Sir William Mount, Commanding Officer of the 61st Reconnaissance Regiment was wounded on D.Day 2 and as his Second in Command I took over temporarily. Every evening I used to go to see General Graham at Divisional Headquarters to report on the day's work. Two days later he said he was arranging for me to take over the command, officially. This made me warm to him as there was a pool of Lieutenant Colonels waiting to take over the command of battalions or regiments that had lost their Commanding Officers.

Earlier when the Normandy Campaign had become virtually static, General Graham put each of the three Squadrons under the command of his three Brigade Commanders. This did not work well in my view. I suggested that the Squadrons should be under my command but be individually 'in support of' the three Brigades so that I was consulted over the tasks they were given. He considered this idea and said 'All right, we will give that a trial and see if it works.' And happily it did. Later on when the advance really began we worked together as a Regiment. He was always friendly and I never recall his once offering a sharp word, except to his ADC saying 'Can't you see Colonel Brownrigg's had a hard day? Get him a cup of tea quickly.' And even that was said in a gentle way.

The informal efficiency of the Divisional Headquarters was superb. One day during the Normandy Campaign our Intelligence Sergeant went to get the latest 'picture' from Divisional Headquarters instead of from the Intelligence Office. As he was walking over to the Intelligence Map the Divisional Commander saw his black beret from his caravan and called out 'Hello, Recce! What do you want?' When he heard he said 'Come in here, I'll show you what's happening. They don't know anything over there.' Was it any wonder that the General's visits to the Regiment were always immensely popular? Sadly General Graham had a nasty fall from his caravan towards the end of 1944 and had to give up command of the 50th Division.'

Soon after he wrote to me, thus:

'Will you tell all your officers and men how grateful I am for all the grand work they have done. They have been simply magnificent and although their battle history is not long as time goes, it has been a glorious one and every one of you can feel justifiably proud of all you have achieved. When much that has happened in this war is forgotten, the memory of your deeds will remain. My heartfelt thanks to you, one and all.'

We were indeed fortunate to serve under the command of such a great General and a wonderful character.

Signed, Philip Brownrigg

Note: Recce – short for Reconnaissance.

## Yalta – Spitfire Presentation Book

When Churchill was to meet Roosevelt and Stalin at Yalta in 1945 the powers that be, thought it would be a gesture of goodwill to give them a book on the Spitfire. It was quarto sized with single pages depicting each Mark with Merlin engines. The top half of each page had a simple perspective drawing (most of them done by myself) and Gerry Gingell wrote the basic details on the lower half. Six copies were made, two bound in red leather to be presented to Roosevelt and Stalin, four others were bound in blue leather, one of which was for Churchill.

On a visit to my local library I found a book which showed a print of a photograph designated to the Imperial War Museum. It showed Stalin cradling a quarto book on his knees, and Churchill was holding another down by his side. The photograph was obviously taken towards the end of the evening as both were in informal dress without hats and beaming broadly at the photographer.

Unfortunately I did not take the name of the book or its author and when I returned to the library it had been removed from their stock. Enquiries at the Imperial War Museum proved unsuccessful for the photograph seems to have disappeared. This has been one of my few unsuccessful searches. If by any chance this photograph is familiar to anybody, or, if the whereabouts of one of the Spitfire Presentation Books is known, I would dearly like to hear.

## Return to Bedhampton

When World War II ended, my work for Supermarine was gradually being superseded by photography so I was prevailed upon to return home to assist Mother who had not been in good health. Father had arranged a part-time job for me as a clerk to run the 'shop' in the College. This, coping with cleaning the house, laundry and the garden, kept me fully occupied. I felt rather bored but looking forward to my marriage kept me going. Back home in my old haunts I missed the companionship of my cat Jinky. Before I went to College he had been put to sleep.

On a visit to Purbrook School I was impressed by the alterations which had taken place over the years. I missed the weeping copper beech and our famous tree which had been such a focal point, had unfortunately been cut down. After 200 years the first stone step of the main stairs had worn very thin. A photograph records the fact I was privileged to be the first person allowed to step on them after the treads had been resurfaced.

## Sydney Donald Rutter

Sydney was born in London on 11th November 1916 where his father was in charge of the railway complex at East Ham. When he was two years old his mother died, his father married again and they had another daughter. His stepmother died shortly afterwards and he was brought up by the eldest of his three older sisters. His father retired and married for a third time, a widow.

At school he had two friends and they remained close throughout their lives, one of whom married his young sister. On leaving school Sydney took a job in Orpington in a shop dealing in postage stamps and he joined the Territorials. At the onset of World War II he was immediately called-up into the Army and his brother-in law with his wife, went into the Fire Service.

In June 1940 he was put on board the cruiser H.M.S. Devonshire which evacuated King Olaf and Government Officials from Norway. On their return he was sent to Gibraltar to be a Radar Operator. After two years he was recalled to England and sent to a Radar Station on a hill above Winchester.

On leave one Saturday evening he walked into Winchester Guildhall where a table tennis competition was being held and entered the male section. He won First Prize. After the competition finished, having seen me play against girls who could only stonewall, he came over and asked me for a game! Some of the other contestants were knocking-about and when we started to play, both being stroke players, they stopped to watch and some of the audience who had remained behind gathered round. I gave a creditable performance against him and they applauded our contest.

He invited me to join him at another competition which was to be held in Romsey the following Friday at 8pm. The only way to get there was to cycle the 10 miles from Winchester. In the summer dusk it took an hour, as only one half of the road along the Straight Mile was free, due to army trucks parked nose-to-tail. I had to keep ringing my bell for soldiers, having been stationed ready for D-Day, were crossing intermittently from one side to the other. I arrived just in time to see him win that competition as well. As both table tennis and cycling were our common interests we became friends and during that summer, finding our ambitions were compatible, we became engaged. Some months passed and he was transferred to Rayleigh along the Thames Estuary to monitor the increasing rocket attacks on London. He joined the army as a Territorial prior to the War. Consequently he was one of the earliest to be demobbed as a Lance Bombardier.

He had been in the field of philately before the War and wished to continue in this occupation and expected to be settled in a secure post within the year. He successfully obtained a position with Mr. H. E. Wingfield, a dealer in postage stamps, whose shop was next door to Stanley Gibbons, renowned in the world of philately, in The Strand. At Christmas his salary was considerably increased and we made plans to marry in the following August. During that summer I met various members of my fiancé's family and spent several weekends visiting places around London.

Soon after our marriage Mr. Wingfield retired and Mr. Michael became head of the firm. Eventually he acquired the firm of Stanley Gibbons and moved all his staff into senior positions but kept the name, Stanley Gibbons, as it was known worldwide. Being very knowledgeable on Canadian and Australian stamps Sydney was made Buyer for the Foreign Section.

In The Strand, two doors away, the original building of Romano's, the famous tea-shop of the 1880s, was acquired by Mr. Michael. The stone staircase, now a fire-escape, rose up to the first floor where Sydney had his desk between the two large windows. The facia of this building has since been altered and a new internal staircase fitted in the Stanley Gibbons present shop.

In 1967 I was unaware for two weeks that a confrontation had taken place between Sydney and Mr. Michael which resulted in Sydney leaving the firm. He went to work for a firm in Whitstable for six months but after three months he decided to work from home as we had a building which could be turned into an office. Within a matter of months he was offered a post in another firm, but despite investing money in it, the business failed. Once again he returned home until Leo Baresh, who lived on the South Coast, obtained a booth in the Arcade in The Strand and appointed Sydney as Manager.

After our divorce he married a Londoner, a lady who lived next door to his boyhood friend. They and their wives played bridge together – this being his passion, until his death from emphysema a few years later.


## Married Life

After the marriage ceremony in Havant we spent our honeymoon in Exeter. The weather was very changeable and we were glad to arrive at his stepmother's house in East Ham where we were to stay for three months. In the East End I took a job as a milliner and it was here I experienced the last thick, yellow 'pea-souper' fog before the 'Clean Air Act' became law. We bought a tandem and spent many Sundays picnicking and exploring the countryside.

Sydney's friend had bought a newly-built terrace house on a bombed area in Crofton Park. He offered us the first floor accommodation with an option to buy the house when he moved to the country. As flats in London were at a premium we were glad to accept and after three months we moved in. Within two years we bought the house.

During our early marriage I had to make every penny count and make the allowance I was given stretch as far as possible. Because I was so alone in my childhood I wanted to be a part of a large family when I married. Although Sydney had several sisters there were unfortunately few children. Sydney was averse to inviting family or friends to stay, so there was little contact and I had no choice but to accept the situation and make the best of it. As Sydney was often playing League Table Tennis in the evenings, I would enjoy a visit to the cinema on Fridays when he would stay at home to look after our children.

Both our daughters were born in this house and when our elder daughter was about two years old, she suddenly threw a tantrum. Her father decided to join her on the floor, kicking his legs in the air and yelling loudly. Her expression at his antics was of horrendous disgust and she walked away in complete silence, never again to display such temper.

Before she was five and old enough to have a tonsillectomy she became ill with repeated attacks of otitis media. Dosages of the drug from the doctor kept it at bay, until one December evening at 10pm the doctor was called to find her very ill. The drug was having no effect. He prescribed streptomycin, this was a new drug and very expensive. As Sydney had a season ticket he volunteered to take the prescription to the all-night dispensary in London. He caught a train just after 10pm and returned home about midnight. Within twenty-four hours this drug was effective and three weeks after her birthday she had her tonsils removed.

Before they were ready for junior school we decided to move to Tonbridge in Kent, that being where the train to London started and Sydney could be sure of a seat. We bought a three storied Victorian house just off the Pembury Road because the Infants School was at the end of the road and the railway station but a further hundred yards.

Sydney's work meant an early start finishing each day by catching a commuter train home. On one memorable evening he boarded his usual train, but as it was very crowded he got off and decided to take the next one. That was the 5.40pm train from Charing Cross to Tonbridge which was involved in the terrible railway crash at Lewisham. Hearing about the accident on the radio I went to the station to find that no train was expected for hours. Eventually he arrived home about 11pm, much to my relief. In the town next day I was shocked to find everybody there was so quiet and restrained. Nearly every street in Tonbridge had been affected by a casualty of this incident.

When the girls were at school I took every opportunity to supplement our income by taking odd jobs to compensate for the lack of visitors, not by my choice. Cycling to a local farm I hoed crops. At another farm in the autumn I picked Cox's apples. In this situation I was able to buy large amounts of apples which were too small for sale. From these I made jars of 'Cox's Apple Jelly' which was delicious and lasted us many years. In the Christmas period I was given a job in the Post Office Sorting Section dealing with the Southern Route, as my knowledge of the South of England was extensive.

In my childhood I received few expressions of affection and only occasional outings. Using the money I earned I took my daughters out on interesting day trips, such as strawberry and raspberry picking, the 'East of England Show', where they were able to become acquainted with farm animals, dogs and horses. Also I was able to buy pretty clothes, books, good presents and, in their teens, a huge box of chocolates each at Christmas time.

When taking a position in the Lingerie Department of a well known store, I was encouraged to go to London and sit the exams for the Corset Guild of Great Britain. I qualified as a Certified Fitter of Corsetry.

When planting bulbs in the garden I dug up a most interesting object. It was only a foot below ground level on the stones of the edge of the ancient flood plain of the River Medway. On consultation with Phil Harding of 'Time Team' he confirmed it was an Auchelian Handaxe. He was most interested because it had been found at the edge of the flood plain of the River Medway. This confirms the knowledge of stone-age man having been in the region. On sending him this information he recorded it in the relevant department of the Kent County Council and wrote 'This additional piece of information will go towards the giant jigsaw that forms the story of Kent. Stone age man not having previously been recorded in this area.'

Whilst in Tonbridge I was delighted to be able to organise some people from the Congregational Church into a musical and drama group. This was very successful and for six years we produced a two hour concert every winter.

One summer day our younger daughter came home at lunchtime in great pain. She had not fallen or banged her leg but her knee was enormously swollen and she had a high temperature. Calling our doctor he examined her, prescribing pain killers and immobilisation. After a few days it had not subsided and she was still in pain. The doctor returned and concluded she had rheumatic fever and required complete bed rest. Bringing her bed down to our front room I nursed her for three months before she could walk again.

No sooner was she back at school at Christmas than her sister complained of neck and back pain also with a high temperature. Within a week the doctor diagnosed rheumatic fever again. She was not allowed to leave her bed as it was imperative to prevent any strain. It was six months and late summer before she recovered sufficiently to be able to go back to school albeit with a heart murmur. This meant that sports and strenuous activity was curtailed.

Having nursed both daughters through rheumatic fever over two years and after getting both settled back to school, I discovered a disturbing fact and found my own health was at risk. Wasting no time I consulted my Doctor who gave me an immediate appointment with the Surgeon. Here, it was baldly stated I probably had a life-threatening disease and if I did not have an immediate operation it was likely I would not survive the year. The removal of one breast was naturally daunting. The prospect of the enormous difference in weight of my other side caused me to request plastic surgery for both with the removal of whatever was necessary. By coincidence I had read about plastic surgery the previous week, which was becoming the recognised solution to certain medical problems and requested a consultation with a Plastic Surgeon.

My Doctor and Surgeon had a quick conference and agreed to contact Mr. Charles Redmond McLaughlin. He had recently succeeded Sir Archibald McIndoe, the famous Surgeon who had pioneered the treatment of airmen badly burnt in World War II, at the Queen Victoria Hospital in East Grinstead. Shortly afterwards an interview was arranged. As it appeared I might be away for some time I felt it necessary for both girls to have a live animal to look after. We bought a tabby kitten called Fluff Puff, and a Pekinese called Chungkee. He was bred from a Champion of Champions and had the most delightful character and they all became good friends.

## The Queen Victoria Hospital at East Grinstead

At the interview with Mr Mclaughlin he told me there was a waiting list for this type of plastic surgery involving two surgical teams. After his examination he drastically reduced the two year list and agreed to treat me under the National Health Act. He asked me to go home, put my affairs in order and stand-by for the date of entry to the Hospital. He requested me to allow a visiting American Surgeon to be present who wished to learn about plastic surgery, it being a very new process. Three months later he sent for me.

I was most surprised my husband did not approve of my having any operation. I could not understand his stubborn resistance to the opinion of my doctor, nor the warning of the Surgeon at East Grinstead. I was fighting for my life!

My memory of returning to consciousness after the operation is, of both Surgeons standing at the foot of my bed in white coats, set faces and hands clasped behind their backs. Mr McLaughlin leaned slightly forward and said 'And how do you feel?' I wanted to laugh, but I couldn't move and replied 'I know where you've been alright!' There was an immediate slackening of their stance. Hands came round in front, smiles wreathed their faces and later he told me that due to my remark they knew I would pull through with flying colours. His comment 'Attitude of mind is 50% of healing' is absolutely true. After five weeks I was transferred to a convalescent unit for a further two weeks.

Mr McLaughlin said all damaged tissue had been removed. His last instruction to me was, if I felt any further discomfort during the following two years to return to him immediately. Providing everything went well I could look forward to a long life, and so it is. My complete recovery is due to his expertise.

## Chase me, Chungkee?

One midsummer morning watching Fluff Puff, our cat, preening herself in a patch of sunlight in our back yard I saw Chungkee, our Pekinese, come out of the kitchen door and trot over to give her a nuzzle. They were great friends.

Expecting Fluff Puff to move away in disdain, I was surprised to see her flick her tail in his face enticing him to follow as she dashed away down the garden path. Following the edge of the flower bed she raced down the lawn and at the end turned and came back along the other side of the flower bed. Chungkee chased her all the way even up the path to come to a stop exactly where they had started from. They stopped, facing each other. It was as though they communicated a decision, for the next thing was that Chungkee ran the same course closely followed by Fluff Puff, with her tail flying.

To see this episode once was magnificent but to my amazement this sequence was repeated no less than SEVEN times before they finally decided – enough was enough and both collapsed.

It was an incredible sight, and one could be excused for thinking it had been an illusion, but the whole astonishing performance had been observed by our neighbour from her bedroom window.

## Lydds Cottage, Ridgmont, Bedfordshire

After my return from hospital we paid a visit to my husband's colleague in Bedfordshire. We were shown a condemned cottage with an acre of ground next door. This was for sale at a very good price allowing us to afford the restoration to current housing standards. We sold our house and bought a caravan to live in whilst the cottage was being redesigned. a period of three years.

Moving day was full of episodes. The girls and I, with Fluff Puff and Chungkee, travelled by train. Sydney, on a motorbike, preceded the van carrying all our belongings. After unloading I was puzzled to be asked 'Have you forgotten anything?' I had left a cooked chicken behind in the cooker! We ate our lunch on the grass and Chungkee began to bark excitedly around the base of the lilac tree. It turned out to be sheltering a stoat! It was speedily sent on its way in the field beyond. Surely this was enough excitement for the day. But no. In the evening two tiny bantam chicks appeared as from nowhere. Where could they have come from? Up in the village we found the owners who said they had just hatched and had obviously escaped through their hedge, trotted down the field to the ditch alongside our land. So ended our first day in the country.

# The White House School, Husbourne Crawley

While my girls were at senior school I took the position of Assistant Teacher to Mrs Wyldbore-Smith in her school at the White House, Husborne Crawley. The history of this house is fascinating. In the mid 1400's it is understood monks from Wooburn Abbey lived in the single stone building which had a large fireplace at one end and a sleeping shelf at the other. After the dissolution of the monasteries it was another 100 years before the then owner made alterations. In the late Georgian period he divided the 'sleeping shelf' space from the original building and added an extension to make a separate cottage. Another extension on the opposite side of the original building made three cottages in all. In the 1800's the three cottages were made into one dwelling and a separate kitchen/brewhouse and cellar was built on the north side of the building. A semi-circular hall with a free-standing staircase was built on the south side. In the Victorian era a fire grate was fitted into the side wall. A three room extension was added and this part of the house became a school. The original wall ladder to the sleeping shelf was removed much later.

During World War II Mrs. Wyldbore-Smith's husband was on board H.M.S. Hood when it was sunk. With two young boys and limited means in a country area, she decided to educate them herself. Shortly afterwards some of her friends persuaded her to educate their children of the same age and so her first class was formed. From this small beginning and throughout further years more teachers and classes were added. As the first group grew into teenagers their younger siblings, amongst others, continued to join the school. I understand both her sons entered university as a result of her personal teaching. The White House became a school of repute.

Mrs Wyldbore-Smith's private dining room dominated by the original fireplace was dark, in spite of two large windows built into the north wall. She held many dinner parties and at one of them Eric Houfe, the architect son-in-law of Sir Albert Richardson of Ampthill who restored the damaged church of St. James's Piccadilly, suggested a small window could be inserted to light the room from the entrance hall. When she told me of his suggestion she was grateful of my offer to design and draw up the working drawings.

Bearing in mind the maxim of C.F.A. Voysey, 'To be simple is the end, not the beginning of Design', I studied the construction of this wall. The original stone had thick plaster on both sides and additional brick and plaster had been added when the present hall was created in the 1800's. A round window set under the free-standing staircase would be appropriate and complement the design of the windows in the hall. It would require a holding frame to support the thick aperture. By themselves this frame with the glazing frame would not have had any design merit. My solution to the problem was to design another between the two frames which made the whole appearance pleasing to the eye. After the completion Eric Houfe came to dinner again and was surprised and very delighted to see it in place. He complimented the design and thought it excellently positioned under the curve of the staircase. Mrs Josephine Lickorish, one of the teachers of that time, recently recalled my drawing of the design and its construction which was undertaken by Mrs Wyldbore-Smith's son with the help of a carpenter and glazier.

A distant relative and a member of the Pitman family of shorthand fame, came to visit Mrs Wyldebore- Smith. He gave her the newly developed i.t.a. Reading Scheme (Initial Teaching Alphabet) for her to examine and comment as to its suitability for teaching in her school. On Friday she presented me with the documents and asked me to study it over the weekend. Monday morning she met me at the door with urgent questions: 'What do you think of the scheme? Could you teach it?' This took me by surprise and I had to think very quickly as to why it was such an excellent teaching tool. My answer was 'It is brilliant, because no one can fail to learn to read.' This method had been offered to the teaching profession and was taken up by the Canadian authorities. Mrs Wyldebore-Smith's decision to change meant I had to be one day ahead of the children, learning it as I went. It was easy to teach and by the end of the year all children in my class could read confidently. One boy's father reported to Mrs Wyldebore-Smith that he was amazed his five year old son could read a paragraph from The Times perfectly. When he and his fellow pupils went on to Public School it was reported back to Mrs Wyldebore-Smith that they were two years ahead of their contemporaries in reading and comprehension.

## Tea with Field Marshal Montgomery

In the Summer of 1962 my husband having only recently passed his driving test requested me to navigate the cross country journey to visit Field Marshal Montgomery at Isington Mill in Alton. I remained in the car reading a book believing my husband to be busy for at least a couple of hours. After a few minutes he returned saying the Field Marshal had spotted me and told him not to leave his wife outside but to bring her in. My husband was insistent I should not discuss the War with him.

On approaching the main door I noticed a very large millstone was used as a step with smaller stones laid beside the path making a feature of the entrance. Having settled my husband to his work the Field Marshal indicated we should take a walk round his garden. Stepping on to the lawn I was dubious as I was wearing high-heeled shoes about leaving holes in the finely cut turf. Drawing his attention to this fact he quickly assured me it was not a problem as 'The gardener mows the centre circle every day, the surrounding two feet every two days and the outer edges once a week.' No wonder everything looked so trim; even the willows, not yet in leaf, marched in ranks along the river edge. At the far end where the mill race parted from the River Wey we discussed what other plants which required little maintenance could be used. Having planted Cornus Alba the previous year in our garden I was able to suggest these could be interspersed so the vibrant red stems would complement the yellow of his willows. On reading the book written by his brother, I note my suggestion had been implemented.

Our conversation continued on the subject of art. Mentioning he had received several amateur portraits of himself he thought it would interest me to see them and we went indoors. Walking into the entrance hall he commented on the fact the floors were made of Tasmanian Oak. The Cedar shingles on the barns came from Canada and Mountain Ash had came from Victoria. All these woods had been presented to him. Climbing up the stairs to the landing several oil paintings were hung along the wall. I gave each but a cursory glance as we walked along for they were not to my taste. At the end he spun round and said, 'Now. Give me your opinion of these portraits.' Startled at his request I was jolted into a considered re-appraisal. My first reaction had been what vulgar colours and treatment of the subject. Giving all of them a second look I strove to define one item on which I could make a positive comment. Fortunately I found, one had captured the tilt of the head, another the definition of the eyes, yet another the set of an ear and one in which the use of a softer palette gave a gentler mood. He was pleased at my remarks and nodded in agreement. Then taking me by the hand he drew me towards his bedroom saying, in a conspiratorial tone, 'Come and look at the only one I can live with.' Skirting the end of the four-poster bed he pointed to another painting hung on the far wall. It was less vibrant and less aggressive in treatment and a much better likeness – I had to agree it was the best of the bunch.

Moving away my attention was caught by two portraits which hung over the bed-head. The left hand one I recognised as that of his father, the large painting of which I had observed in the dining hall before climbing the stairs. The other was of Pope Pius XII. Seeing I looked puzzled, because I knew he was a staunch supporter of the Church of England, he commented, 'Both men have been my great inspiration.'

Returning downstairs to the hall he proceeded to show me the beautiful collection of silver items which had been presented to him. I was very impressed by his Field Marshal's baton which lay in a velvet-lined case. The 'salt' had pride of place on the dining table which had been set for tea. Years later I was very saddened to hear of the burglary when he lost all of these items. Could they not at least have left his baton?

My husband, having finished his assignment, joined us and the housekeeper brought in the tea tray. After a short grace, the Field Marshal turned the tea tray towards me saying 'Stella, will you be mother?'. After tea, when my husband was out of the hall I was much amused by his pointing to a dish of fruit and saying 'Do have a 'nana'. He explained with a smile 'That's what I call them to the children.' He then told me he was in the process of writing his memoirs. At this juncture I felt compelled to let him know of my work with Supermarine and my maiden name.

The instant he heard it, his eyes lit up and leaning towards me with an upraised finger, said 'Ah! Then you must be the young lady who was with Graham.' I smiled and nodded because we could not say anything further as my husband had come back into the hall. I knew he had recalled the situation in which I had been involved on the evening before D-Day for he had to give permission for me to be there. How I wished we could have met again – but it was not to be.

## Weddings and the Psychological Wedge

Joining a local drama society I asked my daughters to persuade some of their school friends to come along and help out. Several boys and girls turned up and they continued to attend the Society even after they left school. Two of these boys became engaged to our daughters.

When the first wedding date was set I looked forward, as mothers do, to entertaining relations at the celebrations. Talking over arrangements with Sydney I suggested we could put up a marquee on our lawn and hire crockery and chairs etc. As we had lots of room to park cars off the lane there would be no problem.

The next day I was taken aback by my husband stating 'I have given our daughter a large sum of money. She will deal with all the arrangements with her sister's help. You are not to interfere!' I was speechless! Feeling hurt and bewildered and not wishing to upset either daughter, I said nothing assuming I would be able to use my talents at the second marriage. Again I was forestalled in the same way! Traditionally it is the bride's mother who organises the wedding breakfast so I was disappointed not to being able to help on these occasions for either daughter. To this day I have never understood his actions. I felt ignored and of no account.

In order to give the second marriage a good start and time to save sufficient deposit to buy their own house, Sydney and I took the decision to let them have sole occupancy of our home for five days a week for twelve months. Sydney and I would find other accommodation and join them every weekend. As I worked in Bedford I found a bedsit and paid the rent out of my salary. Sydney took a flat in Slough and commuted to the City. The arrangement worked well at first but unknown to me Sydney had moved back home before the end of the proposed period. Consequently the newly-weds decided to buy a less expensive house and moved out earlier than expected.

All through our marriage Sydney had refused to take me abroad but after their marriages had taken place both daughters persuaded him to take me to Majorca for a week's holiday! He said he would pay all expenses and I would only need to take some pocket money. Surprised and excited as this was to be my first excursion abroad since visiting Paris as a schoolgirl, I hoped it would improve our relationship. Two days after arriving he informed me he had left his money vouchers behind. We would have to make do with the savings of £25 from my wages, which was not easy. I was disappointed when he did not reimburse me on our return, after having said he would do so. He could well afford it!

I suffered yearly allergic reactions after the birth of my second daughter in early

June. My room had French windows which opened on to a bomb site covered with weeds in full pollen. These reactions started in the spring with tree blossoms, through summer grasses and moulds in the autumn. Now living in town I found most of these attacks ceased but when in my husband's company each weekend, they came back in strength. Antihistamine gave no relief.

For many years my husband had a persistent cough and although I begged him to get advice he adamantly refused to see a doctor. He expected me to return and live at the cottage, but as my doctor had indicated my health was being severely undermined. I had to find a solution.

I realised he had lost all affection for me since my operation and in view of his continual antagonistic attitude to me and his refusal to seek medical advice I realised the marriage could no longer be sustained. Divorce was amicably agreed and our assets were split between us and we went our separate ways.

After our divorce I was told by a business friend that Sydney had been extremely jealous of me. I had no idea of this and considering he was at the top of his profession I found it hard to believe. I appear to have written about many unhappy experiences but there were many happy occasions to balance them.

## On My Own

After our divorce I had to earn my own income. As I could use a typewriter and had reasonable clerical abilities I undertook temporary jobs with an agency. Over some months I increased my speed on the typewriter and learnt to take dictation.

As a temp for three weeks I was asked to take charge of the newly opened Bedford office of Oldham & Son of Manchester. Whilst the Sales Manager was on holiday I was to answer the telephone and record messages for when he returned. To occupy my time I emptied the tea-chest of papers sent from Head Office and organised them into a empty filing cabinet. From the telephone calls received it occurred to me that there was no ledger recording details of equipment. This I endeavoured to do from the information contained in the papers.

When the Sales Manager returned he was accompanied by Mr. J. K. Marshall the Industrial Sales Manager. On viewing the sorting and filing I had undertaken and the ledgers collating the information from the files they saw my working knowledge of their sales and procedures was invaluable. They were so impressed that I was immediately offered a permanent post with the company. After three years when the company was taken over, Mr. Marshall gave me a glowing reference. Together with references from my school and college these enabled me to secure other positions mostly on a short-term basis – filling in for senior secretaries who were on holiday or sick leave.

To take classes in Pitman's shorthand would take a long time so I decided to try Speedwriting. After a little while I developed my own version, omitting any vowels and symbolising the basic shape of the letters. The end result coincided with Pitman's shorthand to the extent that one employer, who could read Pitman's, read my notes with ease.

Early in 1974 after working in London for six months I slipped on a wet floor and dislocated my shoulder. It was very painful until corrected at a hospital and it was a couple of weeks before I could type again. Due to the amount of time spent in travelling I decided to return and work in Bedford, eventually securing an interesting local position within walking distance of my flat. A Land and Property Agent, an Architect and a Builder who occupied offices in the same building, each required part-time secretarial assistance.

There was a garden at the rear which had gone to rack and ruin and I was allowed to clear the debris in my free time. Runner beans were planted that summer and the original brambles gave me many blackberries. The next year I grew radishes, lettuce and tomatoes thus keeping me busy especially over lonely weekends. This was a very interesting and rewarding post.

I have had many setbacks in my life causing me great distress by bullying or by deceit. On the other hand these have been compensated by others who have supported me with their lifelong friendships.


## A Persian Spitfire Pilot

Staying in the house where I lodged was a young Persian girl called Farah. She was attending college and wanted to see places of interest in her free time. As the Queen was expected to drive down the Mall I offered to take her to London for the day.

Just before Christmas she said that she and three friends, schoolgirls, were to meet a Persian gentleman in a London hotel. He was to escort them to their families in Teheran on the following day for the holidays. As he had been one of the Persian pilots of World War II would I like to accompany her to the hotel to meet him? On Friday during our journey she spoke of her family and their close association with the Shah's family. General Ali Rafat, whom I was to meet, was his brother in law.

At the hotel Farah went to contact her party and a few minutes later returned with a very distinguished looking gentleman whom she introduced as the General. He had obviously been appraised of my friendship to Farah during her stay in England for he, with impeccable Eastern politeness, asked me to allow him to express her families' appreciation by taking me out to dinner. He suggested we met in the lounge after he had organised the girls' meal in the hotel restaurant. Being aware of eastern etiquette I had packed a suitable decorous gown for just this sort of situation. After half an hour's conversation he checked that the girls had retired to their suite for the evening.

As he did not wish to eat in the hotel, could I recommend somewhere for us to go? Unfortunately two places I knew of were full. I suggested we got a taxi and perhaps the driver would know of somewhere suitable. He did, and he took us to the Blue Room. As Ali was not wearing a tie, only a white silk T-shirt and blazer, I wanted to be sure he was not refused entry. While he was paying the taxi I asked the doorman to inform the management of the General's arrival, to prevent any diplomatic incident. We deposited our coats and the doorman, having tipped me the 'wink', we started down the magnificent curve of the Hollywood-type stairs.

As we reached the bottom I was pleased to see the Manager, The 'Maitre d' and the Chef lined up to greet the General. We were escorted into the bar and seated on a long settee which had obviously just been vacated by other diners who were now seated at the bar. All very correct.

In the restaurant we were seated at a table by the dance floor and had a very pleasant meal. The music was not so loud as to make conversation difficult. The current topic turned on to the subject of the proposed increase in the price of petrol. What did I think was the opinion of people in this country about this increase? Stating I was not a driver, but I had noted that during the past two weeks many of my friends and colleagues had said, if the price of petrol was raised by more than 6p per gallon, they would sell their cars and use other forms of transport, such as bus or train.

Ali then informed me he was to have a meeting with the Shah on his return to Teheran and he would put my comments before him. On the following Monday all newspaper headlines read: 'Petrol up by 6p per gallon'! Coincidence – or did the Shah take my comments to heart?

## Michael Crawford at Drury Lane

Late on a Friday afternoon when I was working as Secretary to an Architect an unusual situation transpired. It was imperative that certain papers concerning the restoration of a cottage, recently acquired by Michael Crawford, had to be signed by him and presented no later than 10am on the following Monday. There was no way, even by first class post, these could be posted and returned in time. Nor could appointments already made for Saturday and Sunday be cancelled by the Architect. Panic stations! What to do?

Having no plans for the weekend I volunteered to travel to London. By meeting Michael Crawford at the Drury Lane Theatre, and with the papers signed, they could be back at the office by 9am on the Monday. This was the only logical solution to the problem. It also meant I could see the play. Urgent telephone calls were successful and I was given the assignment. As the papers had to be checked they would not be ready until Saturday midday. This allowed me plenty of time to catch the train and travel across London.

Arriving at the Theatre in good time for the evening performance and having collected my ticket from the Box Office, I went round to the Stage Door. There I met the Doorkeeper and explained about the arrangement to meet the Star after the play.

He had already been advised of my visit and told me to join him immediately after the performance.

When the play finished I made my way to the Stage Door to find that a crowd had already gathered. It was a stable door, the top half being open with the lower half secured shut against the crowd. As I caught his eye he signalled me to get behind a very large and vociferous lady who was demanding to be let in. He was quite polite but adamant in refusing entry. Choosing his moment when she moved, he opened the gate sufficiently for me to slip inside. She was absolutely furious and shouted 'WHO IS SHE? WHY HAVE YOU LET HER IN AND NOT ME?' Ignoring her completely he drew his assistant to the gate and instructed him to guard it and not allow anyone entry until he returned.

Taking my arm he led me through dimly lighted passages to the edge of the stage. Pointing to two yellow lines defining the 'safe route' across the stage he said, 'Can you find your way from here? Keep between the lines and you will find Mr Crawford's dressing room at the front. I must get back.' Satisfying himself I would be careful and follow his instructions he sped away to his post leaving me to traverse the stage alone! There was only minimal lighting and it was quite eerie to walk between the massive timber uprights of the stage set of 'Billy' having only seen it from the front of house.

My task completed, I made my way back across the stage down the passages to the Stage Door to say goodnight to the Doorkeeper as he let me out. I was amazed to see the crowd had grown enormously and in the belief that Michael was about to appear, they surged forward completely blocking the way. They were very reluctant to let me pass and it took some pleading from me and 'excuse me' before they parted to let me through. It was a frightening insight into what a Star has to face every day. But what an experience to tread the hallowed boards of the Drury Lane Theatre by someone who was not of the Stage!

Truth can be stranger than fiction. Some months later another incident occurred regarding this cottage. When some old timbers were required for the renovation, transport was arranged with a driver of an open lorry. Early one Sunday morning this driver, with Michael and his Architect as passengers, was negotiating a sharp left-hand bend along a country lane, when the timbers pushed the tailgate open and they slowly slid higgledy-piggledy across the road, blocking the corner. All three jumped out and scrambled to lift these heavy timbers back on to the lorry before any other traffic appeared.

Anyone observing this incident could have been forgiven for thinking he was watching a scene from a Frank Spencer drama. Fortunately no one appeared from either direction to witness the frantic scene. Minutes later, all being secured, the lorry and its load continued on its way.

I had followed all the plans from the beginning with great interest for the Architect had a very sensitive approach to the problem. The resultant completion of the whole project was a delight to the eye. Michael's own description can be read in his book, 'Parcel Arrived Safely Tied with String'.

# Greenfingers

One afternoon a friend took me to hear a lecture on gardening. During the first half of the programme the Speaker remarked 'How do we increase the circulation of gardening magazines and reach those people who are not yet buying one?' From that moment my brain buzzed with ideas formulating an entirely new conception of a gardening magazine.

During the interval I approached the Speaker and was pleasantly surprised at his interest. I proceeded to outline my ideas on the title, presentation of coloured pages and gave three examples of plants for each section and my words for the subtitles. Then suggested a second part could follow as an A to Z index with relevant information. He appeared to think it was a good idea and I requested him to collaborate with me to get a new magazine published. Knowing nothing about publishing I was buoyed up by the hope I had produced a saleable idea for a new gardening magazine thinking it would generate some financial security for my retirement.

About a year later I was horrified to see a magazine entitled Greenfingers advertised on television as being on sale. At lunchtime I bought a copy and showing it to my employers was shattered to discover there was no acknowledgement as to my original concept. This in spite of our verbal agreement confirmed on the shaking of hands! All my ideas and words given to the Speaker were there.

In hindsight I remembered he put a small box on the table with the remark 'We must watch the time'. It was not as I assumed a small clock as my words had obviously been tape-recorded. There was no other explanation for all my words to have been published throughout the edition with such accuracy. No one at that time including myself was aware I had a photographic memory of my brainstorm.

The next day I applied for Legal Aid and set in motion a case against the Publishing Company and Editors of which the Speaker was one. Finally, in November 1979, the publishers were granted a three-day hearing in the Law Courts. Mr. Justice Dillon ruled that there was a case to answer. My Solicitors tried to have my Legal Aid Certificate extended but this was not granted as, in the Opinion of the Barrister, it would be extremely difficult to procure any substantial financial settlement. The result was the magazine was withdrawn from sale and consequently I lost a prospective income. The following year the Publishing Company tried to bring out their own version of Greenfingers but after a few issues it ceased. The shock and trauma of this deception caused my hair to turn white.

## Visit to Robson Lowe of Christies

On reviving memories of my husband's business activities early in our marriage one memorable evening flashed into my mind. In order to confirm this memory I contacted

Mr. Robson Lowe and arranged to meet him in his office on the 18th March 1996. At the age of 91 he was still editing 'The Philatelist'! We spent a very pleasant lunch mulling over previous events and he chuckled over the memory of the party in May 1948. This was the occasion of the Philolympia Exhibition. Mr. Michael had organised an Evening Dance at, I believe, the Cumberland Hotel near Marble Arch for all the firms involved in the Exhibition.

Various Heads and staff of other firms joined our table during the evening. Tables were pushed aside and chairs were positioned around. As the Head of each group joined our extended table, they vied with the previous group with a larger bottle of champagne. We progressed from our original Magnum for 12 people through to a Jeraboam, Methuselah, Salamanazar to a Balthazar.

Some hours later, when we were joined by Mr. Robson Lowe, the number of people had grown considerably. His contribution to the party could not be faulted. In came two waiters trundling a trolley – he had ordered a Nebuchadnezzar!

## Retirement

Now I have time to do my own thing. What shall it be? I want to have another go at watercolour painting and I need to learn something about recording family history as both parents have interesting forbears. In addition I would like to put on record details of my Father's commissioned projects.

I had always wanted to write, probably to emulate my Mother who wrote at her desk every afternoon until 4 o'clock when I came down from the nursery for tea. I tried very hard at school but my English teachers always gave me low marks. I now realise it was probably because I wrote lengthy descriptions of people and places when all they wanted was a brief report. Why was this never explained to me? Convalescing after an illness I wrote again to amuse my husband and children about our cat and dog but their reaction was indifferent and I gave up.

Enrolling in Rothsay College, Bedford I started classes in watercolour painting signing them with the pseudonym Jil Teals. Not being able to afford large sheets of paper I concentrated on small pictures. To my delight within three months I mastered the basic art of painting trees, landscape and water. As my wartime work required precision detail painting miniatures was second nature to me. At the same time I joined the drama class and that Christmas our group performed a mediaeval poem at a Carol Service in St. Peter's Church. Our tutor considered it to be her 'most memorable production'.

At the same time I joined classes in Creative Writing and met Bobbie, a writer of poems under her maiden name Paddy Anne Wilson who had always, as she termed it 'scribbled'. We read each other's writings and became so attuned to each other's thought processes that a wrong or unsuitable word stood out like a sore thumb. My visits became longer and longer to the extent on some occasions I stayed for lunch and the shopping did not get done until the next day. She was very adept at hearing a remark and making up a poem. For example I said 'My tummy is telling me it wants some food' and this was the result.

## Timer Talks

I always wake at seven thirty every day you see,
My tummy has a timer, it's strict as strict can be.
It starts to grumble if I'm ever late for Lunch,
So it really isn't my fault if I have to have a munch.
I'm never late at Tea-time, I wouldn't dare to be
Because my tummy has a timer which really talks to me.
It seems my tummy's sleepy when it's time for Supper
For it lets me get away with just a Bedtime cuppa.
Sometimes in the darkness, I wake up in a fright
It's just my tummy wanting a little something light.

I append below another poem written by her which is in quite a different mode:

## I 'Aint Got No Chance Miss

I 'ain't done me 'omework Miss, I didn't get a chance
'Cos me Dad gave Ma a 'Glasgow kiss', 'Cos she give 'im a glance.
So we're back in the refuge Miss, We're all four in one room,
'Cos me old man's in the poky, And me muvver's sunk in gloom.
We're on the 'Socials' Register, Of children 'O're at risk,
Well me muvver's 'ad a breakdown, And me old man's always pissed.
The baby screamed all night Miss, Me Ma says she's got colic.
Me, I fink she knows, That 'er old man's an alcoholic.
I'm sorry if you're mad Miss 'Cos you caught me sleeping
But it's 'ard to sleep at night To the sound of muvver weeping.
You say I "ain't learning Miss, That I "ain't very bright!
Well it's really 'ard to concentrate When living's such a fight.
Me life's a blinking mess Miss And I just can't see no 'ope
Wiv me sister on the street And me bruvver on the dope.
The T.V. shows me families Miss 'Oo look really nice and sweet.
Do you know where they live Miss? 'Cos it "ain't down our street.
You've looked at me at last Miss You've given me some attention!
I should have known the reason, It's to give me a detention.

She encouraged me to try my hand at writing poetry. As a result I wrote the following under the pseudonym of Jil Teals, an anagram of my initials and name.

## Contentment

Look not on barren walls or peeling paint,
The cheerless hearth or broken window-pane;
But gaze instead on young green leaves
Lightly dusted with sunset's golden glory
And seeing, the troubles of the day disperse
Absorbed within its healing rays.
The fading call of nestling birds, softly
Travels on the quiet of evening's breeze;
Let good humour spread its gentle cloak
O'er aching heart and furrowed brow;
With tender clasp of hands, a soothing kiss
To crown this haven and sweet contentment find.

## Palette

Golden is the sunset Sparkling with splintered light
Taking wing to flying thoughts Masking all in its might.
Blue is the colour bold Far in infinite space
Boosting with endless patience Complicated actions of the race.
Green is the swaying grass That covers all the land
Bending, flowing in the wind Timeless as the road of sand.
Red is the flame of hope That glows within my heart
Engulfing all the lies therein Waiting to play the part.

On joining the local Family History Society I was fortunate to make friends with Harry Arch, a Vice President, and his wife Joan. Hearing of my wish to discover my parents' antecedents and their acquaintanceship with people in the world of Art Nouveau, he encouraged me to research and read about well-known people who were often spoken of by my Father. Gradually I collected information which confirmed his association with them and Harry encouraged my endeavours until his demise.

In Bedford I met a lady who had been a nurse at Haslar, the hospital at Gosport during June 1944. She very kindly gave me her description of that time to include in this book. This meeting caused me to think about contacting former colleagues.

My first quest took me to find Donald Fry, my cycling comrade of H.M.S. Excellent days. Enquiries at his original address proved inconclusive as to his whereabouts.

Two years later I discovered he had moved to Hayling Island and had died just a year before.

In Winchester I searched for my landlady (Mrs. Ward) of wartime years and was successful but it took her a little while to recognise me. I was surprised by her memory of my favourite dress – red poppies on a cream background. She also recalled my dress and jacket of yellow and brown tweed. This was what I wore to the Farewell Party with General Graham on the most traumatic day of my life. David, her eldest son, went on to become involved in the world of flying, namely helicopters. Is it any wonder when all her lodgers were Supermariners!

To find colleagues in Supermarine I discovered the firm had moved to Swindon and I found Gerry Gingell. He told me the Supermarine Association held reunions every autumn in the Social Club of the Evening Echo newspaper in Southampton. At last my search for colleagues of wartime years bore fruit. Having joined this Association and meeting Supermariners at these reunions I was given some stories of their lives and experiences which they agreed could be included in this book.

In my travels I visited Tangmere Museum and was able to give them a picture contributed by the men's outfitters, Burton's, to the Spitfire Fund during the War. This had been given to me and Nick Berrymore accepted this on behalf of Alan Bower, Curator of the Museum. On a recent visit they accepted a thousand-piece jigsaw of aircraft of World War II which I had mounted and framed for display. In addition I gave them the last copy of the poem 'Sub Contracts', produced as a limited edition of fifteen through the Spitfire Society.

A friend required an item to be returned to Her Majesty, Elizabeth the Queen Mother. As Chairman of the Central Region of the Spitfire Society, I contacted a member, Air Marshal Sir Roy Austen-Smith who had recently retired as an equerry to the Queen regarding this commission. He kindly gave me an personal introduction to Sir Martin Gilliatt, the Personal Secretary to Her Majesty. She graciously acknowledged this small service. Sir Martin stated 'How touched the Queen Mother was by the gesture of the return of this photograph which brought back many memories of days gone by.' He also said Her Majesty was grateful for my gift of a copy of the poem 'Sub Contracts' written by a Supermariner. He was most interested in my involvement in World War II and my search for information regarding Mother's family history and thereby became my good friend for many years until his death.

In my free time I attended classes at Rothsay College of Adult Education including archaeology given by Dr. Trump of Cambridge University. At the end of this course he organised a two day trip to the east coast. Our first visit was to view the site of a battle held in 991 at Maldon. We walked along a track by the estuary until we reached the causeway to Northey Island. Here he described the battle and we could visualise the raiders coming across this narrow causeway to meet the Saxons drawn up along the shore. A fatal move for it allowed raiders to get across in numbers. Had the Saxons held the land approach of this narrow causeway by one man supported by others, they could have defeated individual raiders as they attacked. A historical lesson to be learned is: do not allow invaders to secure a landing.

The next day we went to see the ancient chapel of St. Peter's, built by St. Ced, which lies across the ruins of the Roman fort of Orthona. On the way home I persuaded my friend to stop and view Greensted Church, believed to be the only existing church built of split tree trunks. A Templar's tomb lies alongside.

## Recollections - Winchester

During the war years many stage personalities and musical celebrities gave concerts to people who would not otherwise have had the opportunity to visit a theatre or other centres of entertainment. In London musical events were held in the foyer of the National Gallery. This music could be heard by crowds sitting outside in Trafalgar Square. By the same token factories where conscripted personnel were working for the war effort also had visits from various entertainers. At Hursley in 1942 some of these performed in the hut which was the canteen for the Drawing Office.

In the Winchester Guildhall many other events were held including the table tennis competitions mentioned elsewhere. The Guildhall was also the venue for dances with music by the Glen Miller and the Squadronaire Bands. Musical evenings were a great attraction in Winchester and two of these were given by Dame Myra Hess and Benno Moiseiwitsch, both of which I was able to attend. As all transport closed down by 10pm, entertainment centres and the cinema had to close early. I became accustomed to walking the two and a half miles back to my digs at Battery Hill in the blackout. One had to rely upon the slight variation of darkness between the house, skylines and trees if there was no moon. Trailing one's fingers along the walls by the side of the path and the sound of the hedges rustling in the wind would often orientate one's position.

In 1943, to give a little variance to our concentrated routine, a Sports Week was planned – The House versus the Drawing Office. A football match was easy to organise with men. Then someone thought up the idea of a three-legged race of both sexes. Being the only girl in the Drawing Office I was roped-in. At 5 feet 2 inches in height I was teamed up with Noel Mills who was 6 feet tall! We had only a few minutes to practice but came in a close second. We were very pleased with our result but I am sure if we had been given prior notice and a little more time to adjust, we would have won. Many Supermariners who had joined the Spitfire Society greeted me at our stands at Air Shows. On 12th July 1986 at a Spitfire Stand at Middle Wallop one of these was Noel and he was accompanied by his wife.

Visiting old haunts I met up with Mrs. Ward, my wartime landlady, now very elderly. We had a long conversation and she recalled my time with her all those years ago. Her eldest son had become an expert on helicopters, not surprising, when all her lodgers had been involved in the aircraft industry. Finding the address of Mr. Eric

Lovell-Cooper I took a bus to Golden Common and called upon him hoping he would be able to recall certain events. At the age of 82 he was unable to remember them.

Then travelling to Hursley and Ampfield I was able to photograph the site of the 1944 British and American Officers' Mess Hut and the path to Hursley village which I remember from my visit. The telephone cables serving that Camp are still in place.

There were many poems written by people at Hursley but the one I thought the best was 'Subcontracts or The Mad House' by R.B. Bennett and it shows the frustration of trying to produce the numbers of Spitfires required by the Government at the time when our backs were to the wall. Here it is for your perusal:

## Sub-Contracts

This is the home of trouble, we get it day and night,
On the carpet, on the 'phone, Sub-Contracts can't be right.
No matter how we struggle with contracts short or long,
We cannot get the bloomin' reqs – and when we do they're wrong.
There are no rivets at the stores, we cannot get the screws,
They change the mod: on every job and then the drawings lose.
It's true that washers can't be spared and bolts just don't exist
While mild steel and alclad sheet are never on the list.
The typists scream, the 'phones go mad, the din is just appalling,
We've been shot down in flames again – without a chance of stalling.
The shortage list assumes a state of frightening proportions,
Deliveries are down to nil, despite our mad contortions
Production, Spares and the P.R.U, they give us all the shudders,
We can't get struts or Tail Planes, Oleo legs are tricky,
Ribs from Beaton's just as bad, And Wings are awful sticky,
Jettison Tanks and Oil Tanks, we tank they drive us crazy,
We pace the bedroom every night, and come back just as hazy.
Before this war is over, and there ain't no 'Ifs or 'Buts',
We'll find ourselves in padded cells, completely 'slotted nuts'.
But ere this fate befalls us, we'll prove conclusively,
That Spitfires still command the skies – just you wait and see!
Written by R.B. Bennett – Vickers Supermarine – 1942

# Haslar at the Ready
## by
## Peggy Richards, V.A.D. Nurse

Peggy Richards, who was a V.A.D. (Voluntary Aid Detachment) gave me the following story about the Royal Naval Hospital at Haslar, Gosport.

'It was D-Day, we all knew what was happening and I shall never forget the awful sick feeling of apprehension while we waited. A month before, Haslar had evacuated all but a couple of patients who were too ill to be moved. Some of our laboratory S.B.A's (Service Blood Assistants) had vanished to the Naval laboratories at Clevedon to prepare the new drug, penicillin, in readiness for the arrival of casualties. We had been given our specific instructions and stations of duty for when 'IT' happened.

Travel was restricted for we were 'sealed in' on the South Coast and watched the arrival of men, vehicles and guns. On every spare patch of ground, army vehicles and equipment were packed so closely it seemed impossible to walk between them. Local buses had to stop half way down Gosport High Street as the bus station at the harbour was taken over by tanks and lorries. The ferry which normally took a few minutes to get to Portsmouth now took two hours because of the increased naval traffic.

Inside the hospital we turned two ground floor wards into resuscitation units for those needing blood transfusions before operations. In the mean time we packed drums with sterilised dressings and filled hundreds of blood 'giving' sets.

Inside the wall of Haslar there was a raised hump with a seat, called the Admiral's seat. From there you could see across the Solent to the Isle of Wight. In the evening standing there you felt you could have walked across to the Island, if not to France, on decks of the hundreds of ships assembled in the Solent. Later a pilot wrote, that from the air it looked as if the Island was being towed out to sea. We sent our thoughts to the men and crews on board silently wishing them 'God speed' and wondered how long it would be before some of them came back to Haslar.

At dawn we woke to see the Solent grey, empty and waiting. The silence was uncanny. A frightening anticipation of what was to come. From midday on Wednesday the main stream of casualties began to come in. None of us could have envisaged what the next days and weeks would bring. The endless stream of ambulances, the filthy soaking clothing piled in the sluices, bathrooms and even in the corridors as the underground operating theatres worked day and night around the clock. The stench of the terrible wounds we would dress as we would try and comfort the dying.

The Casualty Department received the wounded as they arrived, and their immediate needs were dealt with. Each V.A.D. on duty was given cigarettes and to hold one for a puff was all we could do for some of them. In the wards their filthy uniforms were removed and they were cleaned up prior to theatre. By the next day many were on their way up north to safer areas, or to specialised hospitals such as East Grinstead for burns, in order to free their beds for those wounded who were still coming in. There was no leave for staff for over three weeks and our precious three hours off duty was frequently cancelled.

The tenderness shown by the S.B.A's to those wounded who were unlikely to live, will never be forgotten. In the blackout an S.B.P.O (Service Blood Programme Officer) would play the organ in the Church giving us the comfort and strength to face the next day of horror.'

The description by Helen Long in her book 'Change into Uniform' gives another description of that time.

'Viewed from Haslar, the armada was laid out as it were on a stage beneath the hospital walls... Suddenly there they all were! Above floated a haze of silver balloons attached by gossamer threads to armed merchant cruisers, corvettes, trawlers, minesweepers, destroyers, tank landing craft, M.T.B.s, M.Ls, and ocean going tugs. Each one proudly holding, like a child at a party, its portly balloon. On the top floor a V.A.D glanced out of the window and saw below, a grey sea, grey not with sea but with ships... They formed a solid mass whose limits were beyond her vision. Later that afternoon a rating also looked out but moved quickly away and he too said nothing. This was how everyone kept silent.'

# Lord Beaverbrook to the Rescue
## by
## Ken Miles

The following article is the recollections of Ken Miles's life with Supermarine when he called for help from Lord Beaverbrook.

'When the war started in 1939 my father, a shop keeper, thought I should leave school and get a job. Having received a good business education he naturally thought I should get a job in business but I wanted to be an engineer like my uncle. He was very disappointed but he agreed to my wishes. The first man who came into father's shop wearing dirty overalls was asked if he could get me a job, which he very kindly did – working in a garage.

One evening I came home in a filthy mess after having spent the day crawling under cars. My uncle said 'Good Lord, what on earth have you been doing?' Proudly I told him I was now working in a garage as an engineer. He was extremely annoyed with father and told him I had not received a secondary education to become a motor mechanic which, although an honourable job, was not the place in which to train as an engineer.

My uncle was a staunch Union supporter and brought the matter up at their next meeting. They invited me to attend and asked if I would like an apprenticeship with Supermarine. Such was the power of the Union that an interview was immediately forthcoming. There I was told the Company was not taking on any more apprentices but in view of my education I could start at Eastleigh Works on the following Monday and when I became 16 I could begin as an Apprentice Aircraft Fitter. I was thrilled to be working earning 2d per hour on the final assembly of the famous Spitfire.

One day a boy came up to me and asked if I was an apprentice. I told him I was an Apprentice Aircraft Fitter, at which he said 'Oh' and walked away. 'That's strange' I thought and went after him. 'What do you mean, Oh?' 'Oh nothing,' he replied. So I asked him the same question. 'Oh, I'm an Apprentice Aircraft Engineer.' 'What's the difference?' I asked. 'Oh well, you will be just a fitter when you have finished your apprenticeship but I shall be on the design or technical staff.'

Thinking things over I decided that I did not want to be an aircraft fitter but an aircraft engineer, so banged on the door of Mr. Nelson the Manager. 'Come in!' he shouted 'What do you want?' 'I want to be an aircraft engineer not a fitter.' 'Don't be silly' he said 'You're going to be a fitter and that's that.' and threw me out of the office. I kept thinking about the matter and the next day I knocked on Mr. Nelson's door again and told him I wanted to see Mr. Pratt, the General Manager. 'What for?' he said. 'I want my apprenticeship changed to aircraft engineer' whereupon I was practically booted out of the office. I stewed about this for days thinking as to how I could get to see Mr. Pratt.

All kinds of visitors came to see the new version of the Spitfire which was being assembled by a few selected workmen. A few days later a large limousine arrived with several people from the Government including Mr. Quill the Test Pilot, Mr. Richardson the Chief Inspector, and several high-ranking R.A.F. Officers. They gathered around the new aircraft, some standing on the wing and others on a platform which had been erected at the side. I knew Mr. Quill and Mr. Richardson by sight so I asked another boy who were the others. He pointed out Mr. Pratt but did not know anyone else. Mr. Pratt I thought, that's the man I need to see. Without a moment's thought I climbed on the wing and tapped Mr. Pratt on the shoulder. 'Yes yes?' he said. 'I want to be an aircraft engineer'. Everybody laughed and two security men grabbed me off the wing.

After they left I was called into Mr. Nelson's office and he gave me a terrible ticking off, asking me if I hadn't been taught any manners at my 'posh' school. 'Well' I said 'You wouldn't let me see Mr. Pratt' and once again I was thrown out. Two days afterwards I was called into Mr. Nelson's office once more and this time I was sure that I was going to be given the sack. 'You've caused some trouble you have lad' he said. 'There's a car outside. Mr. Elliott the Assistant General Manager wants to see you.' At Woolston in Mr. Elliott's office I was given a another dressing down. 'What's all this about anyway?' I told him I wanted my apprenticeship changed from fitter to engineer. He said I did not have enough qualifications and I was sent back to Eastleigh where Mr. Nelson stated he didn't want to hear any more of the matter. I was very despondent and felt utterly miserable.

To my horror I was summoned to Mr. Nelson's office again. 'The matter is not over yet my lad, Mr Daniel wants to see you.' He was the Employment Officer and at that time also acted as Apprentice Supervisor. Having met him when I first started work at Supermarine I found him to be a very kind man. This is it I thought, my employment is no longer required. At Woolston I was escorted to his office and there he told me he had been informed of my behaviour and I did not have enough qualifications to train as an aircraft engineer. I stated if I had not left school early in order to get an apprenticeship, I was sure I would have obtained the necessary qualifications. Having given the matter some thought he said that although I had caused a lot of trouble he admired my tenacity. I was to attend a work school which was being set up to raise the education of the shop boys. They did the same work as the apprentices but did not move around to learn other skills. After three months he would assess my progress and if he found it was satisfactory he would break all precedence and change my Indentures to Aircraft Engineer.

None of the boys attending this school had the advantages of a secondary education, consequently I was far ahead of the others at the end of three months. My Indentures were changed to Aircraft Engineer. I had made myself noticed, stood firm with determination and had got to where I wanted to be.

In 1940 my parents went to live with some relatives to escape the constant night bombing. Businesses at that time had to have a Firewatcher at night so father put up a bunk bed behind the shop for me. When the shop was bomb damaged with slates blown off and windows shattered I went to live with friends in Romsey. From there I could still commute to Eastleigh.

The Cunliffe Owen factory was next to the Supermarine Works at Eastleigh. When the sirens sounded we all ran to the shelters on the opposite side of the main road. After the 'All Clear' we saw a pall of black smoke over the Cunliffe Owen factory and I lost my best friend in that raid. Afterwards dummy guns were made from metal tubes and these were put around the hangars at Eastleigh to deter any further dive bombers.

When the main Supermarine works was bombed volunteers were asked to report to the office. As I had trained in First Aid I went along only to be told I was too young. I was sixteen! Mr Bartholomew, a Charge Hand, had sent his family into the country but he was killed when a stray bomb fell on his house. His wife asked that his tools be given to an apprentice and they were given to me.

On 3rd June 1941 I was transferred to Hursley Park. It was a large country estate owned by Lord Cooper and had been taken over by Supermarine after the Woolston Works had been destroyed as their Headquarters. In the garage which had previously held limousines, benches were set up for the Experimental Workshop. Under the archway we worked on an experimental Spitfire fuselage until our work was transferred to the new hangar by the main gate. The day the transfer took place several of us were delegated to carry this fuselage to the new hangar. It was lifted on to our shoulders and we proceeded to walk the half mile to our new home. Our way took us through the orchard and when we arrived the fuselage was full of apples.

On 22nd March 1943 I was transferred to Sewards which was one of the dispersal units. It had been a local garage before it was commandeered by Supermarine. I was to report to Mr. Dicky Earl who was foreman of the Jig and Tool Department. He was an old employee and well-respected although a bit of a character. Outside his office I waited for him to arrive and he greeted me by asking 'What is that box for?' Explaining it was my tool box he said 'You won't be needing that for the job you are going to do. You are to take over the drawing office.' I laughed saying he must have mistaken me for someone else. But no. Introducing me to the draughtsman I explained I did not know anything about drawing but was told that as he was joining the Air Force the following week I was to take over his job. He showed me the work I was expected to do, which was to make drawings of tools and jigs. Some were drawn from tools made in the tool room and others I had to design myself. 'I can't do that.' I said 'Well that's what your job is going to be.' was the answer. Apparently the Management had assessed my potential and decided that I would be suitable to join the design staff at some future date. I had just two weeks to learn the basics before the other man left.

One day I was told a car was waiting to take me to Hursley to meet Mr. Lennox Taylor who had been appointed Apprentice Supervisor. He confided to me that the Earl of Gainsborough was to start work at Supermarine. 'I know what you lads are with new boys and I want you to do your best to look after him but on no account must other boys be told that he is an Earl.' Promising to respect his confidence I returned to my office but another apprentice came up to me asking if I knew a real live Earl was starting. Some secret! Later Tony Gainsborough was transferred to Hursley Drawing Office in the Electrical Section.[1]

Mr. Gooch, the General Works Manager told me to go to Trowbridge and learn the Robinson Process. After many months in the Tool Room Drawing Office I was reasonably confident in my ability to draw. The Process was to draw on matt grey plated aluminium sheet, and these drawings had to be accurate to within 5000th of an inch. These would be sent to the works and used as a template. I took great care with my first drawing, never before having had to be so accurate and submitted it to Mr. Wills the Inspector. He rejected my drawing as it was not within the permitted tolerance. I did it again only to have it rejected a second time. After three rejections I was pretty fed up and just wanted to return to my office at Sewards. A kindly senior draughtsman seeing my misery asked if he could help. On explaining the problem he looked at my rule, which was the usual draughtsman's wooden rule, and told me it would be impossible to draw to the required limits with it. He showed me the correct type which was stainless steel and graduated to 100th of an inch. With a magnifying glass and a chisel pointed 4H pencil you could pinpoint a position roughly half way between the 100th graduations and that would be within the required tolerance.

The next day I called at Lawsons our local tool shop and asked for a Chesterman No.761/3 rule. The salesman laughed and said such a thing had not been seen since the start of the war and was unattainable. How was I expected to help the war effort if I could not get the tool to do the job? Who could help me find one? Lord Beaverbook, the Minister for Aircraft Production would probably know so I wrote to him. Receiving his very nice reply which told me to return to Lawsons where a rule would be waiting. You can imagine the surprise that Lawsons must have had!

I was not happy at Trowbridge and did not get on too well with the boss. One problem was I was a member of 'Staff' and he was still considered 'Works'. So at lunchtimes he would have to go into the works canteen whilst I went to the staff. Out of work we got on fine and the young lady I met in the office, later my wife, and I were often asked to tea at his house. Although he was well respected as a Loftsman I found him a bad administrator and made it obvious. Coming from a young lad this did not go down so well. Eventually I was reported to Mr. Lennox Taylor who put me back on tools and sent me to Shorts in Winchester.

A couple of weeks after starting on 14th August 1944, the Works Manager called me into his office and said 'You're a draughtsman aren't you? I understand you used to run a drawing office at Sewards'. Acknowledging I had been doing drawings but that I wouldn't call myself a draughtsman, he went on to say 'I want to start one here, would you run it?' Agreeing to set up an office I was shown a room with just a table and chair. He agreed I could go to Hursley to get a drawing board, tee square and some other items which I managed to get from Mr. Richardson who was in charge of the Tool Drawing Office.

I worked in this office for several months until Mr. Lennox Taylor heard of it. Summoned to his office I was greeted with the words, 'You are supposed to be back on your tools.' I replied it was not my fault – I was told to do it. 'I'm not having this!' he stormed, 'Back on your tools you were sent and that is where you are staying.' So I was sent to Lowthers in Southampton on 19th November 1944 and put to work on a milling machine. Three weeks later he sent for me again. Now what have I done I thought? 'I can't keep you out of a drawing office, can I?' he said. 'You are to start in the drawing office at Hendys, Chandlers Ford next week.'

The Liaison Officer was Dave Sidley a draughtsman from Hursley who set me to work drawing details which were supplied by him. Soon I was accepted as his assistant, often going to the various dispersal units to sort out problems. At this point I was still 'Works' but on 19th April 1945 I was promoted to 'Staff'. I was on my way back!

Transferred to Hursley Drawing Office on 9th August I continued to work under Dave until loaned to Mr. Richardson the Manager at South Marston to set up a small drawing office on 26th March 1946. There I lived in a hotel and dined with senior staff. Then Mr Lovell-Cooper, having had good reports of my work requested my return to Hursley. Mr. Richardson kept getting it postponed, but eventually I had to go back.

At Hursley I found the 'Glass House', so called because of the secrecy of the work there, had been enlarged. Under the supervision of Jack Davis, a Senior Section Leader, I was to design part of the undercarriage locking system for the Swift. It was very satisfying to see it set up in a rig being raised and lowered proving my design worked satisfactorily.

My father, still running his small electronic component business kept asking me to join him as he was in poor health. I was not interested as he would not have been able to pay the same wage as Supermarine and anyway I knew nothing about electronics. When he became very ill and had to enter hospital he asked me to look after the business. Mr Lovell-Cooper very kindly offered to give me leave of absence when I explained the situation but I was back at Hursley six weeks later. Shortly afterwards father was taken into hospital again. Explaining to Mr. Cooper I would have to resign because mother's livelihood depended on the business. He was very understanding and said he was sorry I had to go, but if I wanted to come back at any time I would be welcome providing it was not too long. I left Supermarine on 18th April 1948 never to return.

My father died and I was left to run a business of which I knew very little. After years of struggle having successfully expanded the business I eventually sold it to a national company before retiring, but that's another story.

During my apprenticeship I experienced many unusual events. Dicky Bird, the son of Commander Bird the previous owner of Supermarine, worked for a while at the Eastleigh Works and kept his light aircraft inside one of the hangars. One day I was told to help him. He explained that he would start it and I was to swing the propeller. I was dead scared and after several failed attempts Dicky told me to get in the cockpit, press a button, shout 'contact', he would swing the propeller and I was to press another button.

All went well until it started to taxi towards the hangar. Dicky grabbed a wing and jumped up into the cockpit and switched the engine off. I was not asked to help again.

On the grass just outside the main hangar the apprentices used to play football and Jeffrey Quill and Alex Henshaw the test pilots, often flew their test flights low over our heads. (Alex has confirmed this fact to the Author.)

The old S6A Schneider trophy plane hung in the roof of the hangar at Eastleigh. The apprentices were given the job of preparing it to be used in the film 'The Life of Mitchell' starring Leslie Howard. Afterwards it was put on display at the Royal Pier before finally being laid to rest in the local museum.

Another film was being made about this time called I believe, 'Men Behind the Guns'. The camera crew came to Eastleigh and shot various processes, one of which was of me working on the undercarriage system. My parents were very excited and when the film came out we all went to see it but my piece had been cut!

Dr. Horace King, a friend of my parents, wrote a song called 'The Hampshire Spitfire Song'. Copies of this song were given to the staff at Eastleigh but it seems these have all disappeared including mine. The sale of this sheet music was designed to raise cash for the Spitfire Fund. Any town wishing to help was given permission to insert their own name in place of 'Hampshire'. Dr. King was later a Speaker of the House of Commons and then became Lord Maybray King of the House of Lords. Since meeting with Ken, the Author has acquired a copy of the words and music from the archives of the Hampshire Chronicle, who received it from the Eastleigh and District Local History Society.

Early on in the Battle of Britain some men from the Royal Air Force came to Eastleigh to give us a course of instruction on servicing Browning machine guns. Working on a bench opposite a Spitfire set up on trestles for minor repair work, someone got in the cockpit and pressed the firing button. This being common practice to blow out the system but on this occasion bullets had been left up the spout! There was a terrific bang and bullets shot just over my head into the electrical conduit causing a small fire and fusing all the lights. A workman who had been leaning on the wing between the guns dropped to the ground and we all thought he had been shot, but I think he was in a dead faint.'[2]

[1] The author confirms the accuracy of this statement as his desk was near hers.
[2] The Author heard of this incident at that time.

# Woolston and Home, Bombed
*by*
*Jack Parnell*

During the bombing of Southampton many civilians lost their homes. Jack Parnell and his family amongst others, experienced more than one destruction. He tells his story as follows:

'I joined Supermarine in 1935 and worked as a Riveter in the Tank Shop (Fuel) before being sent to the old roller mills on the western shore. By 1940 I was working in the Woolston Works and still living with mother and brothers in Radstock Road. The sirens used to go off three of four times a day and we just got on with our jobs between running up and down to the shelters. Once cycling back from Denham with a mate we saw a twin-engined plane flying up Southampton Water, obviously taking photographs of Supermarine. Another time an ME 109 hit a barrage balloon which blew up leaving just a wire!

One day my brother John and I were in our garden and although the weather was cloudy we could see the New Forest across Southampton Water. Coming towards us were several bombers and we heard the click of their bomb doors opening as we dived into our shelter. The ground shook beneath us and we thought our house had gone but we did not even have a broken window!

On Tuesday 24th September 1940 I had gone upstairs to have a bath when the sirens went off and bombs started dropping. Stark naked I fled downstairs and John threw his Mac over me as we ran for our shelter. After the raid it was to find half the house had gone. The bathroom had disappeared and it was impossible to get into my room. John climbed into mother's room and brought out some of her clothes and underwear for me to put on. Mother was in deep shock and stayed in the shelter until Gwen, my fiancée arrived and we all went to Sydney's house (another brother).

The next day when the sirens went off and our guns opened up – there were no bombs! A single plane followed the river obviously photographing the result of the previous day's attack on Supermarine.

Mother got another house, still in Radstock Road, and we moved everything we could salvage. Gwen and I were planning our marriage and Sydney suggested it could take place from his house, but Mother was adamant. She stated 'No way. None of the others have. They will go from here.' meaning Radstock Road. On the day itself my sister's house was also bombed!

She and Mother decided to leave Southampton and move to a bungalow in Chandler's Ford. Gwen and I found a modern flat in Eastleigh. Our neighbour put mattresses into his lorry and took friends out to the country at night. When Eastleigh was bombed one fell between our shelter and our neighbour's house and we were buried alive! So we moved into the bungalow at Chandler's Ford for a short time until Gwen and our son, just 6 months old, went to live in Trowbridge with her parents. When D-Day started we heard the transport planes going over all night.

Soon I was transferred to Trowbridge and there we were far removed from the war. On going to work in the morning we met the night staff who had beds made up in the canteen. We even had a chef to cook for us and had our breakfast in the cookhouse. We returned to Southampton after the war and two years later Norman (our brother) came home after being a P.O.W. for six years.

I observed some American troops who were lined up in the market square and a sergeant was telling them what was happening. He said, 'Left turn. Off we go.' and someone called out, ' Oh Sarg. We don't want to go that way. We went that way yesterday.' Can you imagine a British Sergeant putting up with that? If he told you 'Left turn!' – you did.

Mrs. Morley, my wife's mother, lost her identity card which meant she had to go to the Civic Centre in Southampton and apply for a new one. She was asked to give all the details and information for a new card to be issued and when this had been done she was asked 'Have you anything to prove who you are?' She replied 'Well I've only got my Identity Card from the First World War.' Silence reigned until the officer said, 'Well we needn't have gone all through that Mrs. Morley if you had shown me this card in the first place. I would have given you a new card straight away.' You see all the identification was there. But fancy carrying a 1918 Identity Card in her handbag in the 1939 war! She had only taken it with her, just in case!'

# Target Supermarine
## by
## Bill Fisher

Bill Fisher relates his time with Supermarine before World War II and the difficulties in which the employees worked when the factory was bombed.

'On leaving school in September 1938 a friend of my parents, Frank Wright, a fitter and Shop Steward at the Woolston Works arranged for me to have an interview with the Foreman, Bill Crooks. He took me on as a night shift worker and in the first year I had to do anything from helping fitters on double-handed jobs, cleaning out the hulls of the Walrus flying boats and making tea.

Work on the new factory, known at the Itchen Works, had begun and as soon as the building was ready we all moved in. It was cold as there were no tarpaulins on the waterfront side by the slipway. We had some braziers for warmth but these were soon discontinued as the heat and fumes were harmful to the metal. One of my first jobs was to clean the wings of a number of Walrus flying boats, still in sliver colours. We also refurbished the Stranraers, two-engined flying boats, which were then painted in camouflage. Two experimental Spitfires on floats were built with the idea of using them in Norway, but I don't think they ever flew. Then I was set to work on Spitfire fuselages. As time went by everyone was aware that war was imminent and we steadily increased production.

When war was declared we were enrolled in the L.D.V.s – Local Defence Volunteers. Our uniform was just an armband and some of us were picked to man the Works Fire Brigade. Later we became the 'Home Guard' and were issued with uniforms and a limited number of Lee Enfield rifles. There was an old Vickers water-cooled machine gun mounted in an old boat cabin in the railway embankment and two men manned this all the time. Two Browning machine guns were mounted in sandbagged emplacements on the waterfront. We all took turns to do night patrols along the railway line as far as White's Yard which could be scary. When it was thought wewere going to be invaded we had one period of duty which lasted 24 hours.

During the first few months of the war we had several scares. Everyone had to run to the shelters through a tunnel under the railway built behind the railway embankment. On Tuesday 24th September 1940 we sustained a heavy bombing attack. The factory was not badly hit but the shelters and the nearby houses were bombed. My brother Frank had taken refuge with several others underneath the tunnel because they could not reach the shelters in time. He was lucky not to have been killed as the railway received a direct hit and the embankment collapsed on top of them. Several people died in this attack and Frank was buried up to his shoulders and suffered a compound fracture of his leg amongst other injuries.

That night when we reported for duty we were told that the staff had already moved out to the Polygon Hotel. As no lights could be used due to bomb damage this meant we could not conform to the black out regulations. Now our job was to come in the next morning and help clear up. Everyone was apprehensive but Wednesday passed relatively quietly. Lord Beaverbrook, Minister for Aircraft Production, appeared and gave Supermarine 'carte blanche' to commandeer any garage, laundry or building anywhere which could be considered suitable for the production of Spitfires.

By mid afternoon on Thursday we had moved virtually everything to other sites. Then the warning to Take Cover sounded and with Ted Bridges, one of the Chargehands, we ran through the gap in the embankment, now cleared, to the first shelter. Inside he turned to me and said 'There are too many in here, we'll find another.' Running to the next one we found only a few people inside. Then the bombs started dropping all around and the gunners on Peartree Green were firing their Bofors non stop, which was a comfort to us. Our shelter had a near miss and the blast blew the metal escape hatch off the roof and the concrete floor cracked. To ease our fear we swore and cursed the German pilots. At last we heard the All Clear. No one in our shelter was hurt but we were all badly shaken.

Outside the place was a shambles. The shelters had been built on soft soil which may have saved some lives but it was a mud and clay quagmire. The shelter which Ted and I had first gone into was badly damaged and our work mates were climbing out, many with severe injuries. We did what we could to help until the First Aid people arrived and took over. One young lad was badly shocked and I was asked to see he got home to Hythe. Taking him to our house in Bitterne I made him a cup of tea and when he had calmed down walked with him to Whites Road to catch a bus.

As my wife was not at home I went to the Merry Oak Estate thinking she would be with my parents but my elder brother was the only person there. He told me my wife and sister had gone to visit my younger brother in The Royal South Hampshire Hospital in St Mary's Road. Eventually we all met up and I heard that they had been in a shelter in the town and someone had told them that Vickers Supermarine was wiped out. They were so relieved to see me even though I was covered in mud.

Back at the factory many people were trying to clear up the mess and I was told to find my tools, if they were still there, and report the next day to Hendy's Garage at the back of Woolworth's. We worked there for a few weeks until Southampton had a blitz. Hendy's, having no electric power, I was sent to Seward's garage on the Winchester road and shortly afterwards I was transferred to Reading.

Our house was damaged in the blitz, so putting our furniture into store with a farmer on the Durley Road we went into lodgings with a couple of farm workers. When the factory specially built at Caversham Heights was ready everyone transferred there. Mr. Weedy who had been in the K shop at Woolston was put in charge. Mary and I moved into a large house converted by the local authority into flats. Bungalows being built by the Ministry of Aircraft production specially for the Supermarine workers in

Northumberland Avenue were just like those built at Ampfield near Hursley.

During this time some of us had to go to Benson Airfield near Oxford to convert the fighter fuselages into Photographic Reconnaissance Aircraft. Virtually all the members of the original team at Supermarine spent a lot of time acting as 'teachers' instructing unskilled workers in this modification. There were so many cameras to be fitted that we had to re-route all the flying control cables. A tricky job. When a red alert sounded I was working inside the tail portion and how I got out of the small square door I cannot remember. But I was fairly slim. Our nearest shelters were holes in the ground covered with planks of wood and turf on top. One raider dropped oil bombs and one fell underneath a Wellington Bomber nearby and seconds later it went up in flames.

Before the war a Spitfire (K. 9834) had been built at Eastleigh and prepared for the World Land Plane Speed Record. It had no armament and gleamed with many coats of blue paint with a white flash along the side. It was decommissioned when the war started and in November 1940 was given to the Photographic Reconnaissance Unit at Benson. Wing Commander Geoffrey Tuttle and later his successor, Air Commodore John Boothman both flew this machine. It was fortunate that on a previous occasion our commanding officer was able to get this Spitfire up and well away before the raiders arrived.'

# Supermarine after 1949
## by
## Alf Shorter

These are the memories of Alf Shorter, his employment with Folland Aircraft where they were producing the Gnat, his work at Supermarine and his life.

'After seven years of cycling six miles each way to work every day, I decided to make a change. On the first of January 1956, I joined Vickers Armstrong's Supermarine works at Woolston, Southampton, where my brothers were already working. When the Scimitar programme ended, nearly everyone had to learn new skills for the nuclear submarine space models. I remember with pleasure that I could mark out, cut, roll and weld a lobsterback bend. Other devises were later manufactured for the nuclear programme. The new work demanded a great deal of skill and the use of entirely new materials.

The manufacture of Magnox fuel channel sleeves was one job in which I was involved. There were also monstrous radiation shields in the form of steel tubes about one foot in diameter. These were filled with chilled cast iron and concrete, loaded into a strongback, upended and secured into a huge ballrace situated in the roof trusses of the hangar. These were then rotated and checked for straightness. The jobs that we were required to do were far removed from any that were previously used in aircraft construction. In spite of the difficulty of the work I cannot recall anyone who lacked enthusiasm to tackle the challenges with which we were presented.

My working life ended in a local engineering firm where I was in charge of the inspection department. One day the Quality Manager brought three young lads to me who were participating in the Youth Training Scheme. Whilst giving them basic information I was surprised to be interrupted with the question 'Where are our chairs?' Has the respect given to Senior Managers in my youth changed so dramatically to this causal attitude to work?

During the Miners' Strike I became tired of the television media interviews stressing how hard done by they were, when these were often carried out in working men's clubs where all and sundry were drinking ale and smoking like factory chimneys.

I know that I am an intolerant old man who thinks, as did Oscar Wilde, that youth is wasted on young people. But think on, the basic rate of pay in the fifties was about twelve pounds per week and this was considered good money although the majority of my acquaintances could not afford a car. Cycle racks were more important to the average working man. Perhaps now this is why we have the problem of unemployment.

One incident I recall in my days at Supermarine was on a Sunday afternoon when the Charge Hand came to tell me that my son, a police cadet, had just come off duty and wanted to see me. 'What's up lad?' I asked him. 'The line pole has broken.' was his reply. (Note: Line pole = telegraph pole) 'You haven't come down here to tell me that!' I said. I was earning double pay for the day, plus a 150% bonus, so I wasn't too pleased to be called out for what I considered was a very minor problem. 'Ah! But it fell across the greenhouse' was the next piece of information. After a short silence my son added, 'Mum was in the greenhouse'. Dropping everything I hurried home to find my wife still in one piece but considerably shaken by her experience.'

## Supermariners and the Spitfire Society

At Rothsay College in Bedford I met Squadron Leader Richard Ian Blair. On a visit with him to the Royal Air Force Museum (Hendon) he drew my attention to a poster. It depicted an RAF youth with the words 'CARELESS TALK MAY COST HIS LIFE' and underneath it the instruction 'Don't talk about Aerodromes or Aircraft Factories.' The youth was Ian. On the 4th September 1940 Ian, as an Observer in a Blenheim flying in the Middle East Command, took over the controls when the pilot was killed. Without previous flying experience he flew the aircraft 350 miles back to safety, thereby saving the lives of the Air Gunner and himself plus the Blenheim. For this he was awarded the Distinguished Flying Medal.

Hearing that Jack Davis was to give the 30th R.J. Mitchell Memorial Lecture on 4th March 1986 entitled 'The Basic Design of the Prototype Spitfire' in the Bolderwood Lecture Theatre of the University of Southampton, I mentioned it to Ian. As he was interested we went down together. After the lecture I saw Alan Clifton and spoke to him. He immediately turned to Jeffery Quill with the remark 'Jeffery, you remember Stella?' It was great to speak with them and reminisce with Jack Davis and others of our memories of Hursley Park.

On the following day Ian took me to Eastleigh Airport where the recently formed Spitfire Society was holding a 'Spitfire Fly-In'. This was the Golden Jubilee of the first flight of the prototype Spitfire on the 5th March 1936 from the Aerodrome.

The Spitfire Society was inaugurated on the 6th March 1984 at the Royal Air Force Museum (Hendon) under Jeffrey Quill as President and Group Captain David Green became Chairman. On the 26th May 1984 the R.J. Mitchell Memorial Museum was opened in the Southampton Hall of Aviation.

At Eastleigh I met Mike Baylis, a professional photographer who was taking photographs of various groups. Ian was delighted to meet his colleagues of 602 Squadron of the Tangmere Spitfire Wing namely: Michael Frances, Raymond Baxter and Michael Penny. Some 46 Supermariners were also at this celebration and photographs of both these groups were produced in the Souvenir Edition of the Spitfire Society's Golden Jubilee magazine. The magazine was originally entitled D.C.O. (Duty Carried Out) but since Autumn 2003 it has been renamed Spitfire. Nick Grace's Spitfire trainer had landed on grass at the end of the runway when the undercarriage collapsed and it tipped over on its nose. Peter Arnold, Spitfire historian, and Henri de Meer were to fly this aircraft but were resigned to the fact their flight was cancelled. Also on that day I met Noel Mills and his wife Joan. Noel recalled the 'Sports Day' when we were roped in at the last minute to take part in a three-legged race representing the Drawing Office against the House Team. We came in second which was not bad considering we had no time for rehearsal.

At the Hall of Aviation in Southampton on another occasion I was delighted to meet with Jack Rasmussen and Kenneth Knell, both Supermariners, with their wives. Dr. Gordon Mitchell, son of R.J. Mitchell the famous designer of the Spitfire was also there and Miss Lettice Curtis. She was one of the female Ferry Pilots during the War and now was a Vice President of the Spitfire Society. Meeting with Jeffrey and other Supermarine colleagues after 40 years felt like greeting long lost members of a family.

Jeffrey proposed I should become a Life Member of the Spitfire Society and 'Being a person with the required proven connections' the Committee elected me on the 11th November 1985. I was then persuaded to become Chairman of one of the eight regions, namely the Central Region covering London to Peterborough.

Throughout the next four years I organised the Central Region's stands at various Air Shows. This activity was supported by a committee of Spitfire enthusiasts of varying ages who gave of their time and energy to attend these functions in order to raise funds and interest the general public in the Society. Having no transport of my own I am very grateful to members who made sure that the tent, sales items and myself were able to be present at Air Shows throughout the region. The membership steadily increased and contacts were made in many countries.

At one Air Show I was approached by a German who diffidently asked if it would be acceptable for him and his colleagues, Luftwaffe pilots, to meet with the Spitfire pilots who were signing posters on our stand. Checking that everyone was happy about meeting the Luftwaffe pilots, I introduced the two parties. A unique experience for all.

It was hard work organising the setting-up of stands at various Air Shows throughout the year. After four years of meeting pilots who flew Spitfires, Seafires and the Ferry Pilots plus many Supermariners I felt I had made a good contribution to the establishment of the Society. It had been a very busy time and when I developed M.E. and had to give it up, I concentrated on the research and writing of this book. Since then I have been most fortunate to contact many surviving colleagues of that time.

At the RAF Club in Piccadilly on Thursday 12th December 1991 Jeffrey Quill was presented with a Trophy by the Chief of the Air Staff. Many of our wartime colleagues were present. In conversation with Jeffrey and Jack Rasmussen I said it would be helpful if a book could be compiled listing the names of the Design Staff who had been involved in the development of the Spitfire and that Gerry Gingell would probably be the best source of information. My remarks obviously gave Jeffrey food for thought, because he later discussed the idea with Gerry.

At the Southampton Hall of Aviation on Thursday 8th May 1997 the Supermarine

Spitfire Memorial Book, proposed by Jeffrey Quill and compiled by Gerry Gingell and colleagues, sponsored by Messier-Dowty and Dowty Aerospace, was presented to the Director of the R.J. Mitchell Memorial Museum by Alex Henshaw. This hand-made edition records as many names as possible of those who were involved in the original design of, and subsequent development on, the Spitfire from 1932 to 1945 under R.J. Mitchell and later Joseph Smith. Two other hand-made books have been presented to the Royal Air Force Museum (Hendon) and Imperial War Museum (Duxford). Copies of this book were given to other dignitaries. The Southampton Daily Echo reported this occasion and photographed most of the 36 members of Supermarine who were present. Jeffrey, who was to have been the principal guest had, regretfully, died a few days earlier.

Watching a programme about Art on the television in the 1990s I saw two people walking away from the camera. There was no mistaking one of them. His distinctive walk reminded me of Ken Sprague, a colleague at Supermarine. Looking through pages of my autograph album I found his colourful entry. After making some telephone calls I got in touch with him hoping he would be able to be at the next reunion. Unfortunately this was not possible but on the day he rang me at the venue and Gerry was able to chat with him. When staying near Exeter some years ago I took the opportunity to meet him as he was in Exeter Hospital overnight. His comments to his surgeon and the people in the ward was 'Can you believe it! We worked together 60 years ago!' And he illustrated another picture opposite the one in my album.

At meetings of the Central Region we were very honoured to have prestigious speakers such as Sir Rex Hunt the former Governor of the Falkland Islands and Air Marshal Sir Ivor Broom former President of the Pathfinder Association. The latter became a close friend and learned of my involvement with General Graham and the D-Day Commanders. Hearing that an Officer who was present at the Farewell Party had written to me and confirmed my presence, he persuaded me to record my memories as 'It was such a unique episode in the annals of Military history.'

## M.E. Attacks

I wonder if due to the massive nettle poison received in my childhood and the birth of my second daughter in early June, when the grass and weed pollens were at their height, caused me to develop allergic reactions. These increased over a series of years to finally result in an attack of M.E. (Myalgic Encephalitis) after being bitten by a horse fly.

One morning I found that both my legs refused to lift off the floor! From my waist to my knees all my muscles had seized up. My doctor diagnosed I had developed M.E. At that time very little was known about this virulent illness. There was nothing the Medical Profession could do other than to prescribe pain killers and advise rest.

From the beginning I was housebound and my life was limited by visits of my doctor, home-help, meals on wheels and alternative weekly visits by both daughters. My telephone was my only means of communication with the outside world. Support from the library in changing books, was a Godsend. The prospect of being enclosed in my flat was, to say the least, frustrating.

Realising that enforced rest would probably result in muscles gradually atrophying, I endeavoured to prevent it. Having read about and met some of the pilots for instance, Douglas Bader, Geoffrey Page and Ginger Murray, who had overcome their injuries and faced up to life in spite of burns and amputations, I was determined to rise above my predicament. Every hour of every day I kept up the routine of never staying in one position for any length of time. After six weeks, knowing that too long a rest would result in muscle wastage I devised a recovery programme. In my youth Father had instructed me in anatomy and I realised this had to be by my own efforts. There was no one to help me.

For weeks I persevered taking one or two steps between bed and chair by using the lifting muscles and gauging the number of steps between chairs. Over a period of several months finally succeeded in walking from bed to the living room by lunchtime. At the same time, having read of an experiment where a group of people crippled with arthritis were given cod liver oil and another group, a combination capsule of cod liver oil and evening primrose oil, the latter group was observed to exhibit considerable improvement. So I started taking the same medication of the  combined capsule of cod liver oil and evening primrose oil every morning.

My principle was to walk a few steps but never taking one step too much, otherwise I found this could be a set-back.        Throughout these years I struggled to keep active but found if I stumbled slightly my muscles would not hold me upright and I would find myself flat on the floor. By  gradually increasing my mobility programme I could walk confidently relying on my muscles to keep my upright. Of course there were many setbacks including several months of suspected arthritis which turned out to be negligible. By the end of August the illness had travelled up into my head giving me three months of mental confusion. Then it disappeared only to travel down my arms and both hands became very swollen to the extent I could only hold a tea spoon. It was not until Christmas Day that I could actually use a knife and fork again. It was a year later when I noticed a small lump had appeared on one wrist and some weeks afterwards it was gone. I felt that the illness had at last left my body.

For three years I kept to my rigorous programme and eventually succeeded in reaching the front door! The next stage was to get to the front gate. A year later I actually achieved the end of the road to catch a bus. The first bus ride, only one stop, was shattering. It only took a few minutes but on getting off the bus had to enter the nearest shop and ask for a chair. During the next couple of years on every journey into town this shop keeper allowed me to rest even though I made no purchase of their goods. Stopping every so often to regain a resurgence of energy by resting on public seats I managed to move around to the bank, library, café or any other shop – although it took hours. Now even at my age, it still does!

Eight years after the onset of this illness I started to travel again in spite of the ongoing residual weakness left by the attack of M.E. which continues to this day. On these journeys the provision of a wheelchair and assistance by railway staff has been much appreciated. I have met other sufferers who tell me it took them the same number of years before they could get around and take part in normal life.

As there was little known about this wretched condition and many people were inclined to think that sufferers were 'not pulling their socks up' I wrote an article to describe just how a sufferer of M.E. felt. This has been published in the Bedfordshire Housebound Special by Bedfordshire County Council. I thought Dr. J.G. Hawkes, another Spitfire pilot, a Consultant at the Arthritic Clinic I was attending in Bedford Hospital, might be interested in my articles entitled 'M.E. and ME'. On reading it he persuaded me to send a copy to Dr. A.M. Denman, Consultant Physician in the Rheumatology and Clinical Immunology Department at Northwick Park Hospital, Harrow. His reply was very prompt and I quote:

'Thank you very much for sending me your essay on the ravages of 'M.E.'. The best people to comment lucidly on this kind of problem are patients themselves. Your beautifully written description of your symptoms will prove far more helpful and instructive for me, my colleagues and our patients than standard text-book descriptions. I will make sure that your thoughts are widely shared; I do hope that your health improves in the near future.'

Signed Dr. A.M. Denman

His comments on my writing ability encouraged me to further endeavours in researching and writing this book. The article was written to interest other M.E. sufferers and their families and is reproduced below:

## M.E. and ME

From the Greek: 'Beyond his strength may no man fight, howsoever eager he be.'

'The above maxim is what a sufferer of Myalgic Encephalitis, M.E. for short, should take to heart. M.E. is a long name for an insidious virus infection which can be equally exasperating for the sufferer, their relatives and friends. Whilst M.E. can attack any age group it appears, in many cases, to attack those who may be under stress and/or who have recently had some illness which has lowered their bodies' immune defences. Is this why perhaps, this disease seems to have become apparent in the late 1900's when most people's lives are under stress?

I would like to put on record the precepts which I believe helped me to combat the virus and its subsequent effects enabling me to lead a relatively normal life many years afterwards. In the 1950's Mr.C.R.McLaughlin, successor to Mr. A. MacIndoe of the Queen Victoria Hospital at East Grinstead, stated to me before operating 'that attitude of mind is 50% of the healing process.'

So I say, when everything seems hopeless and you are in continuous pain with what appears to be no end to your suffering, this is the time to mentally 'gird up your loins' in the biblical vernacular, (Luke Chap. 12.v.35.). Lower the speed of your breathing, relax as much as possible, ignore your fears and doubts, concentrate and believe that no matter how you feel, the future WILL be better – this is a fact – just give it time.

What can you do to cope with this illness? I think the clue is pace yourself, that is, think of your body energy as being two tanks of water. The first tank is what keeps the heart and lungs working and cannot be drawn upon for emergencies. The main tank is that which gives the body energy to do everything else – stand, sit, walk, move every joint, think and even talk. Therefore if the virus turns on the tap which drains the tank completely you can understand just how an M.E. sufferer feels at that moment.

In order to allow the body to refill the tank and gain sufficient energy to continue movement, it is vitally necessary that the sufferer should NOT ATTEMPT to force themselves to take one further step because by so doing they are liable to cause damage to the tap permanently. It is only the M.E. sufferer who can estimate exactly how much energy is in reserve.

To refill the tank after the complete exhaustion takes place, the sufferer needs to rest, sit, lie down or even sleep for 10-20 minutes. This allows the body to regain energy. To prevent this extreme condition it is necessary for each individual to recognise their own limitations – that is their mental and physical energy levels. If the sufferer feels the flow of energy being drained and takes immediate action the after effects can be considerably lessened.


## DO AND DO NOT

DO recognise your limitations and accept them.

DO NOT hanker after past achievements.

DO take medication to alleviate pain

DO NOT ignore breakfast or supper. The first gives energy for the day, the latter the ability to sleep.

DO eat and drink at regular intervals. Small amounts, if necessary several times a day.

DO NOT let the virus settle in one place.

DO gently keep all muscles and joints moving every hour.

DO NOT sit or lie down for lengthy periods. Stand, walk or move every so often.

DO learn about posture. Sit upright against a firm back with upright on both sides.

DO NOT sit sideways curled up or cross your legs and ankles.

DO dictate your own pace.

DO NOT push yourself to please others.

DO look forward and change direction, sometimes this can be to your advantage.

DO NOT despair. Remember, time is a healer.

DO think on the positive side. Use your thoughts to give you a forthright attitude to life.

REMEMBER continual small steps not big jumps are the signposts to regaining your good health.

I trust the above principles will inspire all sufferers and show them, there is a light at the end of the tunnel.'

'What is mind, never matter.

What is matter, never mind.'

R.A. Emerson

## What does the Future hold?

Time to complete many projects which have been 'on hold' during the writing of this book. Firstly I look forward to a long holiday by the sea, then having recharged my energy levels, start painting pictures planned so long ago. Alongside this activity complete an embroidery only partly designed. Another project is to sort out a collection of past scribblings containing odd items of interest which may result in articles or even a book!

The prospect of meeting up with people, or the family of those no longer with us, mentioned in my life fills me with anticipation. Perhaps to see the Edinburgh Tattoo and the Trooping of the Colour events. Visits to Whale Island Museum which I have never seen and revisiting H.M.S. Belfast in order to assist their proposed programme on the creation of the four inch gun protection skirts.

In my remaining years, if I am fortunate to eventually live down in Hampshire once again, I hope to be able to be of assistance to Tangmere Museum. Perhaps to enjoy the company of friends of like interests and play Mah-jong, Halma and Bezique.

# Index of Names

Quill, Jeffrey, Chief Test Pilot, 118, 119, 166, 170, 177, 178, 179.

Rafat, General Ali, 153, 154.

Randall, Miss, Teacher, Bedhampton School, 75, 78.

Randolph, Thomas, Ambassador to Scotland, 43.

Rasmussen, Jack, R.A.F. Liaison Officer, Supermarine, 114, 118, 123, 127-178.

Rennie, Thomas, Major General, C.O. 3rd British Division, 133, 139.

Reynolds, Sir Joshua, Artist, 27.

Richards, Peggy, V.A.D Nurse, Haslar, Gosport, 163, 164.

Richardson, Mr., Chief Inspector, Supermarine, 166, 168, 169.

Richardson, P.H., Lt. Col., C.O. 7th Bn., The Green Howards, 133.

Richardson, Sir Albert, Architect, 148.

Riley, John, Artist, 30.

Roosevelt, Theodore, President U.S.A., 141.

Roubiliac, Louis François, Sculptor, 27.

Ruskin, John, Poet, 102.

Russell, John, 13th Duke of Bedford, 83, 84.

Rutter, Sydney Donald, Philatelist, 142, 144, 147, 151, 152.

Rutty, Mary, wife of J.B [3], 18, 22.

Ryan, Pugilist, 28.

Ryland, Fred, Chairman, West Bromwich Municipal Instruction Committee, 31.

Rysbrack, John Michael, Sculptor, 27.

Schofield, Mrs. L.M.P., 36.

Scott, Septimus E., Artist, 34.

Scott, Sir Walter, Author, 72.

Scragg, Mrs., 'Auntie', 79.

Senior, R.H. Brigadier, C.O. 151st Infantry Brigade, 133.

Seve, Stanley, Experimental Workshop, Supermarine, 117.

Shah of Persia, 154.

Shepherd, Jack, Villein, 22.

Sherlock, Bishop, Master of the Temple, London, 19.

Shiel, Brigadier, C.R.A. to General Rennie, 139.

Slack, Jack, 28.

Shorter, Alf, Supermarine, 176, 177.

Sidaway, Frank, Alice, 14, 49.

Sidley, Dave, Supermarine, 169.

Simpson, Arthur, World War I Memorial, 35.

Slatter, Dudley Malins, Pilot Officer, son of W.S., 98.

Slatter, Valetta, wife of William, 98, 99.

Slatter, William, Chemist of Emsworth, 98, 99.

Smith, H.D.N., Lt. Col., C.O. 1st Bn.The Hampshire Regiment, 133.

Smith, Joseph, Chief Designer, Supermarine, 117-121, 124-127, 135, 179.

Wellington, Duke of, 20.

Wentworth, Lady, Author, 36.

White, G.W., Lt. Col., C.O. 5th Batallion East Yorkshire Regiment, 133.

Widdington, Ralph, President and University Orator of Christ's College, 18.

Wilbore, Jeremiah, brother to Mary, 17.

Wilbore, Mary, wife of Broughton [1], 17.

Wilcox, Mr., Barrister, 20.

Wilde, Oscar, 176.

Willmott, Elizabeth, wife of J.B [4], 28.

Wills, Mr., Inspector, Supermarine, 168.

Wilson, Paddy Ann, 157.

Wingfield, H.E., Philatelist, 143.

Wolsey, Cardinal Thomas, 33, 34, 35.

Wood, G.I., Major, 133.

Wooton, John, Artist, 36.

Wright, Frank, Shop Steward Supermarine, 173.

Wyatt, M.D., Architect, 89.

Wyldbore-Smith, Rachel, Headmistress, White House School, 90, 148, 149

Young, Irene, Author, 114.

Young, Mary, mother of Mary Rutty, 22.

## Index of Places

## Poems

1. Words      by Paddy Anne Wilson
2. The Littlest One      by Marion St. John Webb
3. The Laws of the Navy      by Rear Admiral Ronald A. Hopwood
4. The Unpayable Debt      by Joyce Lucas
5. A Moth Eaten Rag      by Sir Edward Hamley
6. Timer Talks by      Paddy Anne Wilson
7. I 'Aint Got No Chance Miss      by Paddy Anne Wilson
8. Contentment      by Jil Teals
9. Palette      by Jil Teals
10. Sub Contracts or The Madhouse      by R. B. Bennett

## Books and Records Consulted

| General | Author |
| --- | --- |
| Who Was Who? and Who's Who? | |
| The Complete Peerage | |
| Kings and Queens of Great Britain | Eric R. Delderfield |
| Kings and Queens of Great Britain | David Williamson |
| The History of The King's Bodyguard | Colonel Sir Reginald |
| of the Yeoman of the Guard | Hennell |
| The Yeoman of the Guard. History 1485-1885 | Thomas Preston |
| William Augustus Duke of Cumberland | E. Charteris |
| The English Court in the Reign of George I | John M. Beattie |
| Foster's Yorkshire County Families | |
| Fasti Ecclesiae Anglicanae 1541-1857 | John Le Neve |
| Fosters Alumni Brigienses | |
| Alumni Cantabrigienses | |
| Eton College Register | |
| Fawcett Index of Clergy | |
| The Victoria History of the Counties of England | |
| Yorkshire Archaeological Society – Journal. Vol. 4 | |
| Dictionary of National Biography | |
| Oxford Dictionary of National Biography | |
| Greater Oxford Dictionary | |
| Pear's Encyclopaedia | |

| | |
|---|---|
| Roget's Thesaurus | Betty Kirkpatrick |
| Kellys Directories | |
| Sketches of Burley | Alan H. Bird |
| The Gentleman's Magazine | |
| Morning Post – January 1789 | |
| Daily Advertiser | |
| Awards of Honour | Aurthur Joceleyn |
| British Orders & Awards | |
| Major Lawrence Gordon | |
| The Company of Watermen & Lightermen – Records | |
| The Walpole Society. Vol. 22 | |
| The Studio – First Issue | |
| Queen Victoria Was Amused | Alan Hardy |
| Tate & Lyle Times | |
| The English Way Of Death | Dr. Julian Litten |
| The Cabinet War Rooms | Imperial War Museum |
| H.M.S. Belfast | Imperial War Museum |
| Salisbury Cathedral – Library | |
| The Kinver and Enville Collection | Robert F.Clarke |
| Railway Accidents of Great Britain and Europe | |
| Peacehaven | Bob Poplett |
| Chichester Remembered | Kenneth Green |
| Chichester, the Valiant Years | Bernard Price |
| The King's English | Arthur Mee |
| Smitten City | Portsmouth Evening News |
| Purbrook Park High School Magazines | |
| Tools of the Old and New Stone Age | Jacques Bordaz |
| More or Less | Kenneth More |
| Parcel Arrived Safely Tied with String | Michael Crawford |
| Bedfordshire Housebound Magazine | Beds County Council |
| A Silver-Plated Spoon | John Russell – |
| | 13th Duke of Bedford |

## Art, Artists, Sculptors and Architects

| | |
|---|---|
| The Oxford Companion to Art | Harold Osborne |
| Who's Who in Art | Algernon Graves |
| The Royal Academy of Arts 1769-1904 | Algernon Graves |
| The Art of Illuminating Practised in Europe | W.R. Tymms |
| from the Earliest Times | & M.D. Wyatt |
| English Art 1724–1800 | Joseph Burke |
| Dictionary of British Sculptors 1660–1851 | Rupert Gunnis |

| | |
|---|---|
| Sculpture in Britain 1530-1830 | Margaret Whiancy |
| Landseer, the Victorian Paragon | Campbell Lennie |
| Dictionary of British Artists | Grant M. Waters |
| Dictionary of Contemporary British Artists | Bernard Dolman |
| Dictionary of British Artists – 1880-1940 | J. Johnson |
| Dictionary of Victorian Painters | Christopher Wood |
| Dictionary of Portrait Painters in Britain up to 1920 | |
| Burne-Jones | M Harrison & B Waters |
| The Stained Glass Windows of William Morris, | David Bond |
| & his circle in Hampshire and Isle of Wight | & Glynis Dear |
| Past Into Present | Rebecca Lowe |
| MacMillan Encyclopaedia of Architects, Vol. 4. | James M. Maclaren |
| A Biographical Dictionary of British Architects | H.M. Colvin |
| (1600-1840) | |
| C.F.A. Voysey | Duncan Simpson |
| C.F.A. Voysey | Stuart Durant |
| C.F.A. Voysey 1857-1941, Exhibition Catalogue | Brighton 1978 |

## Boxing

| | |
|---|---|
| Eighteenth Century Boxing | Randy Roberts |
| The Complete Art of Boxing | An Amateur of Eminence |
| Poor Fred & the Butcher | Morris Maples |
| William Augustus, Duke of Cumberland | Hon. Evan Charteris |
| The Art of Boxing | David Mendoza |
| Book of Boxing | Henry Cooper |
| The Encyclopaedia of Boxing | Maurice Golesworthy |
| Capt Godfrey's Treatise | Pierce Egan |
| On The Useful Science of Self-Defence | |
| The Bare Knuckled Breed | Louis Golding |
| Flying Post | |
| Pugilistica | |
| Boxiana | |
| Fisticania | F. Dowling |
| The History of British Boxing 1719-1863 | Henry Downes Miles |
| Up to Scratch | Tony Gee |
| Fresh Light on Jack Slack | Tony Gee |
| The Road to Tyburn | Christopher Hibbert |
| Weekend – Article | Ian Brown |

### D Day 1944

| | |
|---|---|
| The Path of the 50th | Major Ewart W. Clay |
| The Battle of D Day | William McElwee |

| | |
|---|---|
| Three Assault Landings | Major A.E.C. Bredin |
| The D Day Landings | Philip Warner |
| D Day | Robert Collier |
| D Day | Lesley Burton |
| D Day 1944, Voices from Normandy | Robin Nallards |
| D Day the 50th Anniversary | Southern Newspapers of the Normandy Landings |
| | |
| The Longest Day | Cornelius Ryan |
| Gold Beach | Simon Trew |
| Gold Beach | Christopher Dunphie & Garry Johnson |
| | |
| Assault 3rd Division | Norman Scarfe |
| The Faithful Sixth, | Harry Moses |
| The Sixth Battalion, Durham Light Infantry | |
| All in the Day's March | Major General David Belcham |
| | |
| Victory in Normandy | Major General David Belcham |
| | |
| Victory in the West. Vol. 1 | L. F. Ellis & Others |
| The Sign of the Double T | Major Ian English |
| The Sign of the Double 'T' | Barrie S. Barnes |
| A Field Marshal in the Family | Brian Montgomery |
| Montgomery Vol. 2 | Nigel Hamilton |
| Montgomery – His Life | Lady Peacock |
| The Lonely Leader | Alistair Horne |
| A General's Life | General Omar Bradley |
| A Soldier's Story | General Omar Bradley |
| Travel & Trade & Veterans Newsletter November 1993. Issue 3 | Southern & Normandy Tourist Boards |
| The Deception Planners | Dennis Wheatley |
| The World We Fought For | Robert Kee |
| Battle over Britain | Francis K Mason |
| Ultra | F.W. Winterbotham |
| Pillboxes | Henry Wills |
| Jeeps | Ray Walker |
| Enigma Variations | Irene Young |
| Change into Uniform | Helen Long |

## Scotland

| | |
|---|---|
| Scotland Encyclopaedia | John & Julian Keay |
| Monarchs of Scotland | Stewart Ross |

| The Stewart Dynasty | Stewart Ross |
| The Scots Peerage | J. Balfour Paul |
| Biographical Dictionary of Eminent Scotsmen. Vol 2 | University of Glasgow |

| Fasti Ecclesiae Anglicanae | John Le Neve |
| Knox Genealogy, Chart and Text | William Crawford |
| John Knox | Rosalind K. Marshall |
| John Knox | Edwin Muir |
| John Knox | Jaspar Ridley |
| Ochiltree | Alexander Murdoch |
| Ochiltree House & Its Romances | Kilmarnock Standard |
| Barony of Avendale | John Hastie Museum |
| History of Strathaven and Avondale | William F. Downie |
| Stra'ven Castle | William D. Howat |
| The Castellated and Domestic Architecture of Scotland | David McGibbon & Thomas Ross |

## Music

| Grove's Dictionary of Music and Musicians | Eric Blom |
| Handel | R. A. Streatfield |
| Handel and the Harris Circle | Rosemary Dunhill |

## London

| The London Encyclopaedia | B. Weinreb C. Hibbert |
| An Encyclopaedia of London | William Kent |
| The Survey of London | John Stow |
| London Street Names | Gillian Bobbington |
| The Guilds and Companies of London | George Unwin |
| The City of London Livery Companies | Bryan Pontifex |
| London Signs | Bryant Lillywhite |
| London Coffee Houses | Bryant Lillywhite |
| London Inns and Taverns | Leopold Wagner |
| More London Inns and Taverns | Leopold Wagner |
| The Coachmakers | Harold Nockolds |
| Westminster Abbey Library – Records | Historical Memorials of |
| Westminster Abbey | Arthur Penrhyn Stanley |
| Account of Worshipful Company of Tallow Chandlers | R H Monier-Williams |

### Supermarine - Spitfire

| Spitfire – A Test Pilot's Story | Jeffrey Quill |
| Sigh for a Merlin | Alex Henshaw |

| | |
|---|---|
| Testing Times | Harry Griffiths |
| The Forgotten Pilots | Lettice Curtis |
| It Came To Pieces In My Hands | David Sweeting |
| The Spitfire Story | Alfred Price |
| Spitfire | Morgan & Shacklady |
| Clean Sweep | Tony Spooner |
| D.C.O. – now – SPITFIRE | Spitfire Society |

## List of Illustrations and Photographs

**On front cover:**

General Bernard L. Montgomery
Air Marshal Sir Ivor Broom
Spitfire by Pat Owen, aviation artist